LEGENDARY LOCALS

OF

BRISTOL

RHODE ISLAND

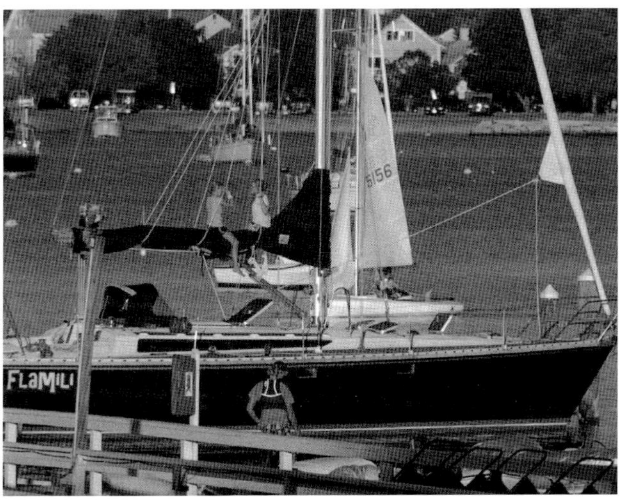

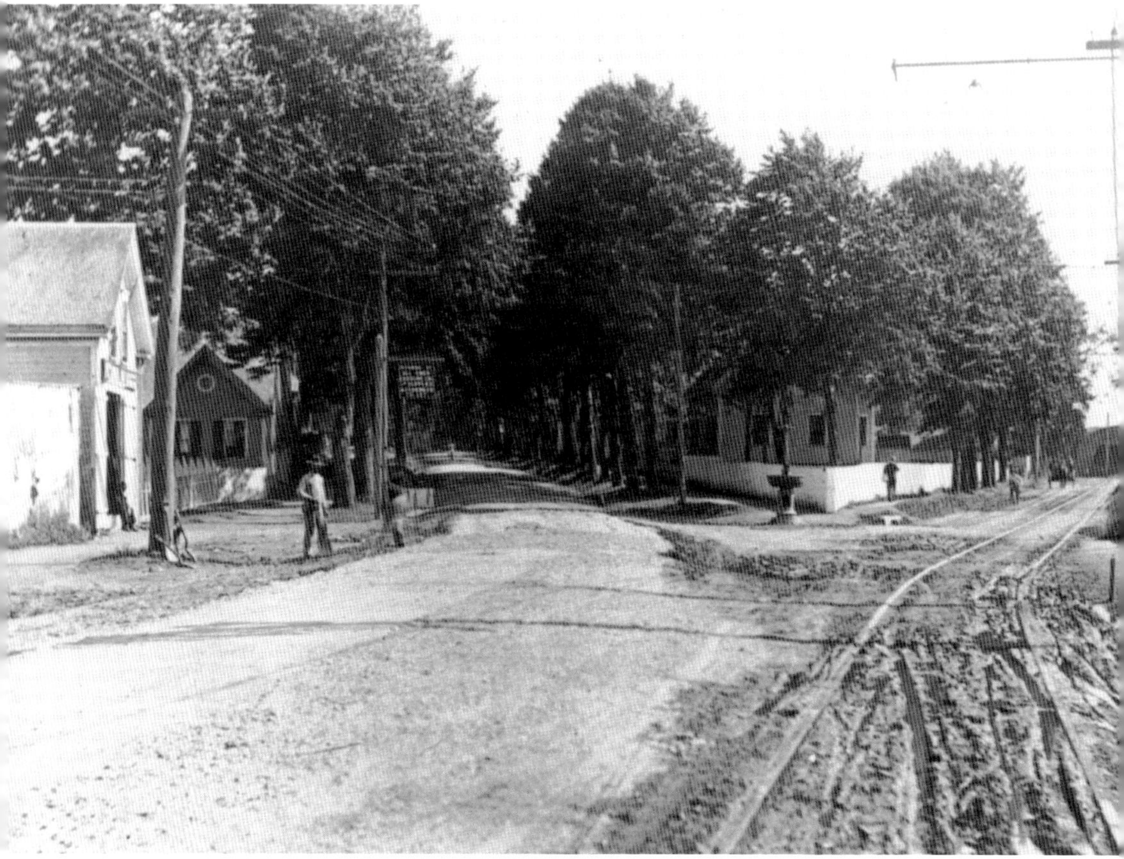

Hope and Thames Streets
In spite of all that has changed in the 100 years or so since this photograph was taken, this intersection is instantly recognizable to anyone who has ever spent any time in Bristol; for the southbound traveler, this fork in the road marks the beginning of downtown Bristol. (Courtesy of Linden Place.)

Page 1: A Favorite "Waste" of Time
For more than 300 years, Bristolians have known that there's nothing better than a warm summer evening spent with a good friend on a boat overlooking Bristol Harbor. (Author's collection.)

LEGENDARY LOCALS

OF

BRISTOL

RHODE ISLAND

CHRISTY NADALIN

LEGENDARY LOCALS

ISBN 978-1-4671-0139-4

Legendary Locals is an imprint of Arcadia Publishing
Charleston, South Carolina

Printed in the United States of America

Library of Congress Control Number: 2013951273

For all general information, please contact Arcadia Publishing:
Telephone 843-853-2070
Fax 843-853-0044
E-mail sales@arcadiapublishing.com
For customer service and orders:
Toll-Free 1-888-313-2665

Visit us on the Internet at www.arcadiapublishing.com

Dedication
This book is dedicated to the people of Bristol's past, present, and future: legendary, every one.

On the Front Cover: Clockwise from top left:
Marjorie and Augustine Van Wickle, socialites and philanthropists (Courtesy of Blithewold; see page 70), Ethel Barrymore, actress (Courtesy of Linden Place; see pages 122, 123), Samuel Pomeroy Colt, industrialist (Courtesy of Linden Place; see pages 28, 29), Joan Roth, educator, preservationist, and community activist (Courtesy of Joan Roth; see page 76), Gil and Sarah Almeida, business owners (Courtesy of Lisa Sienkiewicz and Gail Parella; see page 38), Cable Car, band (Courtesy of Cable Car; see page 108), brothers LeBaron Bradford and Samuel Pomeroy Colt, lawyer and industrialist, respectively (Courtesy of Linden Place; see page 22), George Sisson and Thomas Byrnes, community activists, preservationists, and philanthropists (Courtesy of Michael Byrnes; see page 68), Chris Santos, chef (Courtesy of Chris Santos, see page 118).

On the Back Cover: From left to right:
Gil's Television and Appliances (Courtesy of Lisa Sienkiewicz and Gail Parella; see page 38), members of the Bristol County Medical Center (Author's collection; see pages 36, 37).

CONTENTS

ACKNOWLEDGMENTS

I would like to thank the following people for their assistance: Susan Battle, Joyce Black, Ed Castro, Maggie Church, Jim Connell, Manny Correia, Jock Hayes, Cathy and Garry Holmstrom, Cindy Johnson, Kris McDonagh, Mary Millard, Scott Pickering, Joan Prescott, Norene Rickson, Betty Vargas, Erin Vosgien, Ronnee Wasserman, and Margaret Whitehead. Where not otherwise noted, images are courtesy of the author.

INTRODUCTION

Bristol has always been an American archetype. This small town has borne witness to the same historical touchstones that have shaped our nation from the very beginning, with each event playing out on an intimate, local scale.

This most patriotic of towns has, at one time or another, been home to some of the most remarkable people in American history. Yet for many more people, Bristol has been a great place to quietly go about the business of life: raising a family, volunteering at a house of worship or for a youth sports league, and sharing an occasional meal with good friends.

Yes, Bristol has hosted a number of presidents, and major Hollywood names like Barrymore and Quinn have called Bristol home at one time or another. The town's great sailing tradition brought the America's Cup home many, many times. During the Revolution, Bristol's patriots so annoyed the British that our enemy specifically targeted the town not once but twice. Bristol's sons have also been central figures in conflicts and commerce that engender less pride, most notably as key players in the African slave trade. And it was a son of Bristol who ordered the assassination of the son of Massasoit, one of the natives who welcomed the Pilgrims to Plymouth.

These people—some of them, anyway—will be mentioned in the following pages. So will a lot of people who spend most of their days simply living their lives while at the same time using their unique talents to make Bristol a better, more beautiful place for all who enjoy it now and in the future. Unfortunately, only some of those unsung friends and neighbors are in the pages of this book. That is by necessity; it is, as you can see, a small book. Like anywhere, if you listen, you will learn that everyone has a story—a great one—one that ought to be told. That is certainly true for Bristol, and if everyone whose story warranted it had been included, this book would be multiple volumes, thousands of pages, and eternally unfinished.

In Bristol, the ordinary and extraordinary coexist in ways that can be difficult to define. Bristolians know their home is unique but when pressed for reasons why, they will probably trot out the same few valid but trite replies: beautiful harbor, historic downtown, oldest continuous July Fourth celebration in the nation. But there is more to it than that, even if locals are not always able to articulate it as originally as amateur bard and educator 'Fessor DeWolf did with this c. 1809 verse that bristles with (perhaps) unintentional hilarity:

> "Hail, Bristol, happiest village, hail;
> What rich produce is thine.
> Girls, geese and onions thou canst boast;
> O triad most divine!"

CHAPTER ONE

Patriots, Privateers, and Politicians

When Bristol's story began, of course, it was not even an incorporated town, or even part of Rhode Island, which did not exist at the time. The swampy, forested lands south of the Pilgrims' settlements were part of the Massachusetts Bay Colony but slightly farther afield—a perfect place, the Puritans seemed to think, for religious radicals like Anne Hutchinson and Roger Williams to go off and do their own, odd thing. And they did.

As time passed and the area became more and more populated with European settlers, the "Rogue's Island" moniker stuck, and at times seemingly with good reason. The "you go your way, I'll go mine" mentality in part explains why Rhode Island was the site of the first major act of rebellion against the British crown but the last to ratify the US Constitution.

Bristol has been home to minutemen, soldiers and sailors, and jurists and politicians who have served with great honor. Bristol has also been home to men who had no trouble disregarding the rule of law. And occasionally, those men were one and the same.

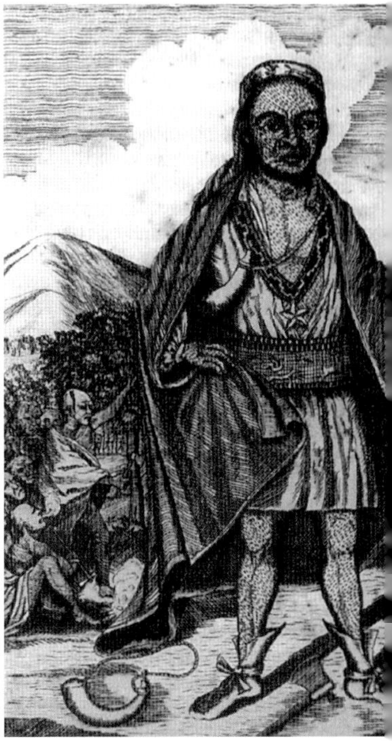

Death of a King

The Wampanoag sachem Metacomet rose to power on the death of his brother Wamsutta and father, Massasoit (of Plymouth Colony fame), in 1662. His seat of power, shown below, is a natural rock formation located on land near the base of Mount Hope. The historical record suggests that Metacomet (c. 1638–1676) initially straddled the line between hostility and assimilation, going by the European name of Philip when dealing with the colonists and buying his clothes in cosmopolitan Boston. Relations soured in the 1670s. Pushed by the leaders of the Plymouth Colony for one too many concessions, Metacomet leveraged his tribal relationships and took the lead in a widespread effort among the Native Americans to force the Puritans out of New England.

In August 1676, outgunned and cornered by Capt. Benjamin Church and his rangers, Metacomet was assassinated by a "praying Indian" (one who had converted to Christianity) in a swamp not far from his seat on Mount Hope, as dramatized in this illustration. His body was quartered and his head sent to Plymouth, where it remained on a spike for many years. Triggerman John Alderman was awarded one of the hands, which he retained, reportedly displaying it for guests when the mood struck. King Philip's seat on Mount Hope remains, a stone monument to the first "Bristolians" on historical record. (Both, courtesy of Linden Place.)

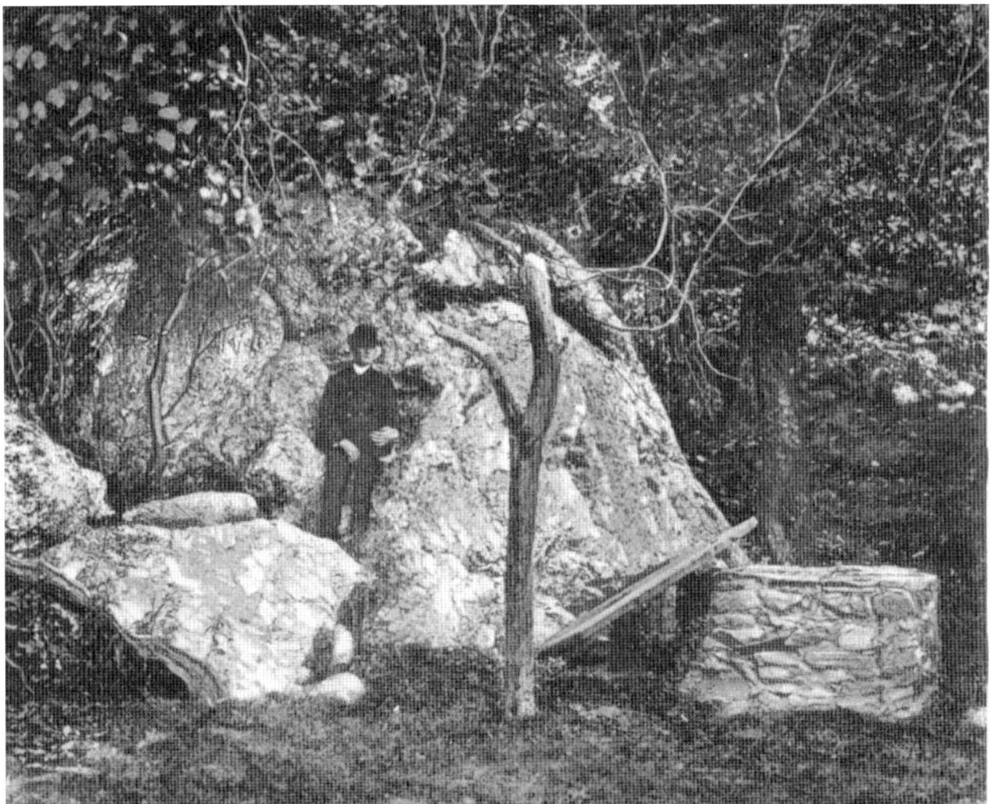

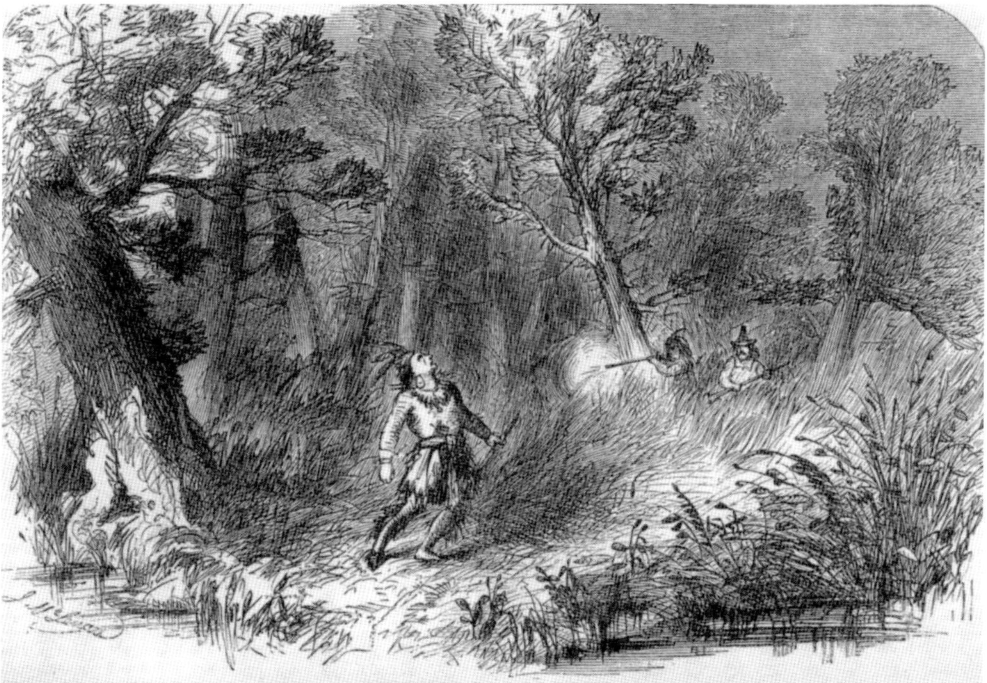

THE DEATH OF KING PHILIP.

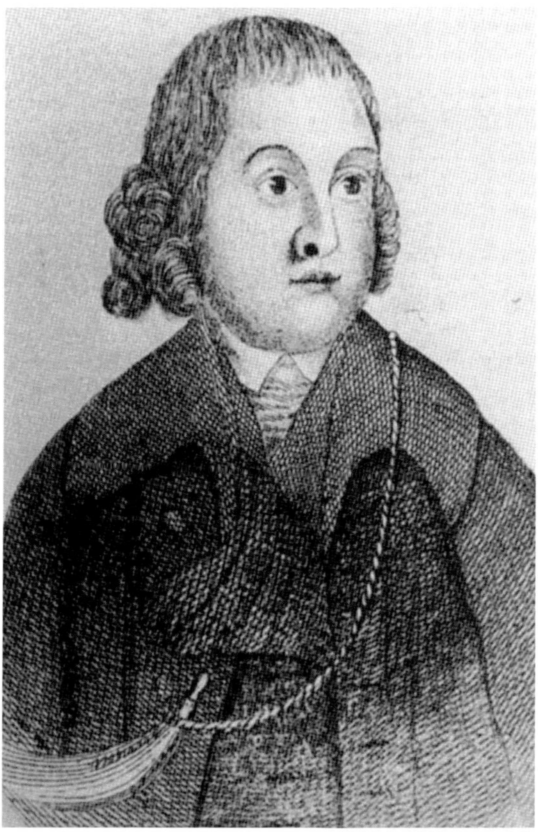

Deadly Tactician

Capt. Benjamin Church (1639–1717) was born in Plymouth, Massachusetts, and died in Little Compton, Rhode Island, but in the intervening years, he became one of the first inhabitants of Bristol when it was settled in 1680 and served as the town's first representative to Plymouth from 1682 to 1684. More notably, Church was the veteran of several Indian battles, raising a local company in 1675 to defend the colonists. Using tactics that were unfamiliar to colonial militia at the time, Church incorporated friendly Indians, whose hunting and tracking skills were unmatched, into his company. He also quickly learned to think (and fight) like an Indian, traveling in loose formation and maintaining the ability to quickly encircle the enemy. Church utilized both these strategies to good effect, particularly on the day his company assassinated King Philip. History regards Church as the first American ranger.

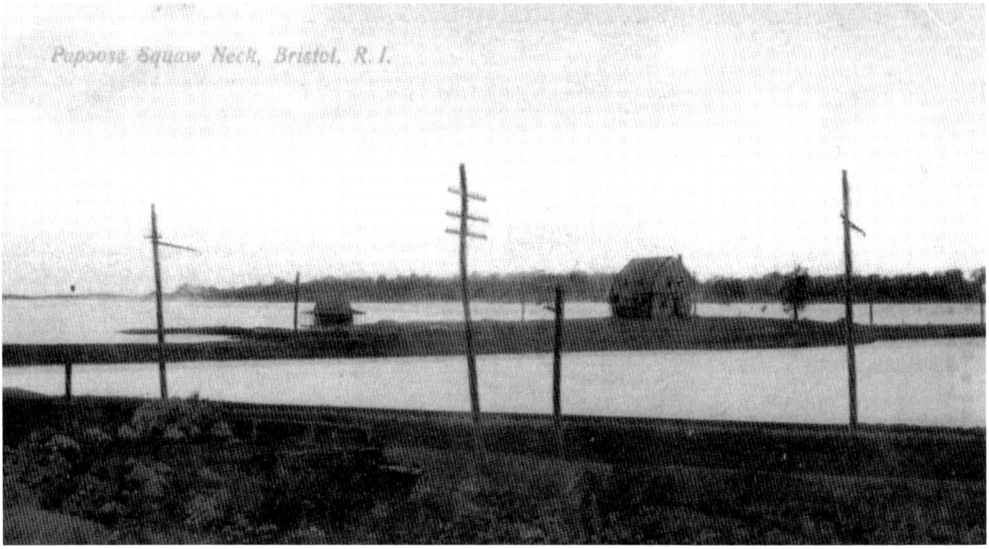

First on the Neck

John Gorham, a man about whom relatively little is known, was granted 100 acres of land north of the "Neck Burying-Ground" by the Plymouth Colony General Court, provided the Indians agreed to the sale. The purchase went through and was ratified by the court in July 1677, making John Gorham most likely the first Caucasian settler in Bristol.

The Four Founders (OPPOSITE PAGE)

In September 1680, for the sum of £1,100, four Boston merchants purchased Bristol. According to the original deed, it included "the lands, pastures, meadows, feedings, marshes, swamps, ways, easements, creeks, coves, harbors, mines, stones, beaches, flats, fishings, fowlings, woods, underwoods, trees, bushes, fences, profits, priviledges, rights, commodities, hereditaments, emoluments and apiurtenances whatsoever, growing, standing, lying, being, arising or issuing forth" from the roughly five acres of land that constituted the original township.

Nathaniel Byfield (1653–1733) hailed from a prominent English family; his father was a pastor, and his mother's brother was bishop of London and a close friend and advisor to Charles I who comforted the ill-fated king on the scaffolding the morning of his execution. Byfield arrived in Boston in 1674 and quickly became a successful merchant. He made his home on Poppasquash Point and was an active legislator and jurist until old age forced his retirement.

John Walley (1644–1712) was born in London; his father a rector who followed his son to Boston some time before 1664. According to historian Wilfred Munro in his book *The Story of the Mount Hope Lands*, Walley is remembered as a "man of uncommon sweetness and candor of spirit" who appeared to be universally well liked. "His gentle and retiring disposition never allowed him to put himself forward as a candidate for office, and yet office after office was continually thrust upon him." Walley lived in Bristol until advanced age and an unspecified painful and debilitating disease drove him back to the more civilized confines of Boston, where he died in 1712.

Little is known about Stephen Burton (d. 1693) beyond the fact that he was educated at Oxford before arriving in Boston. Despite his apparent intellect, he took on a bit role in the founding of the town due to a "disorder in the head."

Nathaniel Oliver (1652–1704) is credited with the role of fourth founder despite "flipping" his share of the Mount Hope real estate not long after the signing of the Grand Articles. Oliver sold his share to Capt. Nathan Hayman, another wealthy Bostonian, who was recorded as one of the four proprietors in the records of the first town meeting. Sadly, Hayman did not live long to enjoy his new town, dying in 1689.

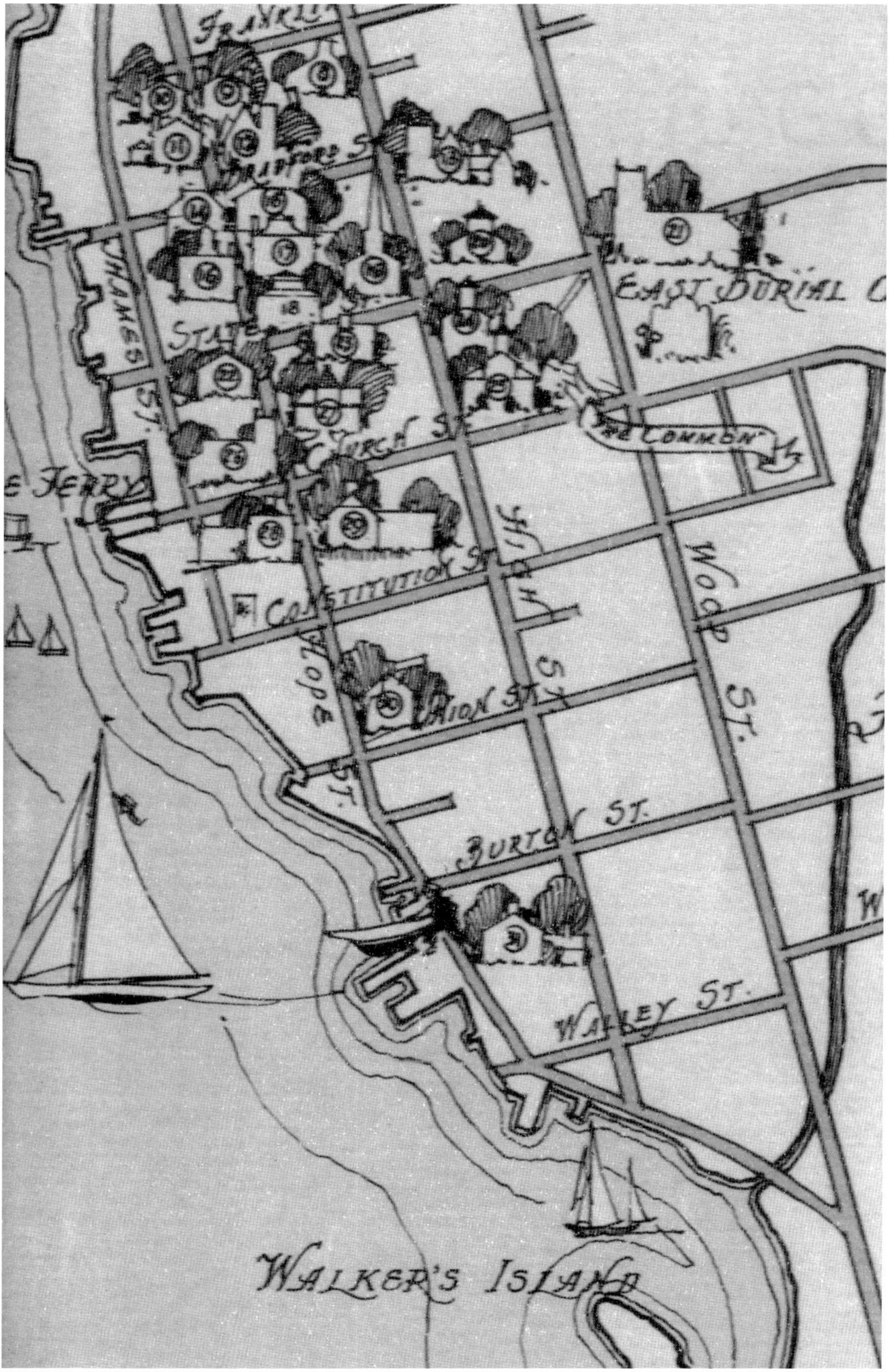
BRIDGE ST.
EAST BURIAL
THAMES ST.
STATE
CHURCH ST.
THE COMMON
CONSTITUTION ST.
HIGH ST.
WOOD ST.
HOPE ST.
UNION ST.
BURTON ST.
WALLEY ST.
WALKER'S ISLAND

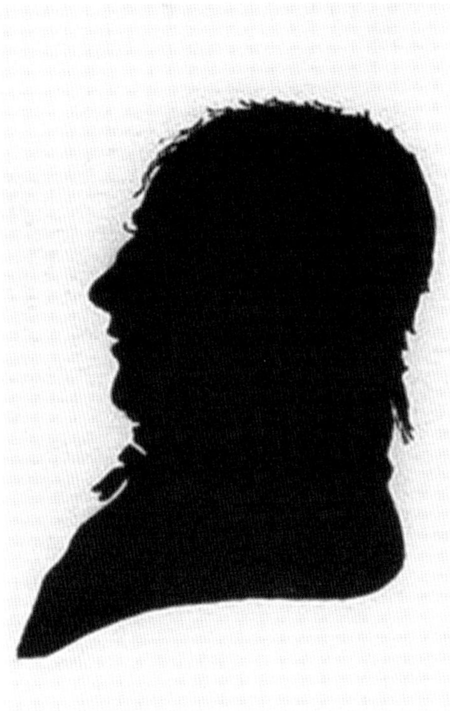

Constitutional Champion

Benjamin Bourne (1755–1808), who was born and died in Bristol, is credited with a key role in Rhode Island's eventual ratification of the US Constitution. A Harvard Law School–educated attorney, Bourne joined the 2nd Regiment of Continental Troops during the Revolution. He became Rhode Island's first representative to the US Congress, resigning after four terms to sit on the bench of the US District Court of Rhode Island, a position he held until his 1801 retirement.

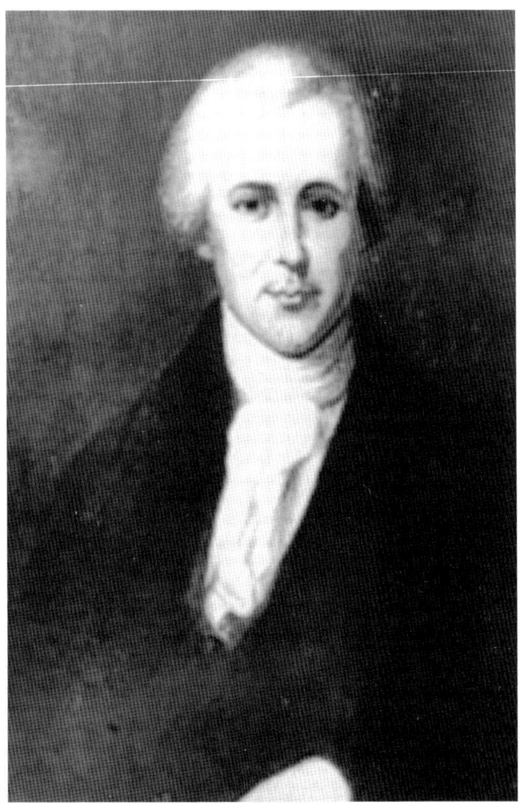

Plymouth's Prodigal (Great-Great-Grand) Son

As colonial pedigrees go, blood didn't get much bluer than that of William Bradford (1729–1808), whose great-great-grandfather of the same name was the first governor of the Plymouth Colony. A physician, Bradford practiced medicine in Warren before moving to Mount Hope Farm in the mid-1700s. Bradford entered politics, serving in both the Colonial Assembly and eventually the US Senate. When the British bombarded Bristol in 1775, Bradford's house was destroyed along with many others, and he has been credited with being instrumental in negotiating the ceasefire. He was elected to (but failed to attend) the Continental Congress in 1776. He resigned from the Senate in 1797 and enjoyed a decade in retirement in Bristol until his death.

Command Center

Though only a "local" for a brief period of time, the French Marquis de Lafayette and his staff set up shop in Bristol, using the Joseph Reynolds House as their headquarters during the Battle of Rhode Island in 1778. According to the National Park Service, the home, which was built in 1700, is the "oldest known 3-story upright structure in Rhode Island, and perhaps the earliest wooden structure of its form extant in New England." The Reynolds House was given National Historic Landmark status in 1983.

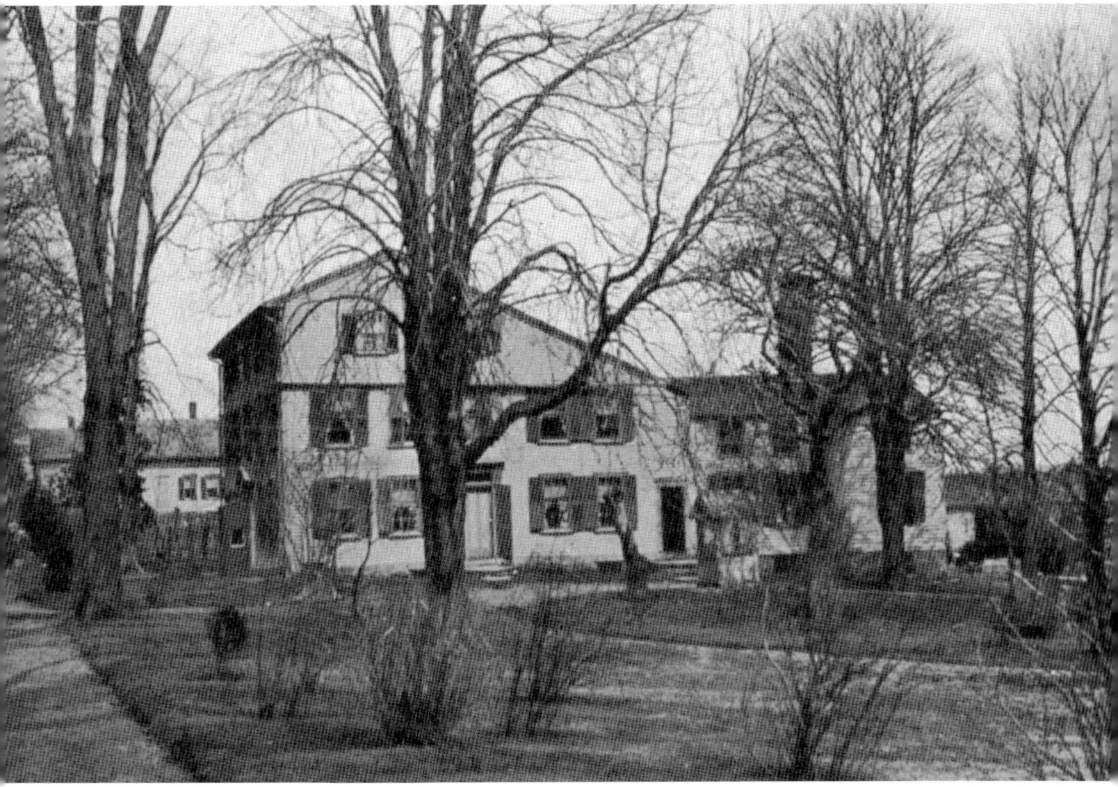

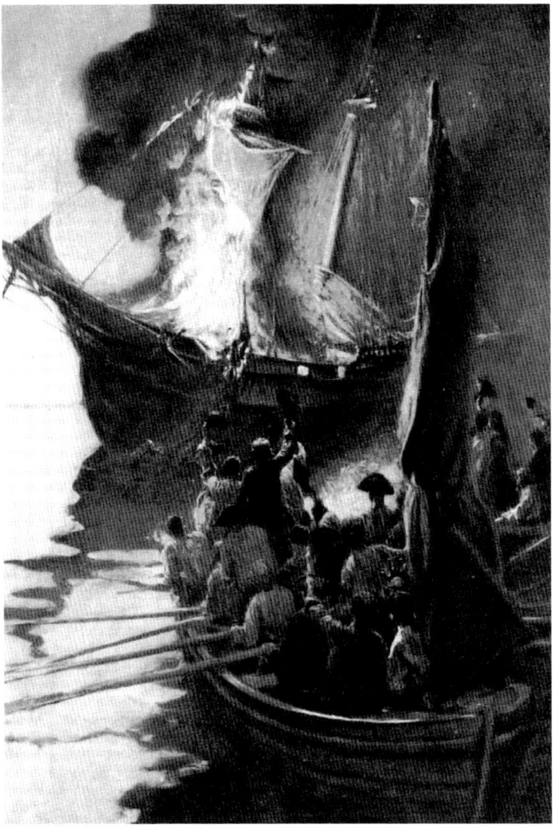

Revolutionary First Responder
Known for claiming that he would "plow the sea into pea-porridge to make money," Simeon Potter did just that. An illiterate but intelligent and resourceful ship captain, Potter was a slave trader and privateer who was a key figure in one of the earliest acts of revolution in the American Colonies when, in 1772, he captained a longboat full of Bristol sailors at the burning and sinking of the British tax ship HMS *Gaspee*. In his travels, Potter met and apprenticed a young Mark Antony DeWolf of Guadeloupe, who would marry Potter's sister Abigail and father several children, eventually forming the nucleus of the largest family of slave traders in American history.

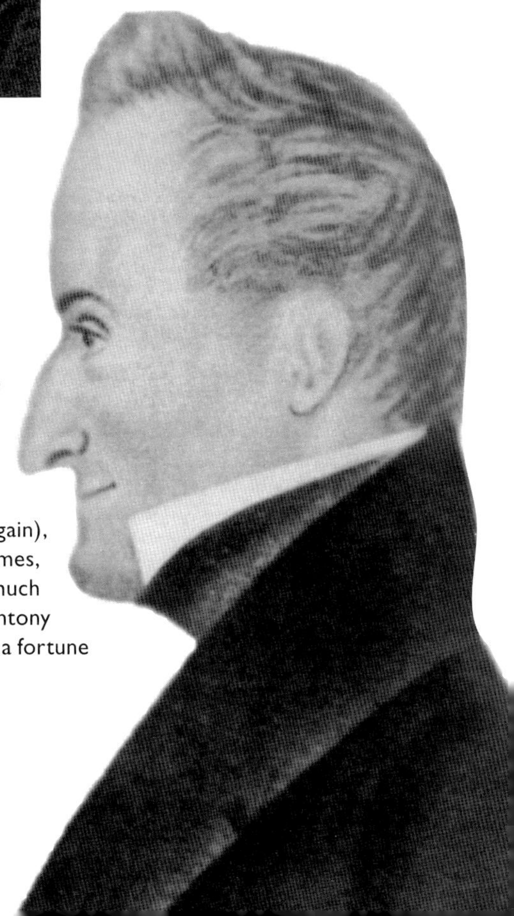

Potter's Apprentice
Mark Antony DeWolf (1726–1793) was born in the French West Indies on the island of Guadeloupe. He died in Bristol. In the years in between, he apprenticed under Capt. Simeon Potter, married Potter's sister Abigail, and had 15 children: Charles, Mark Antony, Margaret, Abigail, Simon, Abigail (yes, again), Samuel Potter, Nancy Potter, John, Lydia, William, James, Levi, Mary, and Elizabeth. Though he never attained much personal wealth himself, the male children of Mark Antony and Abigail who survived into the 19th century made a fortune in the slave trade and tangential business interests.

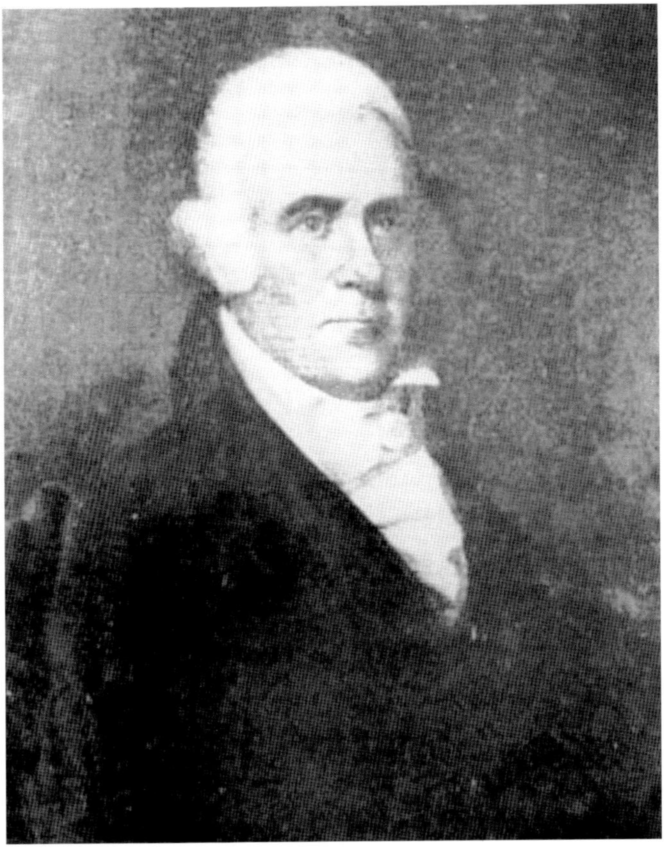

Family Values

In the late 1790s, James DeWolf found himself at the epicenter of a highly profitable syndicate in a business that changing times—and both the state and federal government—were seeking to ban. But with access to untold wealth, ships, a rum distillery, a sugar plantation, and everyone (including the president) in his back pocket, he simply battened down the hatches, further centralized operations, and kept doing what he'd been doing: making obscene amounts of money engaging in one of the most reprehensible businesses in 18th-century America—trading slaves.

Though one of the younger brothers, James (1764–1837) would become the wealthiest by far. He began his career working on a slaving vessel owned by John Brown of Providence, and by the age of 26, he had one of his own. He married Nancy, the daughter of William Bradford, who had an interest in a local rum distillery. He owned a plantation in Cuba, which served as both a source of sugar and an off-loading point for the slaves traded for rum in Africa.

The tighter restrictions of slaving became, the more James circled the wagons. When the federal government cracked down on the trade, he got his friend Thomas Jefferson to appoint his brother-in-law as customs collector at Bristol. When the feds confiscated one of the family ships, he kidnapped their agent and rowed him around to the other side of Mount Hope so he wouldn't be able to prevent one of DeWolf's loyal captains from reacquiring the vessel at auction.

Indicted for murder for throwing a slave infected with smallpox overboard, James was never charged, thanks to a federal official in Newport who claimed for four years that he could not find one of the most high-profile figures in a town less than 15 miles away.

James continued in the trade long after most Americans had renounced it, with recent research by historian Cynthia Mestad Johnson suggesting he never fully quit. James DeWolf served in the Rhode Island General Assembly from 1803 to 1820 and the US Senate from 1821 to 1825.

The Supporting Actor
William DeWolf (1764–1829), the supposedly pudgy and affable DeWolf brother, is on record as a co-owner (with James) of the waterfront warehouse that served as the center of the family slaving operation in Bristol at the end of the 18th century. William owned a number of ships in his own right as well as underwriting DeWolf family slaving expeditions as the principal of the Bristol Insurance Company.

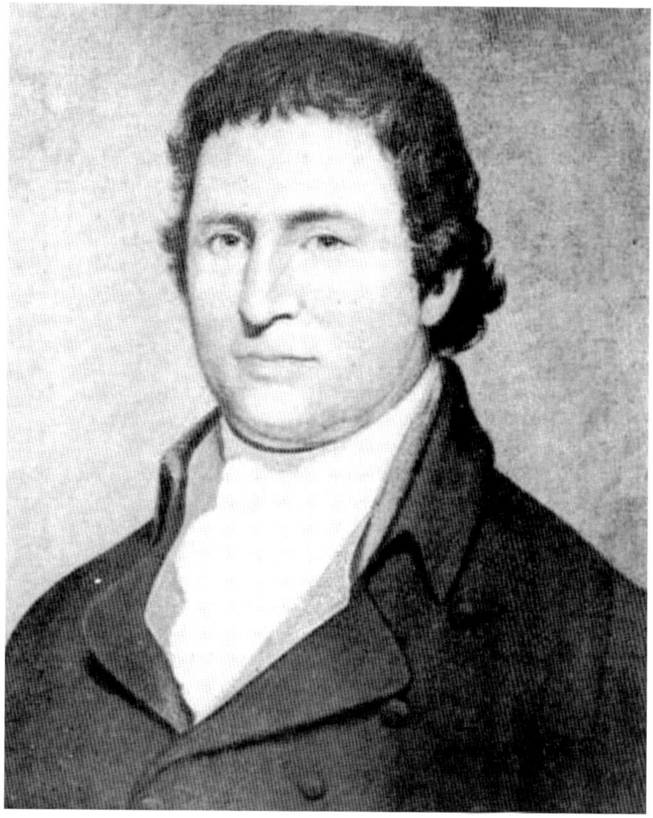

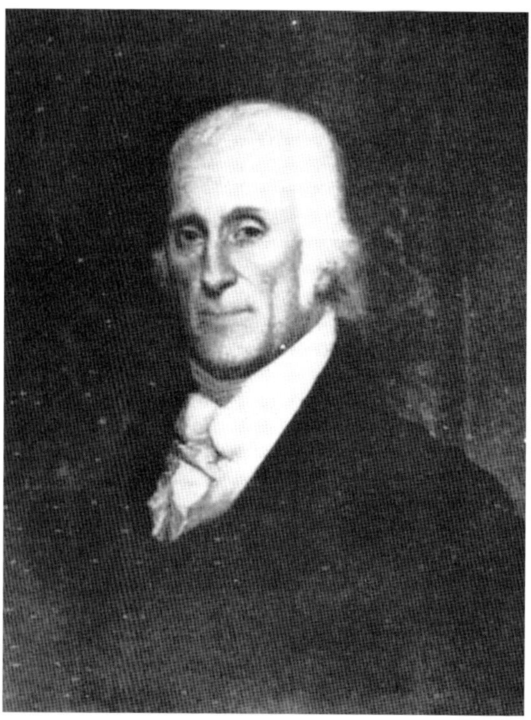

Rolling in It
Remembered by family chroniclers as even more greedy than James, Charles (1745–1820) is said to have once proved it, literally rolling in gold in his counting house in the company of the local Congregational minister.

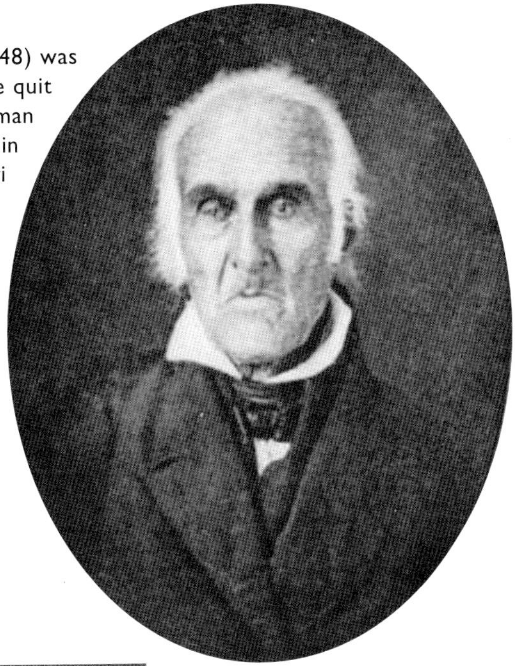

Quaker Levi?

Though family lore suggests that Levi (1766–1848) was so revolted by his single slaving voyage that he quit immediately, recent research suggests that the man his brothers called "Quaker Levi" was involved in the trade for much of his life. In his later years, Levi spent a good deal of time tending to the onions on his farm, which became the site of Juniper Hill Cemetery, the family burying ground.

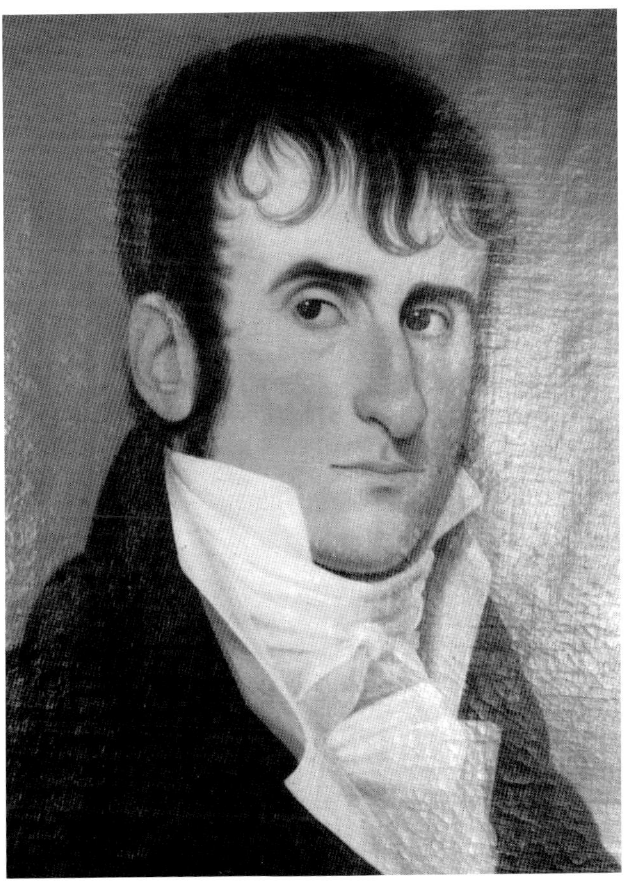

Carrying the Family Mantle

George (1778–1844) was the next generation: a son of the avaricious Charles and, like his father, a wealthy merchant, ship owner, and slave trader—though he never actually served on a voyage himself. His main interest was a sugar plantation in Cuba that he called Noah's Ark, where he personally held slaves. The fortune of Bristol was tied heavily to Noah's Ark, as many of its residents and relatives had invested in George's sugar empire. In 1825, George's crop failed, and banks and lenders called in their notes. George went down and took his family and Bristol with him. In December of that year, George packed his family and fled to Cuba in the middle of the night. When the news got out, the townspeople swarmed Linden Place, George's home, and left with everything that was not nailed down. (Courtesy of Linden Place.)

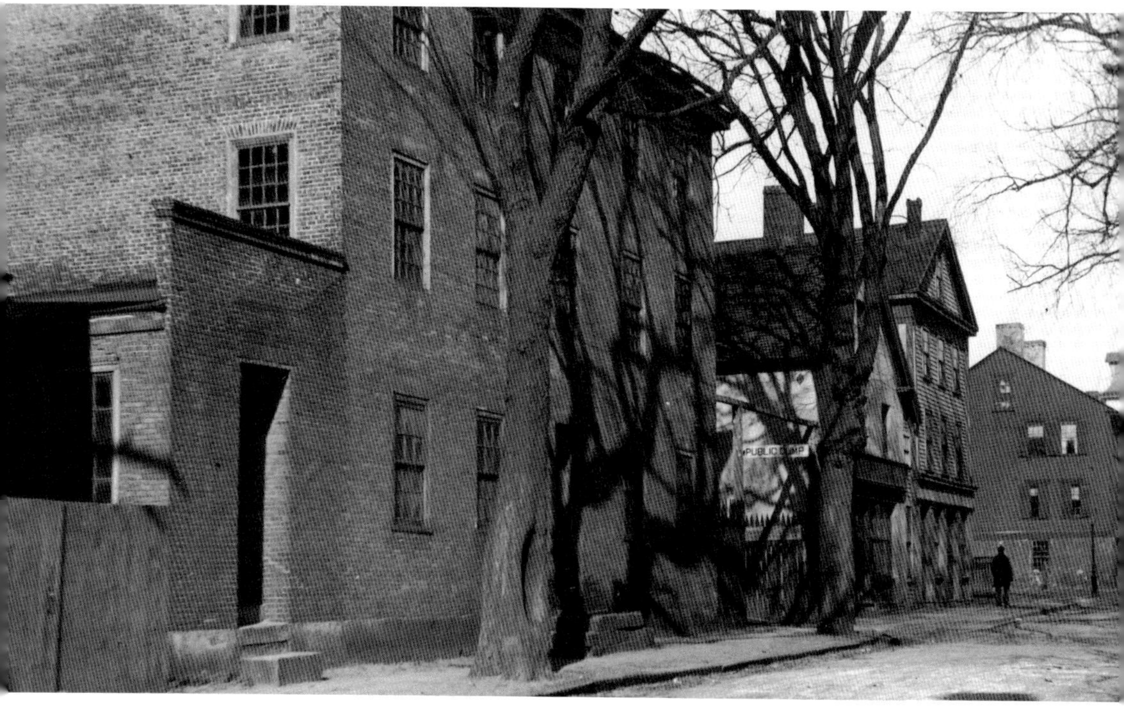

The Headquarters

The operational heart of the DeWolf family business was along this row of Thames Street buildings, as photographed around 1910. Here, the DeWolfs operated a rum distillery, a counting house, and a warehouse.

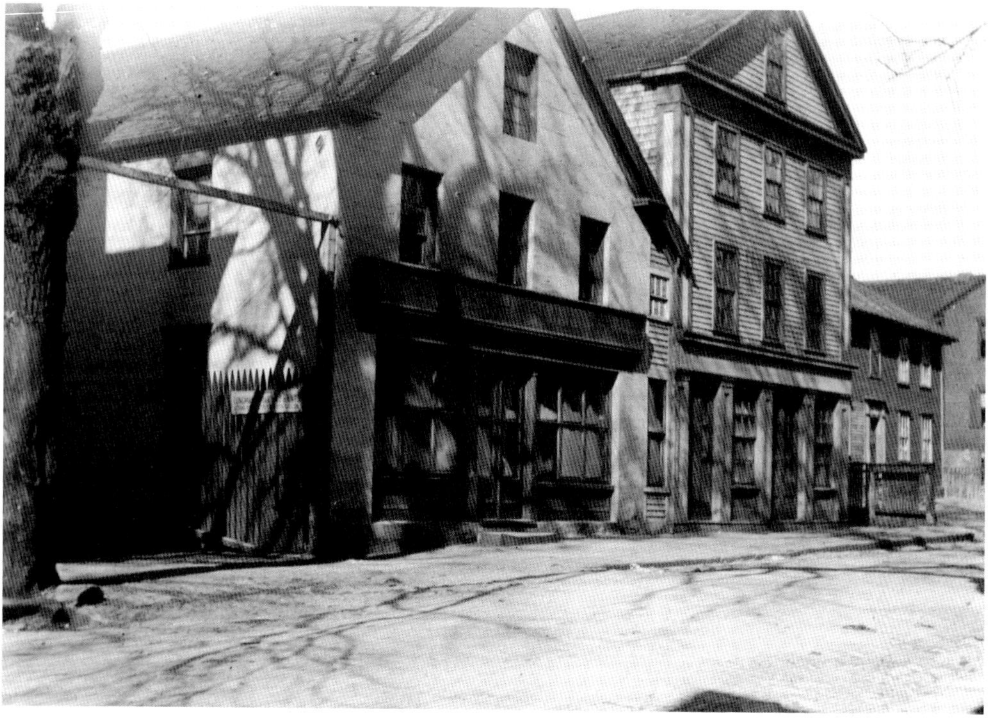

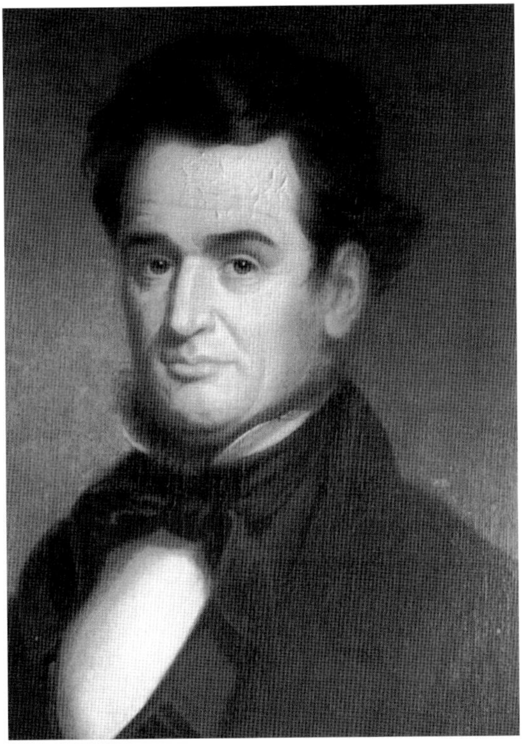

The Governor

Bristol-born Byron Diman (1795–1865) was a one-term Rhode Island governor, multi-term member of the Rhode Island House of Representatives, and a brigadier general in the state militia. A Law and Order Party candidate, Diman's election was shrouded in controversy when he was selected by the General Assembly after neither he nor the incumbent candidate received an electoral majority. Following his term as governor, Diman served three years in the state senate. In business, he prospered in mills and whaling, and prior to that, he worked for more than 20 years in a counting house—a skill that should have left him leaps and bounds more qualified than the average politician.

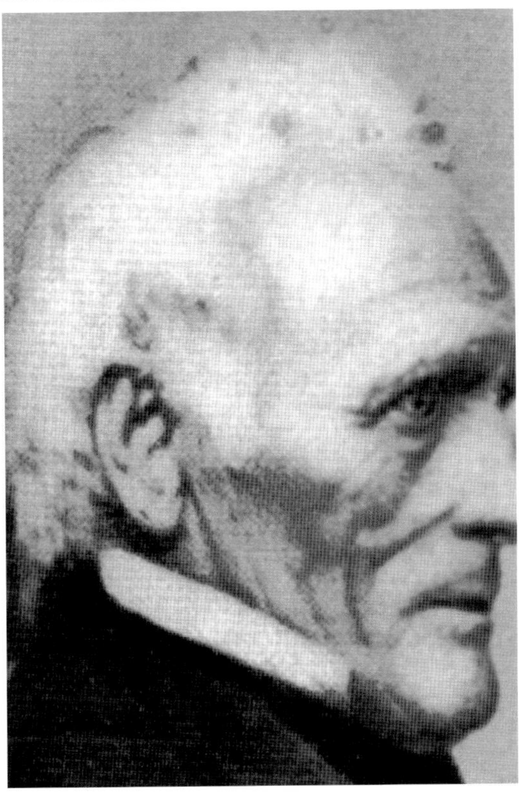

Melville's Muse

John DeWolf, who went by the swashbuckling nickname "Nor'west John," was a sailor, adventurer, and the first American to cross Siberia. He left Bristol in August 1804 and returned in April 1808. In the interim, his travels on board his ship *Juno* took him from Bristol around Cape Horn to Sitka, Alaska, and across Siberia. Reaching St. Petersburg, he caught a ship to Copenhagen and then another to Portland, Maine. Later in life, he married Nancy Melville, whose nephew Herman summered with the couple at their home at 620 Hope Street. It is said that Herman was very much influenced by his uncle's stories of maritime adventure, inspiring him to take his own whaling voyage and immortalize it in the novel *Moby Dick*—which references "Nor'west John" in chapter 45.

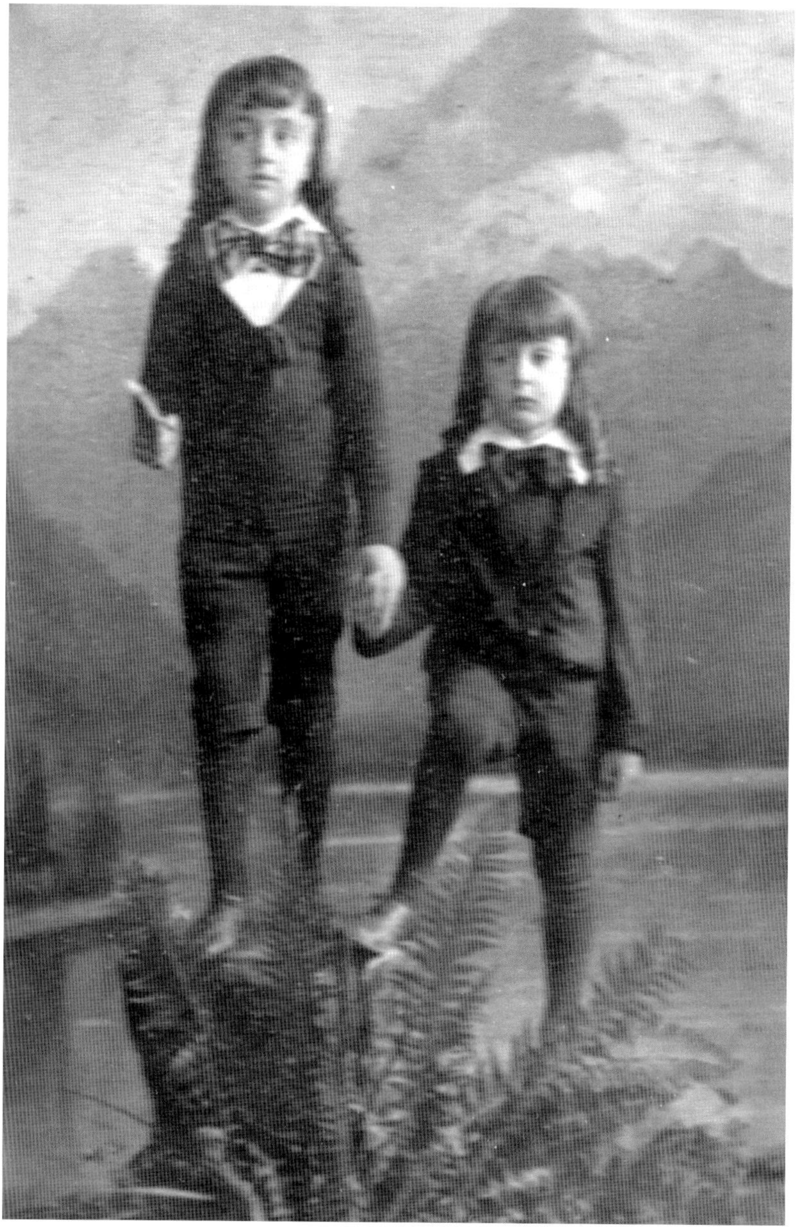

The Other Colt

Despite the enormous shadow cast by his successful younger brother, Samuel Pomeroy Colt, elder brother LeBaron Bradford Colt was a very accomplished man in his own right. Receiving an undergraduate degree from Yale and his law degree from Harvard, LeBaron did the obligatory year abroad before moving to Chicago to practice law. Before long, he returned to Bristol, established a firm in Providence, and began to serve as a state representative from Bristol in 1879. President Garfield selected him as judge of the federal court for the District of Rhode Island in 1881, then in 1884, President Arthur named him as the presiding justice for the First Circuit Court of Appeals. He was elected to succeed Nelson W. Aldrich in the US Senate in 1912 and reelected in 1918. He served in the senate until his death at Linden Place in 1924. Samuel (left) and LeBaron are pictured above as young boys. (Courtesy of Linden Place.)

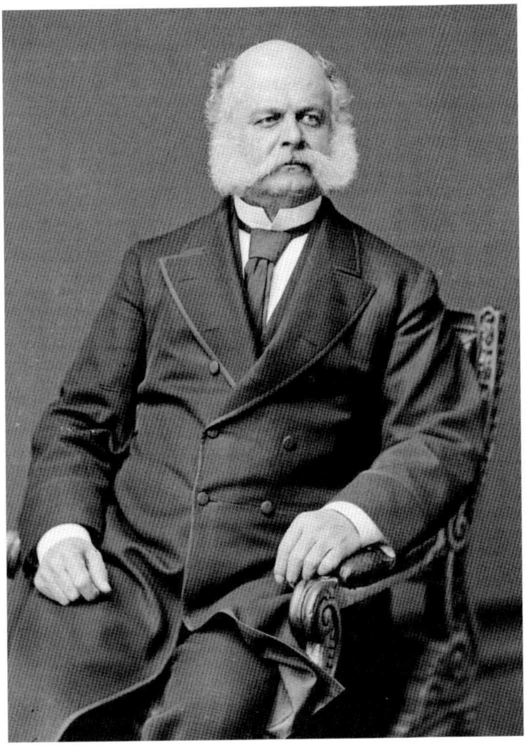

Major General, Governor, Antebellum Trendsetter

The world—and the 1970s in particular—thank him for his iconic contribution to facial hairstyles, but Ambrose Burnside (1824–1881) did more with his life than show off a hirsute jawline. Originally hailing from Indiana, Burnside settled in Bristol after serving in the Mexican-American War. He was commissioned colonel of the 1st Rhode Island Infantry at the start of the Civil War, rose to major general by March 1862, and took command of the Army of the Potomac in November 1862, a command he lost following a disastrous campaign at Fredericksburg. After the war, Burnside distinguished himself in both manufacturing and railroad concerns and served as governor of Rhode Island from 1866 to 1869 and as a Republican US Senator from 1874 until his death. The sideburns changed color from brown to gray to snowy white, but he wore them loud and proud until the end. (Courtesy of Cathy and Garry Holmsrom.)

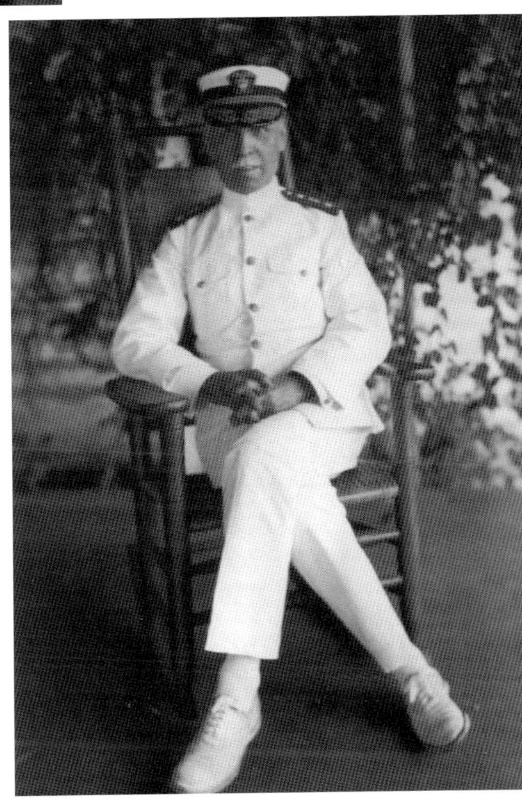

Naval Scientist

A native of Pennsylvania and a graduate of the Naval Academy at Annapolis, Rear Adm. John R. Edwards was a skilled and knowledgeable officer whose expertise in mechanical and steam engineering made him an invaluable asset to the Department of the Navy. He saw active duty during the Spanish-American War on board the *Puritan*, and in 1900, he was detailed to the Navy's Bureau of Steam Engineering. In the years to come, he would serve as chief engineer of the Portsmouth (New Hampshire) Navy Yard; inspector of machinery with William Cramp & Sons Company in Philadelphia, where US Navy vessels were constructed; and general inspector of machinery for the Navy on the Atlantic coast. He took mandatory retirement in 1915 due to his age but continued to take on special assignments from the Navy Department. He retired to Bristol with his wife, Harriet DeWolf Allen, becoming very involved in local affairs and serving as president of the Bristol School Board for several years.

Mr. Clean

John R. Edwards Jr. followed his father's path into the military, enlisting in the Army as a private. He would go on to become a first-class aviator and was sent to Tours and later to Assouan, France, where he attained the rank of first lieutenant in the 99th Aero Squadron and took part in extremely dangerous observation work. He also served as liaison officer for the French and American air forces. Older Bristolians will remember John as "Mr. Clean," an eccentric man-about-town who cleaned obsessively around the Hope Street home he shared with his wife, the former Marion Paull. The couple enjoyed regular meals at the Lobster Pot, where Edwards would keep his young nieces entertained by coloring on the place mats, much to his wife's (feigned) horror.

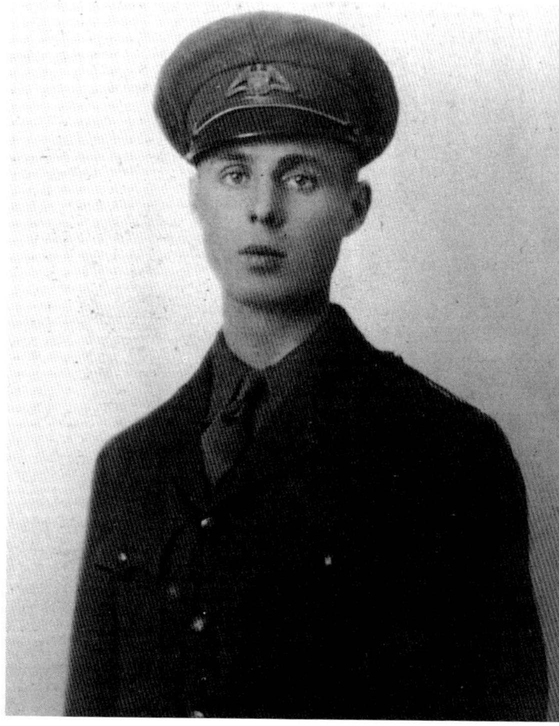

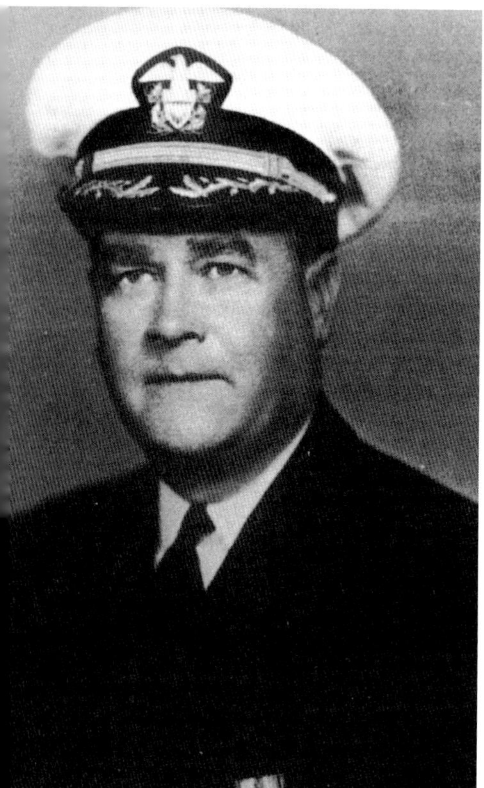

An Impossible Choice

Adm. Gilbert Hoover was a highly decorated US Naval veteran of two world wars and one of the first Americans involved in the development of the atomic bomb. Unfortunately, it was something he did not do that threatened to overshadow his otherwise sterling career. As Captain Hoover, he was at the helm of the light cruiser *Helena* alongside the ill-fated *Juneau* in the South Pacific in early 1942. Their task force engaged a Japanese submarine, which inflicted crippling damage and sank the *Juneau*. As acting commander of the task force, Captain Hoover led the remaining ships from the area and did not report their location, as he was operating under orders to maintain radio silence. An overhead B-17 failed to report in as well, resulting in the deaths of all but 10 members of the *Juneau* crew, which included the five Sullivan brothers of Waterloo, Iowa. For this action, he was removed from his command and ordered to New Mexico to work on the Manhattan Project. Nonetheless, it was conclusively determined that Captain Hoover acted appropriately under the circumstances and his decision to maintain radio silence was instrumental in the subsequent naval victory in the Pacific. The men who served under him remembered him as an honorable and skilled commanding officer. (Courtesy Naval Archives and Records Administration.)

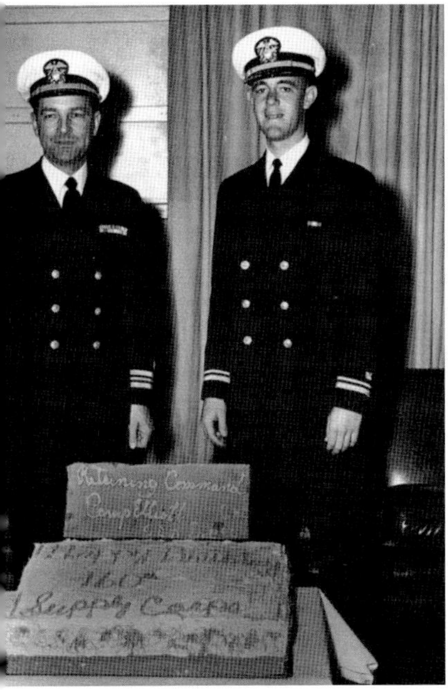

Lifelong Supporter of Education and the Arts
A native of San Francisco, Lt. Comdr. Alfred James Shepherd (1916–2006) joined the Navy as an apprentice seaman. He served in the Pacific in World War II and in Key West as an on-board communications officer during excursions with Pres. Harry Truman. After leaving the service, he became a counselor at Roger Williams University, beginning on the Providence campus in 1956 and moving with the college to the Bristol campus, recently established with land given the university by the Fulton family. Shepherd would retire in 1985 but remain supportive of the university throughout his life. Shepherd was also a financial supporter and member of numerous local causes and organizations, including Linden Place, Friends of Rogers Free Library, Redwood Library, Salve Regina University Circle of Scholars, Rhode Island Shakespeare Society, Blithewold Gardens and Arboretum, Herreshoff Marine Museum, Haffenreffer Museum of Anthropology, and the Bristol Historical and Preservation Society. He is shown here as a young offer, at left, with an unidentified colleague. (Courtesy of Cathy and Garry Holmstrom.)

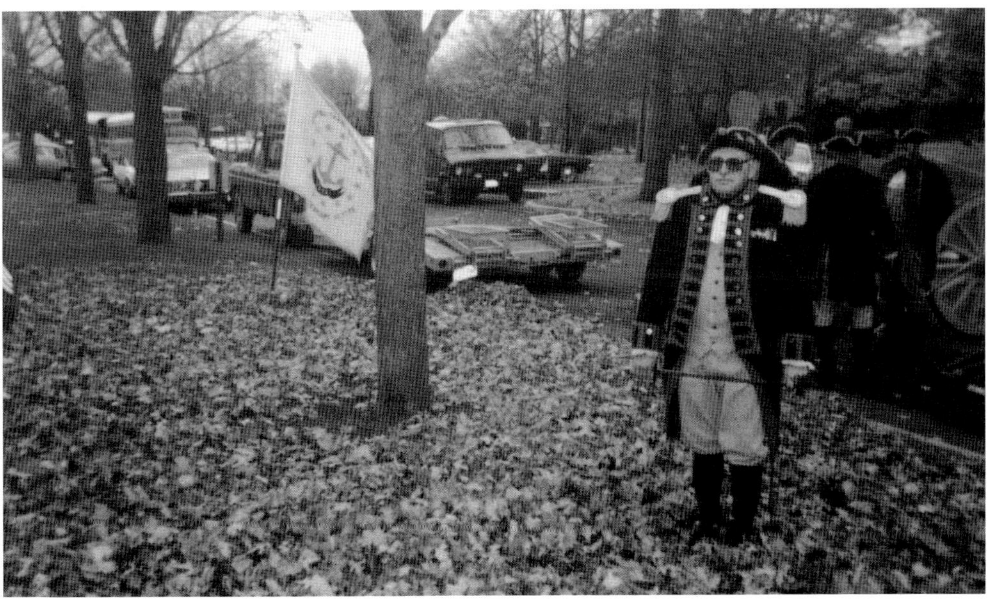

Seven Decades in Uniform
For years, Brig. Gen. Everett T. Francis (1921–2011) was the face of the Bristol Train of Artillery, a Rhode Island militia artillery unit chartered on February 12, 1776, and active since its inception. Born in Bristol, Francis served in the Pacific during World War II with the US Army 295th Assault Signal Company and was awarded the Silver and Bronze Stars and a Purple Heart. He was also a successful local businessman, and he owned and operated Francis Brothers Reality; ELJ, Inc.; A-Blast, Inc.; and the Bristol Golf Club. But Bristol will always remember his bearing and the figure he cut in his uniform, presiding over countless parades and veterans' events over the years, such as this one on the grounds of the Veterans' Home around 1980. (Courtesy of Rogers Free Library.)

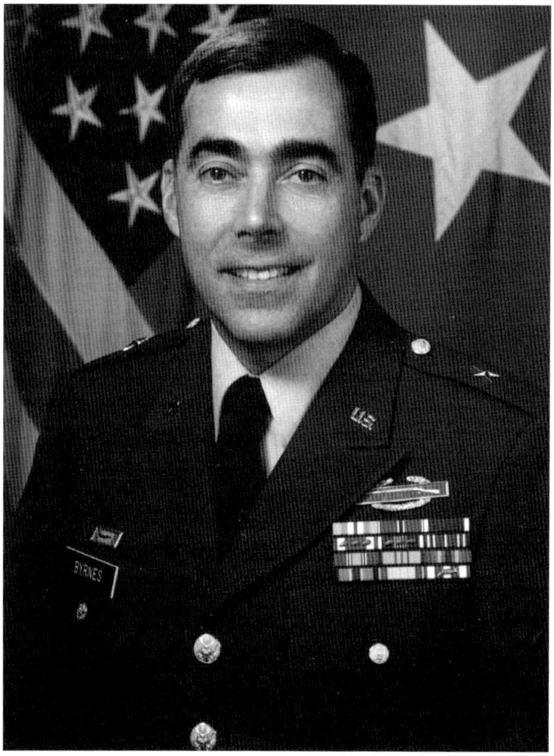

Bristol's China Connection
Michael T. Byrnes has made a career out of Chinese-American relations and business. After 30 years in the US Army, some of which was spent assigned to the US Embassy in Beijing as the defense attaché to both China and Mongolia, Byrnes retired as a major general. Since his retirement, he has served as the president for Tyco International, China, and prior to that as vice president for China operations at Rockwell Automation. Byrnes was active in community affairs and served on the board of the Beijing-American Chamber of Commerce as well as the boards of several US-invested enterprises in China. He has been no less active since returning to his hometown, where he and his wife, Marie, have made a business dealing and consulting in Chinese decorative arts, and Byrnes has taken on a leadership role in local economic development, spearheading the Explore Bristol initiative. (Courtesy of Michael T. Byrnes.)

Homecoming King
Navy pilot Porter Halyburton was 24 years old with a wife, infant daughter, and 75 combat missions under his belt when his F-4B Phantom was shot down near Hanoi in October 1965. His daughter would be seven years old before Halyburton finally returned to the United States in 1973, following years as a prisoner of war in both the "Heartbreak Hotel" and "Hanoi Hilton." A native of the South, Halyburton was imprisoned with Fred Cherry, the first black officer to be captured by the North Vietnamese. Their captors hoped racism would help break the two cell mates; instead, the Americans forged a bond, recounted by author James S. Hirsch in the book *Two Souls Indivisible*, that would sustain both men throughout their captivity. Halyburton and his wife, Marty, had two more children following his return, and they raised their family in Bristol while he taught at the Naval War College in Newport until retiring to North Carolina in 2006. (Courtesy of Porter Halyburton.)

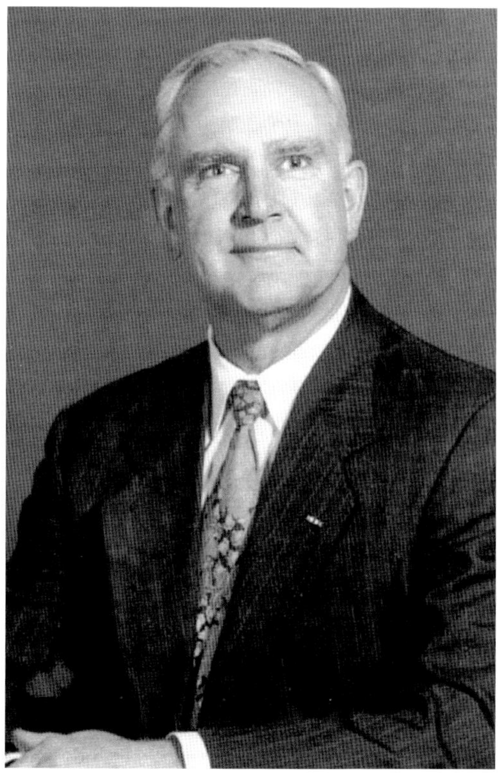

CHAPTER TWO

Business, Great and Small

When it comes to community cohesion, business is the business. Whether it is Samuel Colt, whose factory's labor demand lured employees from Europe, or a little kid with a lemonade stand and a dream, the community is better off for the commerce created. Bristol has benefitted tremendously from the harbor, which provided ready access to trade routes in past centuries and today draws the profitable tourist trade. Both Bristol Harbor and the waters beyond have been a gold mine of fish and shellfish and an indispensable proving ground for boats ranging from classic Herreshoff yachts to superfast offshore racing boats. Still, some of the oldest businesses in Bristol could just as easily be in Omaha, but they have thrived here for generations, and in a couple of cases, more than a century. The most enduring businesses will always be the ones that are organically part of the community, and by blooming where they are planted, they strengthen their community's bottom line—and hopefully their own as well.

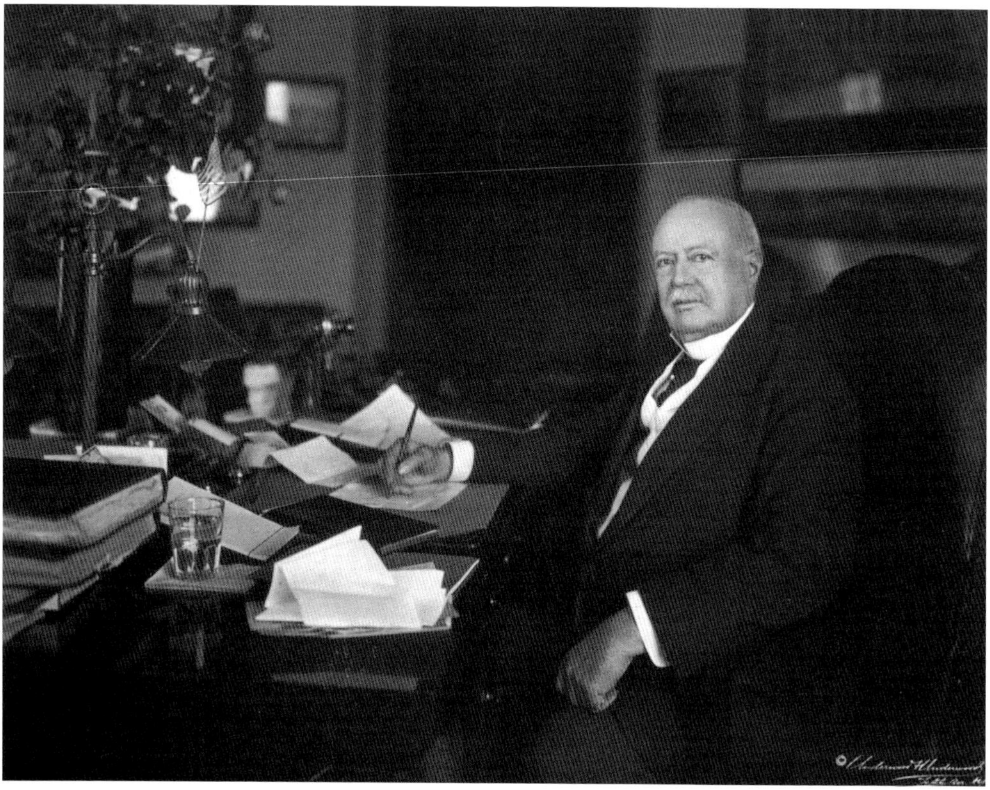

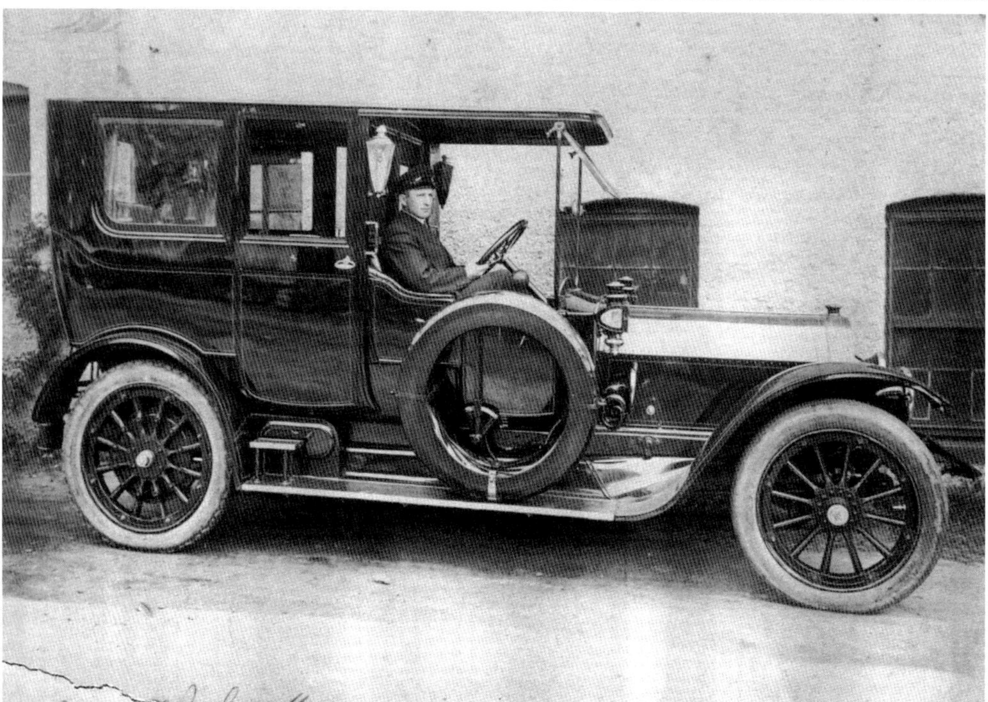
Samuel J Smith · S P Colt 1912 FIAT

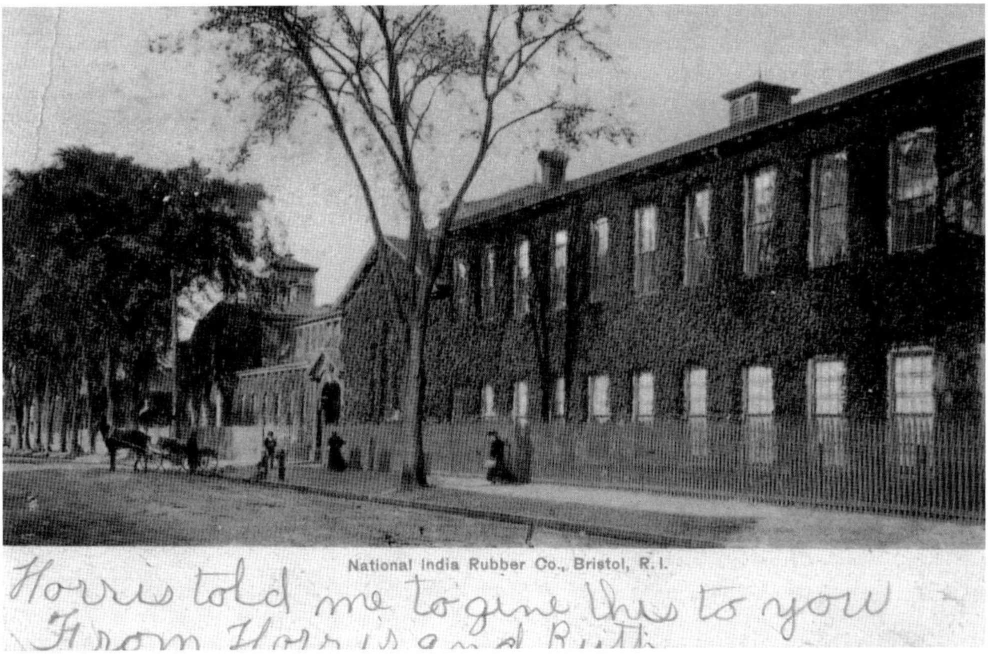

The Rubber Baron

Samuel Pomeroy Colt (1852–1921), seen at his desk and the epicenter of his empire, was a very impressive man. Born into privilege, he was blessed with a formidable mind and an abundance of business acumen. Graduating from the Massachusetts Institute of Technology in 1873 and from Columbia Law School in 1876, Samuel (or "Pom" as he was known) entered private law practice in 1877, partnering with his brother LeBaron and Francis Colwell.

A foray into politics met with limited success, but it was in business that Colt truly excelled. He established the Industrial Trust Company in 1886 and grew it into the state's largest financial institution (it would eventually become Fleet Bank after Colt's death and was acquired by Bank of America in 2004.) Appointed receiver for Gov. Augustus O. Bourne's bankrupt National Rubber Company of Bristol in 1887, Colt had other plans. He took over, reorganized, and renamed it the National India Rubber Company. Through a series of mergers, it soon became the US Rubber Company. As the head of one of the world's largest rubber interests, Colt could afford to indulge his hobbies, including collecting luxury automobiles.

Samuel Colt shared much of his wealth with the people of Bristol, building and endowing the Colt Memorial High School in memory of his mother, Theodora, for whom he also purchased Linden Place, her childhood home. (All, courtesy of Linden Place.)

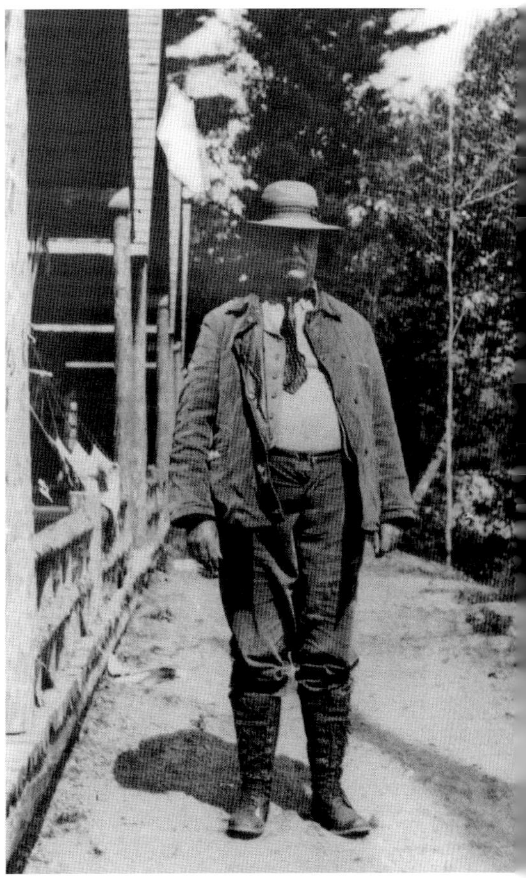

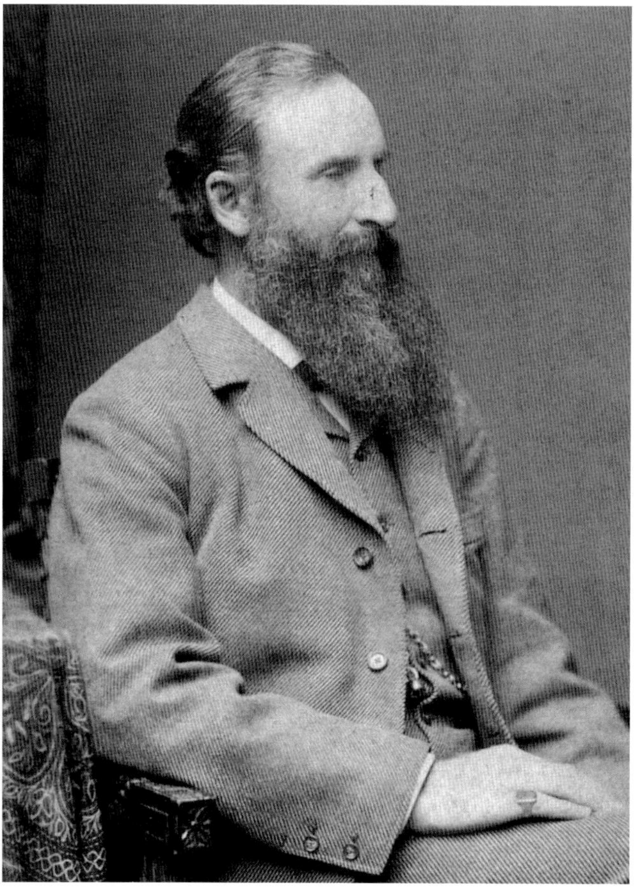

The Boatbuilding Visionary
Though Nathanael gets majority credit for being the principal designer of seven America's Cup defenders, it was his elder brother John Brown Herreshoff (1841–1915) who ran the business end of the Herreshoff Manufacturing Company for 37 years after the brothers cofounded the firm in 1878. "J.B.," as he was called, laid the foundation for the Herreshoff Company with early technical work on US Navy craft, and he also built boats on his own for 15 years prior to teaming up with his brother. An excellent administrator, J.B.'s accomplishments are impressive, and even more so when one learns that he was blind by the age of 14, losing one eye to disease and another to an accident. (Both, courtesy of the Herreshoff Marine Museum.)

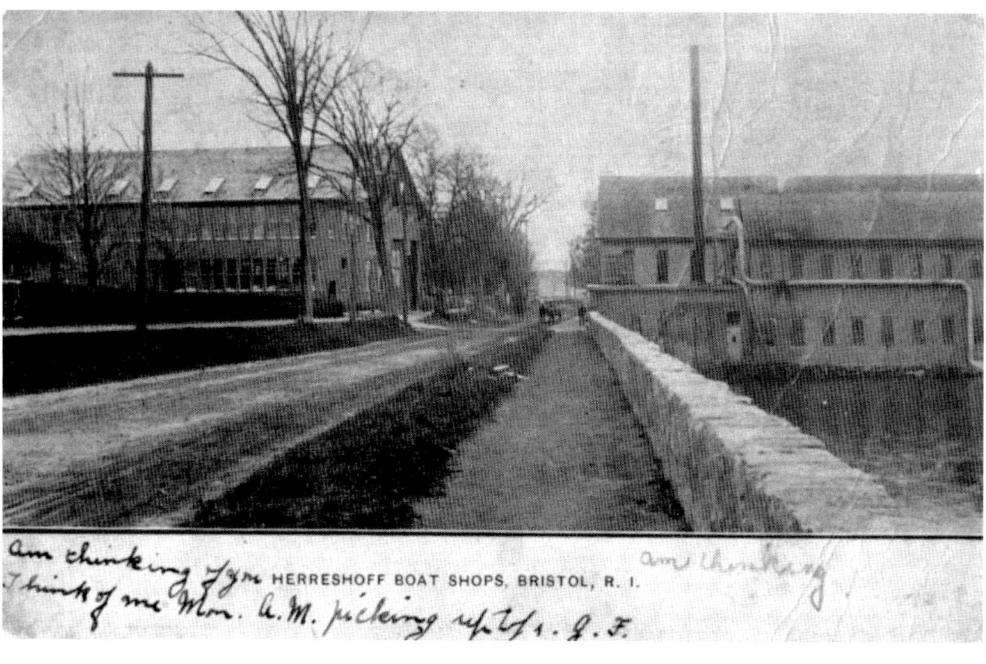

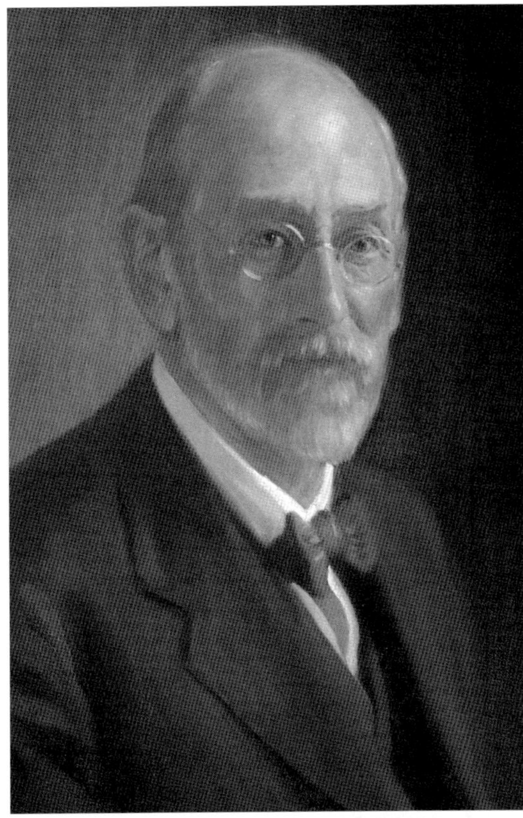

The Wizard of Bristol

Capt. Nathanael Greene Herreshoff designed every defender of the America's Cup from *Vigilant* in 1893 to *Resolute* in 1920, and the Herreshoff Manufacturing Company, owned with his brother J.B., built them all. Herreshoff was not just a good yacht designer, he was the first and last word in yacht design, and his innovative creations earned him the moniker "the Wizard of Bristol." Trained as an engineer at the Massachusetts Institute of Technology, Herreshoff was equally successful in designing boats large and small, power and sail, even receiving the first American patent for a catamaran.

Herreshoff Laborers

While J.B. and Nat were the brains behind the Herreshoff Manufacturing Company, the brawn was the hundreds and hundreds of workers, skilled and unskilled, who toiled on the docks year after year building Bristol's storied Herreshoff legacy. (Courtesy of the Herreshoff Marine Museum.)

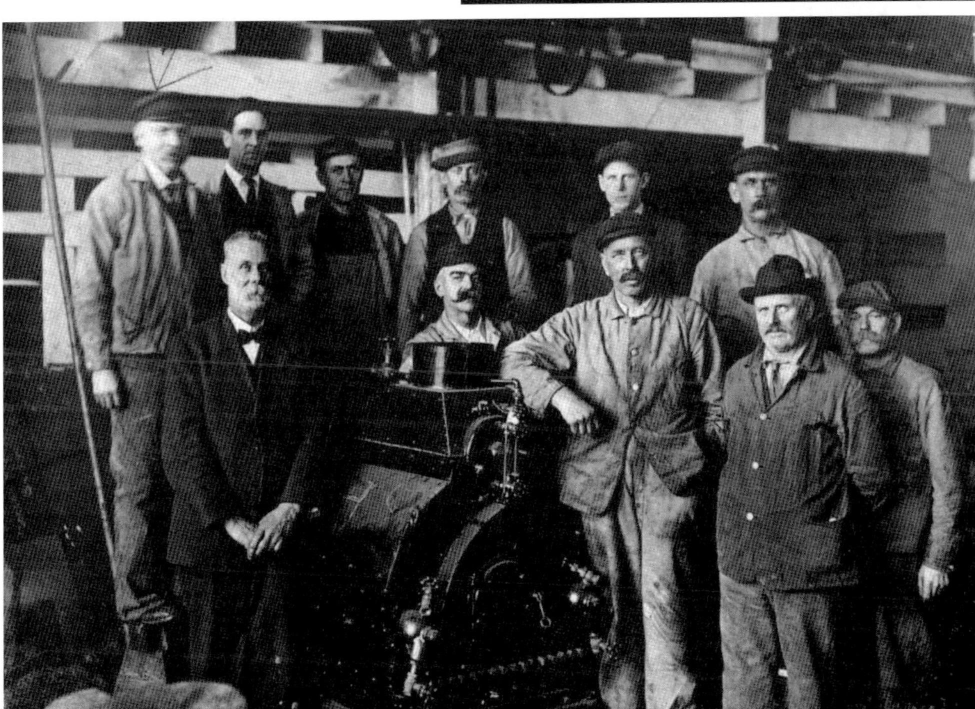

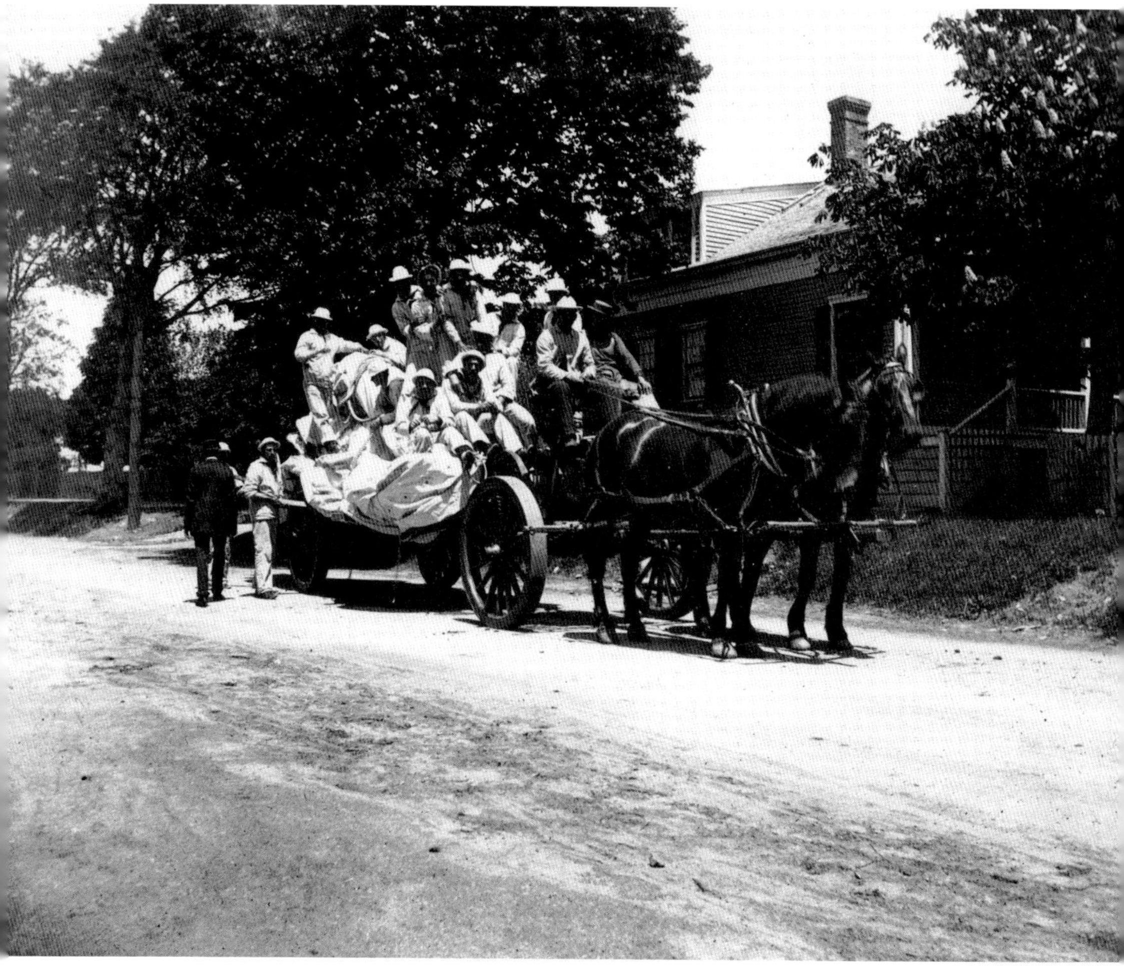

Taking Out the Laundry

Herreshoff-built America's Cup yachts were enormous, and enormous boats have enormous sails—sails that, when wet, need to spread out on a sunny lawn to dry. Back in the day, there was only one accessible piece of property that had the footage to dry an outsized sail, and that was Blithewold. Happily, the Van Wickle-McKee family was glad to help a neighbor. It is unclear if the sail pictured above was on its way to or from Blithewold. The photograph may have been taken during the 1899 *Columbia* campaign, when a collapsed mast sent the mainsail into the water, or during the 1920s campaign when the sail of *Resolute* needed to dry out. (All, courtesy of the Herreshoff Marine Museum.)

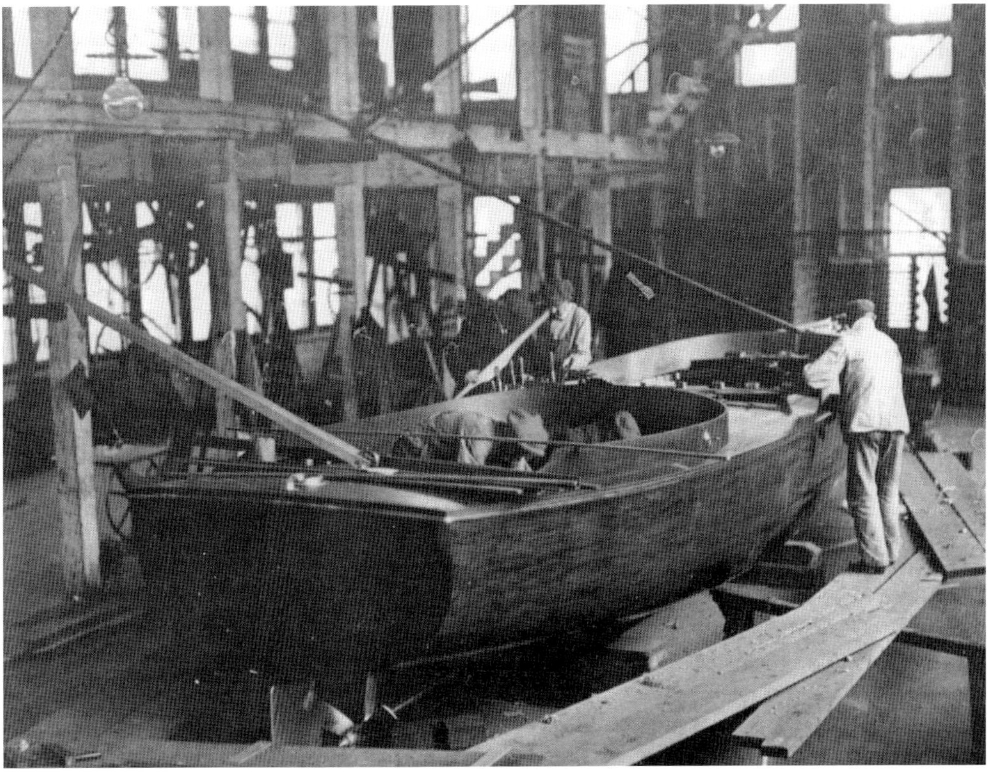

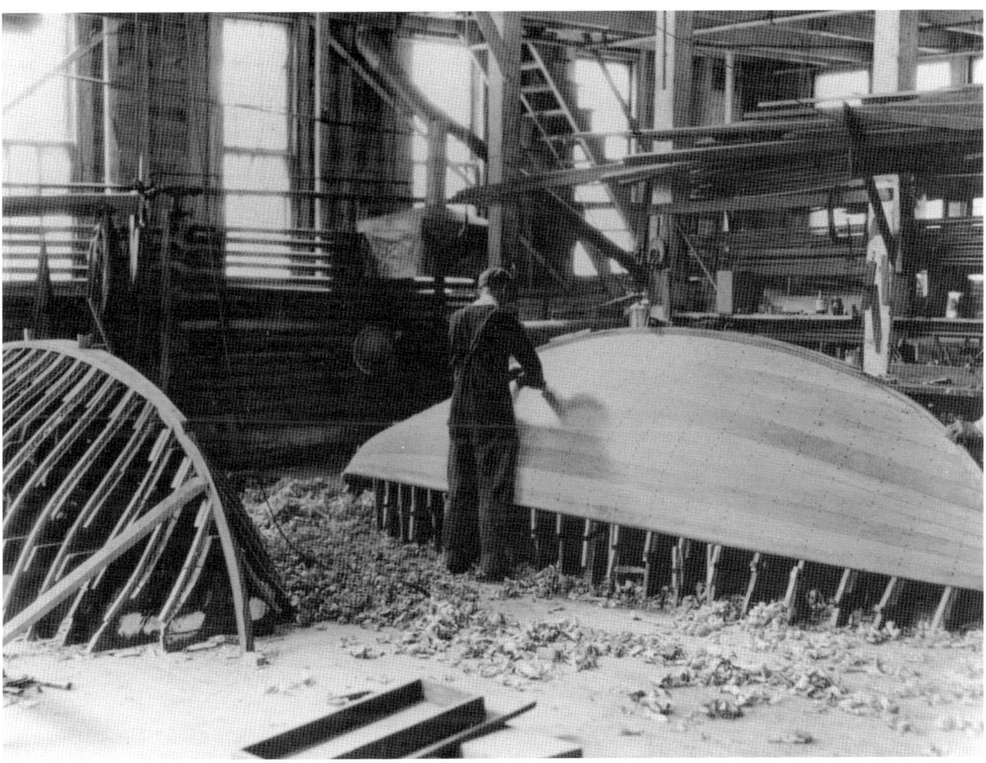

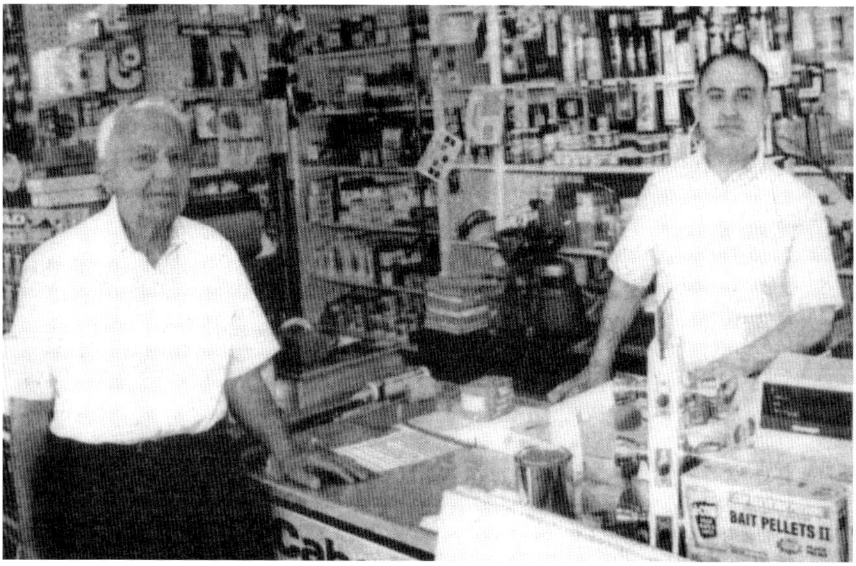

What You Want, They've Got

Union Commercial opened its Wood Street doors on August 10, 1910. The name came from a commercial union of five emigrants from Atriani, Italy, of which Thomas Pansa was one. The bottom image shows Thomas and his son, Andrew, in the 1930s, and the above photograph, considerably more recent, shows Andrew with his son and current proprietor, Andrew Jr. It's one place where time does seem to stand still a little bit, and that's a wonderful thing. Union Commercial's storefront is small, but as anyone who shops there regularly can attest, looks are deceiving. Go in and ask for something. Pansa may turn around, vanish stage left, or step out a back door, but he will be back in a flash—and not empty-handed, either. How does he do that? Pansa shrugs. "Once you have been in business a few years, you tend to know what people want," he smiles. (Both, courtesy of Andrew Pansa.)

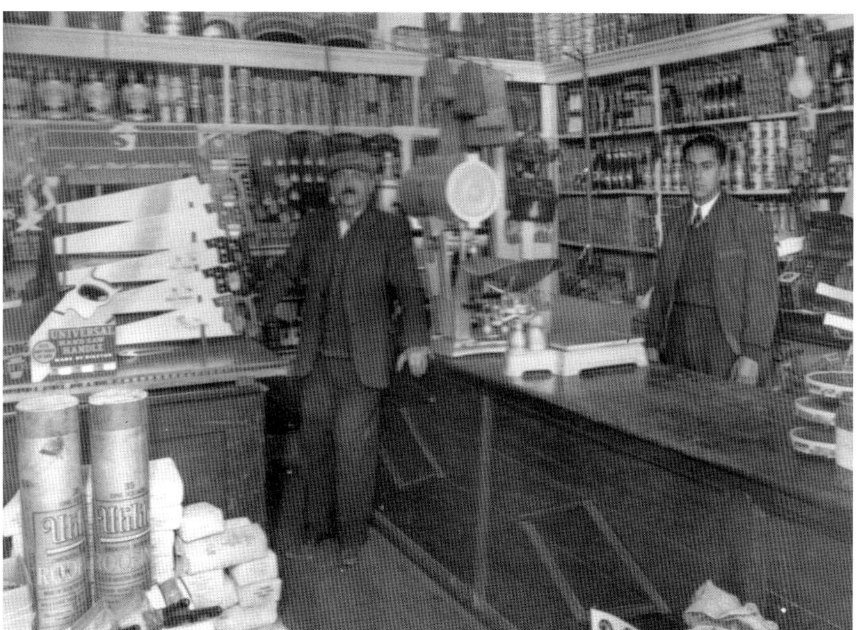

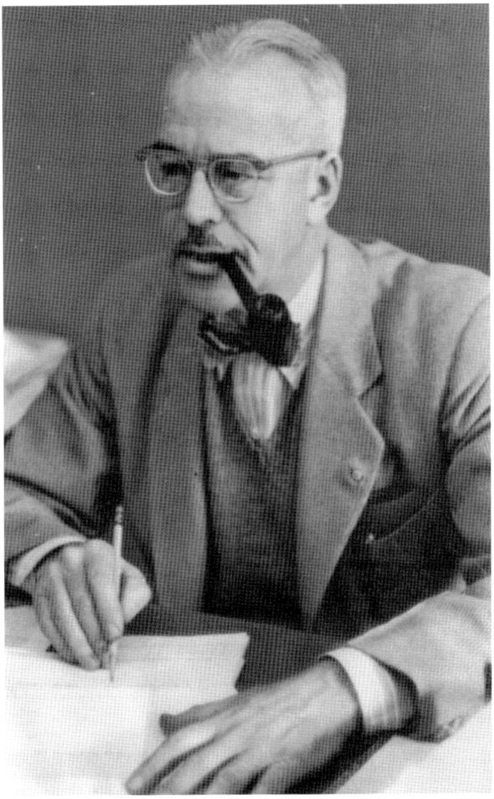

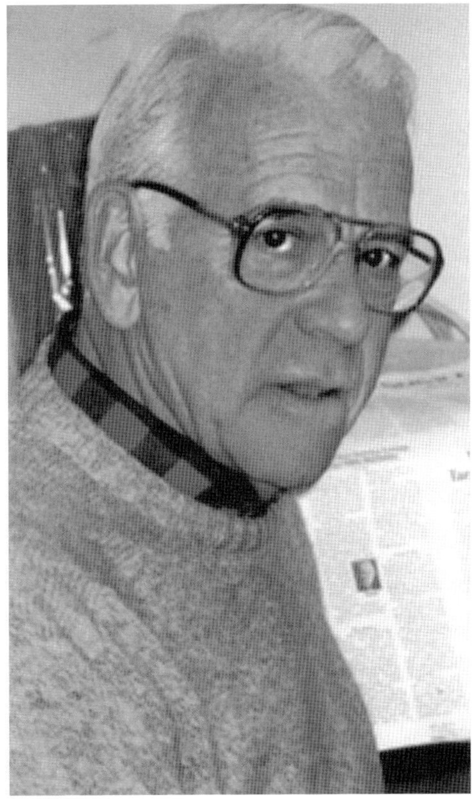

Great Communicators

Roswell Bosworth Sr. (left) was editor of the *Bristol Phoenix* for 44 years and publisher of East Bay Newspapers until his retirement in 1973. Bosworth moved to Rhode Island from Bangor, Maine, as a child; his first job was delivering papers. A teacher and principal, he worked for the *Phoenix* for many summers before purchasing the company in 1929.

Bosworth's son, Ros Bosworth Jr. (right), likewise spent 50 years with East Bay Newspapers and was publisher for more than 25 of them. Under the younger Bosworth's leadership, the *Barrington Times*, the *Warren Times*, the *Sakonnet Times*, and the *East Bay Classifieds* were added to the brand.

Both men were founding members of the New England Press Association, and Bosworth Jr. was cofounder of the Rhode Island Newspaper Group. Bosworth Sr. has been named to the Rhode Island Journalism Hall of Fame. (Both, courtesy of Ros Bosworth Jr.)

An Idea Whose Time had Come

It used to be that there was no such thing as a group medical practice. General practitioners lived in relative isolation, taking office visits and making house calls. For Dr. Charles Millard of Warren, by the late 1950s, the practice of being on call 24 hours a day, seven days a week, had become exhausting—so much so that Millard would occasionally drive out of town and check himself into a hotel so he could catch up on sleep. Then one day he approached Dr. Paul Botelho of Bristol, and they talked about forming a medical group, bringing in Dr. Robert Drew of Barrington and a surgeon, Dr. John Bernardo. They also hired Dr.

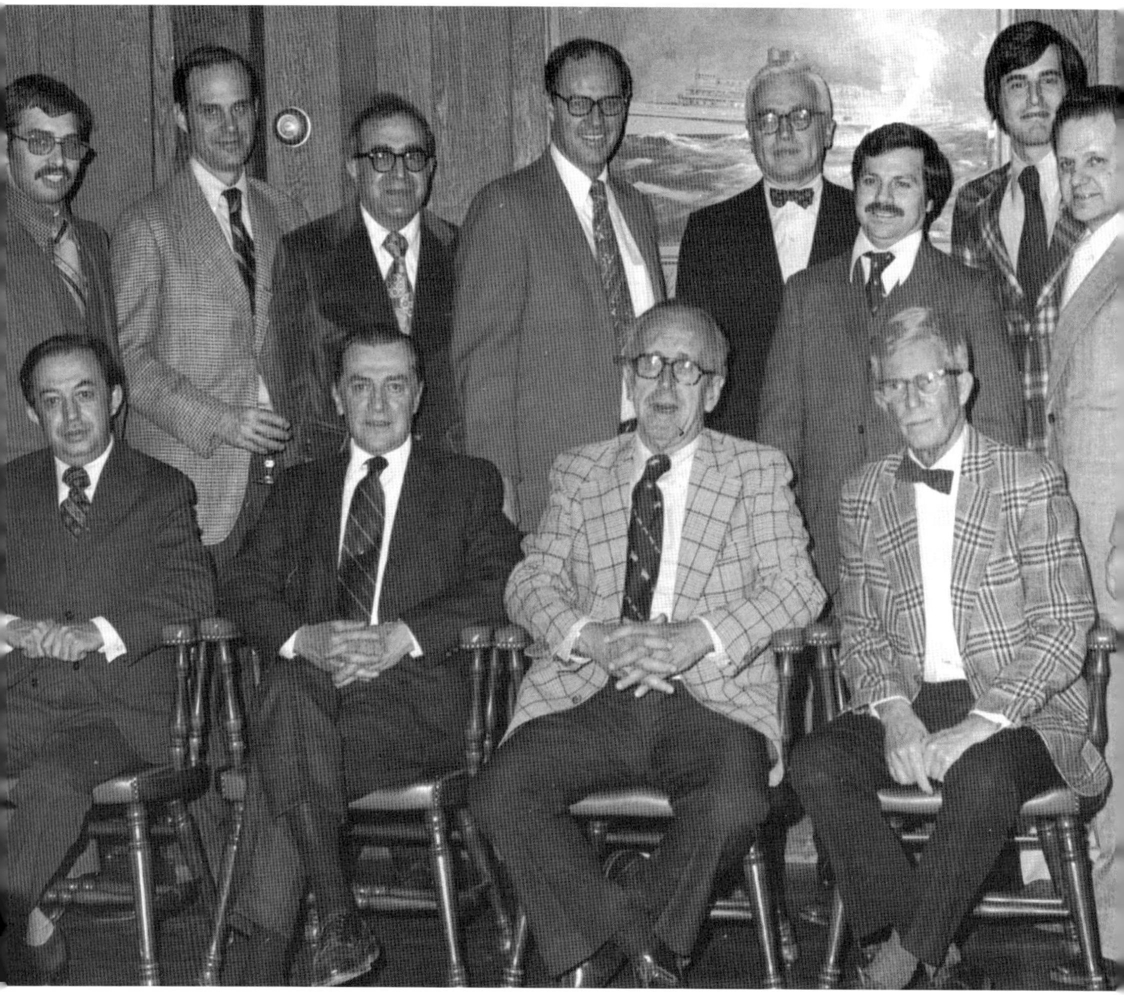

Victor de Medeiros, who was fluent in Portuguese, and opened their doors on Saturday, February 16, 1963. Dr. Manuel DaSilva joined the practice that July. That was 50 years ago, and the rest is history. Today, the Bristol County Medical Center is the largest private clinic in the state of Rhode Island, with more than 50 practicing physicians. The photograph at left, taken around 1980, includes (first row) Dr. Botelho, Dr. Holdsworth, Dr. Millard, and Dr. Drew; (second row) Dr. Reuter, Dr. Scott, Dr. Darakjian, Dr. Gibson, Dr. MacKenzie, Dr. Capezian, physician assistant Joseph Massaro, and Dr. DaSilva. In the photograph below, Dr. Millard is consulting with unidentified members of the Bristol County Medical Center staff.

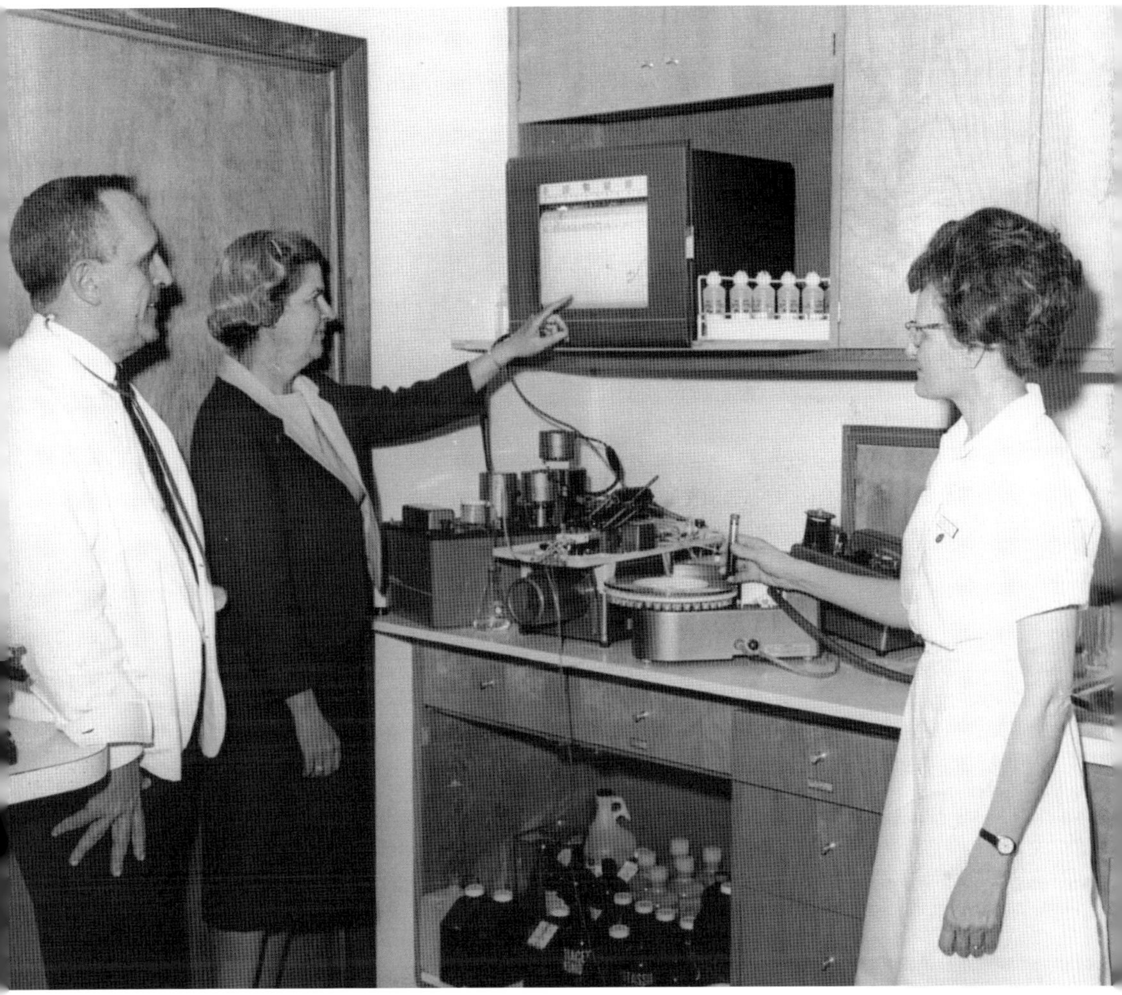

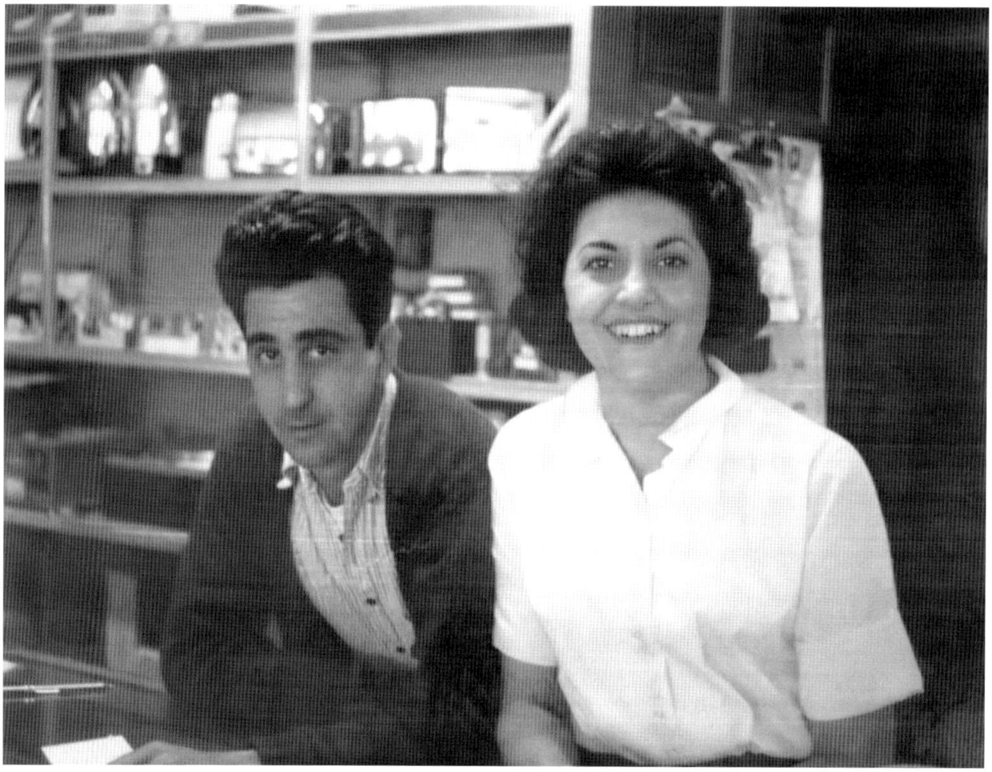

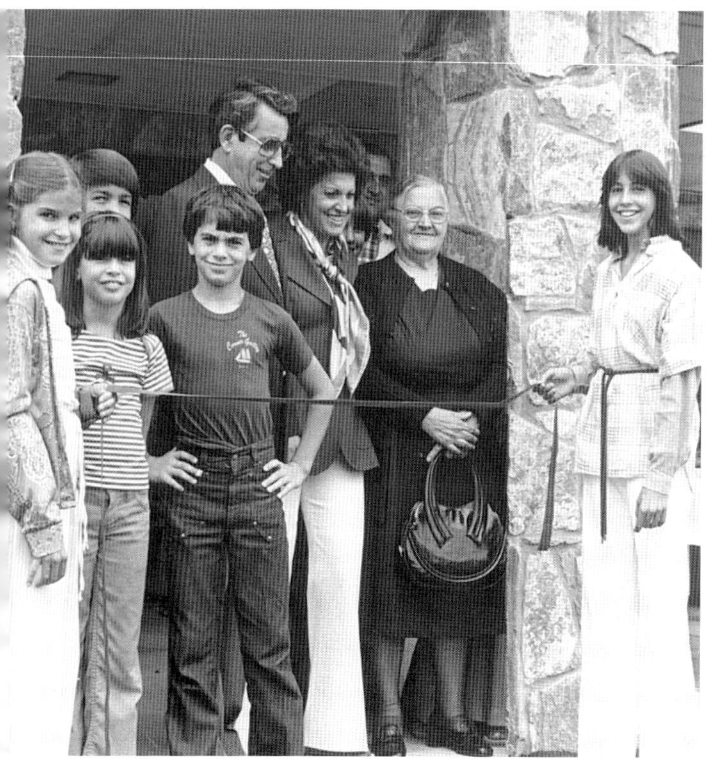

Family Business
Sisters Lisa Sienkiewicz and Gail Parella are co-owners of Gil's Television and Appliances, a business started by their parents, Gil and Sarah Almeida (above), in 1961. Lisa and Gail grew up in the business—often right in the store—taking it over in 1997. Ever since their doors opened, Gil's has been an integral part of the community, providing customers with the best-priced products and superior service. Gil's has consistently assisted local nonprofits with sponsorships, donations, and support. The people of Gil's—Lisa and husband Frank Sienkiewicz, Gail and husband Joe Parella, and their children—are engaged neighbors and friends, active in their school communities and local sports and civic organizations. At left, Gail is pictured far left and Lisa is far right. (Both, courtesy of Lisa Sienkiewicz and Gail Parella.)

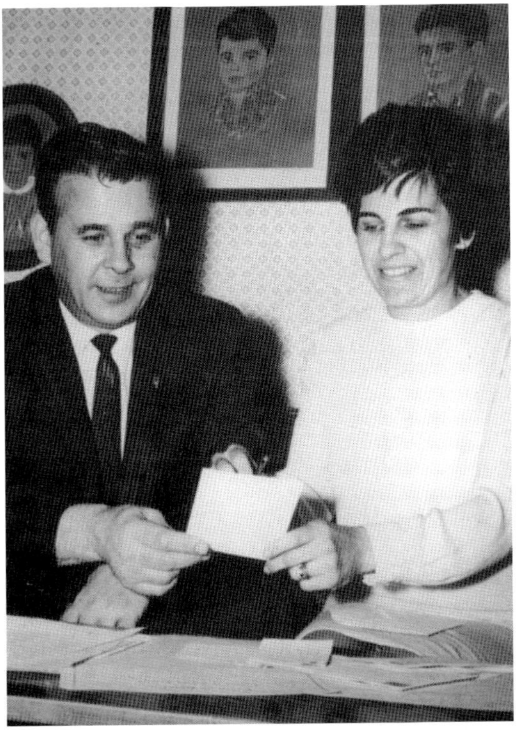

Anchoring Downtown for More Than 30 Years

Edward and Leonora Costa married in 1946 after meeting in classic Bristol fashion. Walking home from lunch following the morning shift at the former Collins & Aikman factory, Leonora saw something that caught her eye outside the YMCA. Back at work, she described this "handsome guy" to her coworkers, one of whom announced, "that's my cousin" and facilitated an introduction. The rest is history. The couple bought Duffy's in 1956. Ed was tending bar at the Belvedere Hotel when he saw that a barbershop was for sale next door to Duffy's. Duffy was an old man with a soda fountain, very little inventory, a shop that was falling apart, and one contingency: he wouldn't sell unless they kept the name. The Costas agreed, combined the two properties, and opened Duffy's as a newsstand and variety shop, selling hobbies, newspapers and magazines, and a little of everything else, until they retired in 1987. (Both, courtesy of Leonora Costa.)

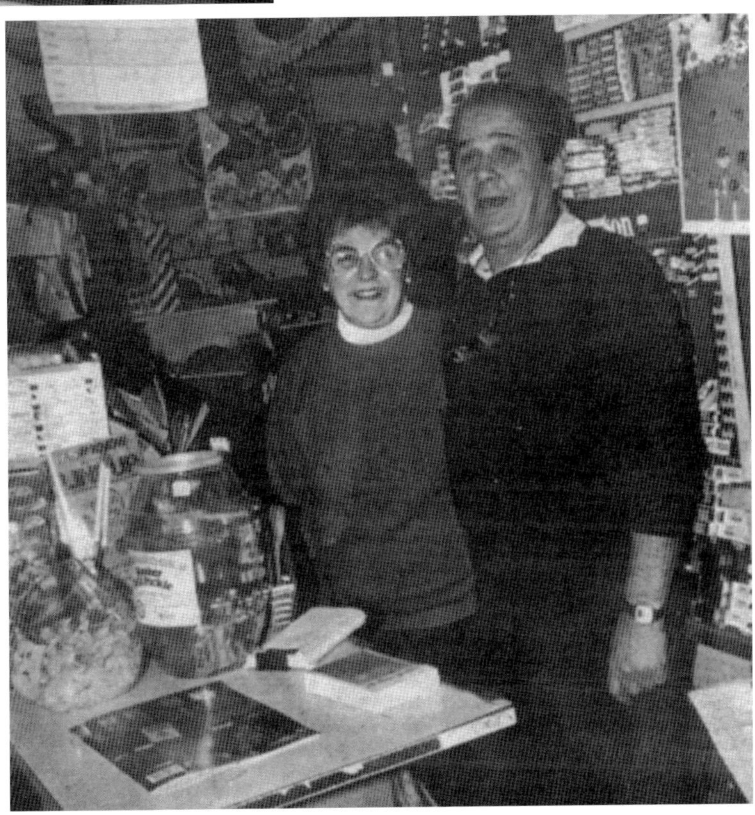

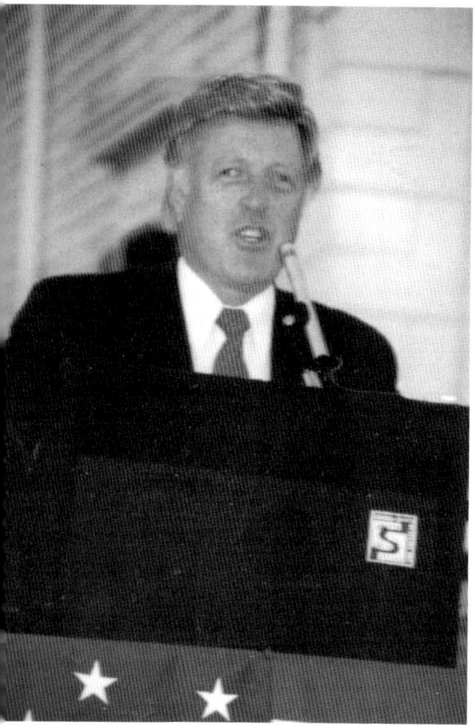

An Iron in Every Fire

The youngest person ever to attain the rank of full professor at Providence College, Dr. Patrick Conley also practices law and manages a real estate development business. He has served as chairman of the Rhode Island Bicentennial Commission (ri76), chairman and founder of the Providence Heritage Commission, chairman and founder of the Rhode Island Publications Society, and general editor of the Rhode Island Ethnic Heritage Pamphlet Series. In 1977, he founded the Rhode Island Heritage Commission as a successor organization to ri76. Dr. Conley was also chairman of the Rhode Island Bicentennial (of the Constitution) Foundation and chairman of the US Constitution Council. In May 1995, he was inducted into the Rhode Island Heritage Hall of Fame—one of a handful of living Rhode Islanders who have been accorded that honor. Presently he is president of the Rhode Island Heritage Hall of Fame, president of the Heritage Harbor Museum, and chairman of the Rhode Island Senior Olympics. Conley has published 18 books and written more than a score of scholarly articles on history, law, ethnic studies, religion, and political science. (Courtesy of Patrick Conley.)

Great Food, Great Prices

When people are in the restaurant business, Manny Rego will tell them, "You can do anything you want, have any gimmick you want. But the people will make the decision for you." Rego, the proprietor of Van's Spa on Wood Street, has his gimmick—and it's not this funny plastic wig (no, that's not his real hair). Van's serves good food cheap—that's it. To call this establishment unassuming is an enormous understatement. Customers seat themselves, pour their own coffee, and bus their own tables. That's not part of anyone's gimmick though, it's just out of consideration for Manny, who spends enough time on his feet as it is. The college crowd fills the message boards with praise. "If there's a better place to go in the Bristol area on a lazy Sunday or to handle a hangover, I haven't found it," one regular claimed. "Frankly, I don't think I ever will." (Courtesy of Manny Rego.)

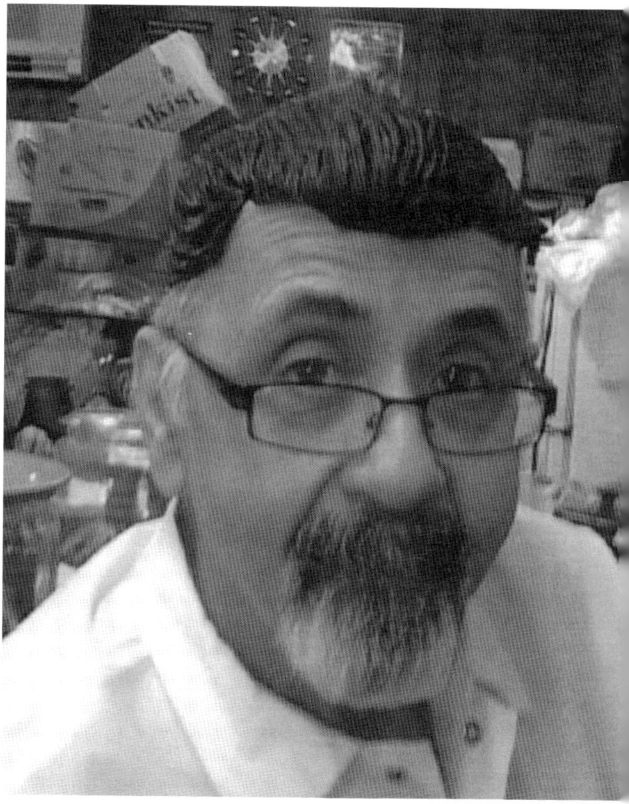

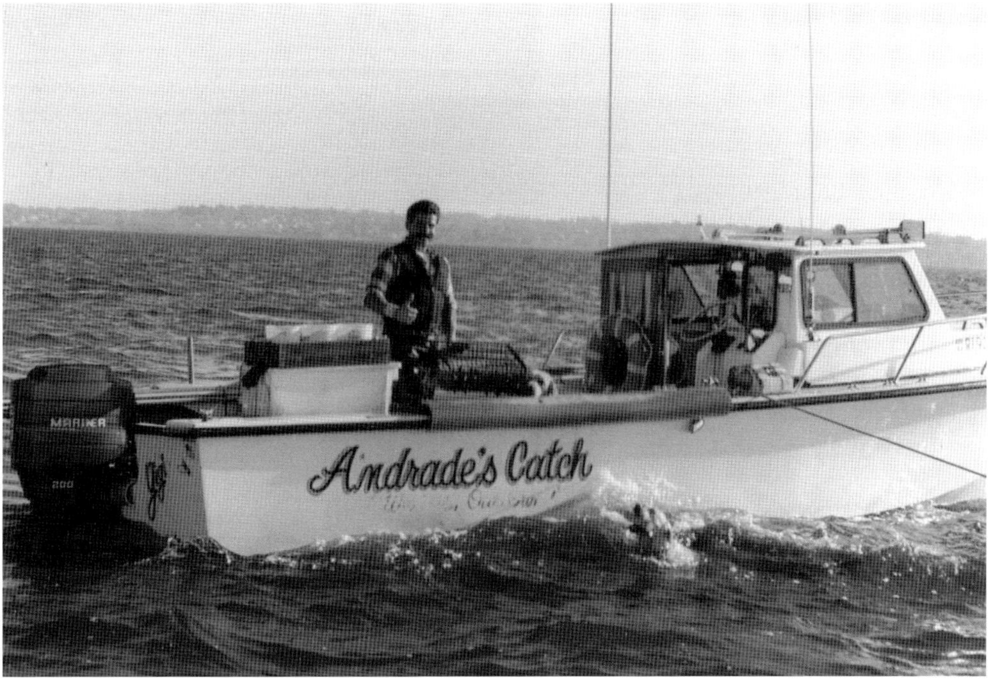

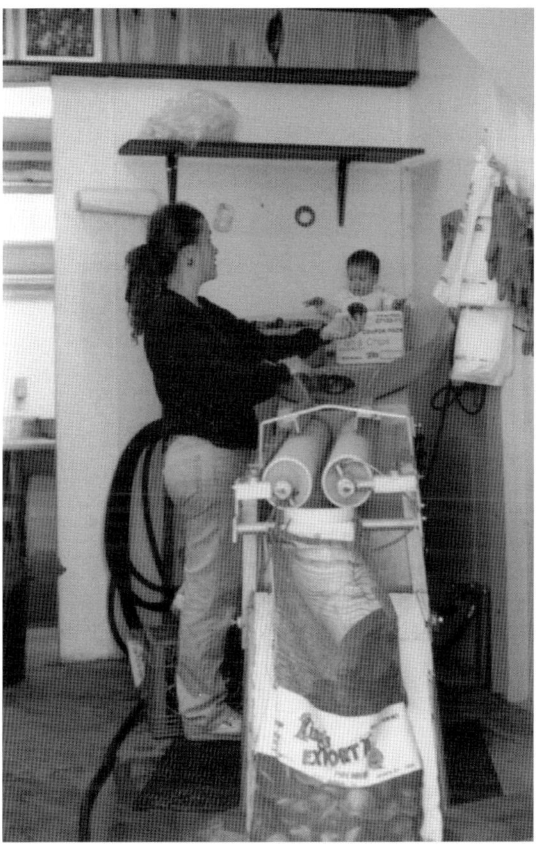

Clam Aficionado

David Andrade started shell-fishing in 1977 when he was 15 years old, and he and his fiancée Gisele ("Gigi") bought the building that became their retail market, Andrade's Catch, when he was 22. "I would go quahogging all day, then at night Gigi and I would be down here, fixing the place up," he said. In addition to their retail sales, Gigi would cook and sell fish and chips from their Wood Street location. That ended when Gigi (pictured at left with their daughter Chelsea on the quahog sorting machine) lost her battle with cancer in 2006. "She was the one with all the magnetism," David says. "Customers loved her. I was just the guy who drove the truck." Andrade's next generation, including daughters Chelsea and Nikki and son Davy, are available to help when they can. It's primarily a wholesale/retail operation these days, with some of the freshest shellfish to be found anywhere. Sadly, customers will still have to go somewhere else for fish and chips—and good luck finding any as good as Gigi's. (Both, courtesy of David Andrade.)

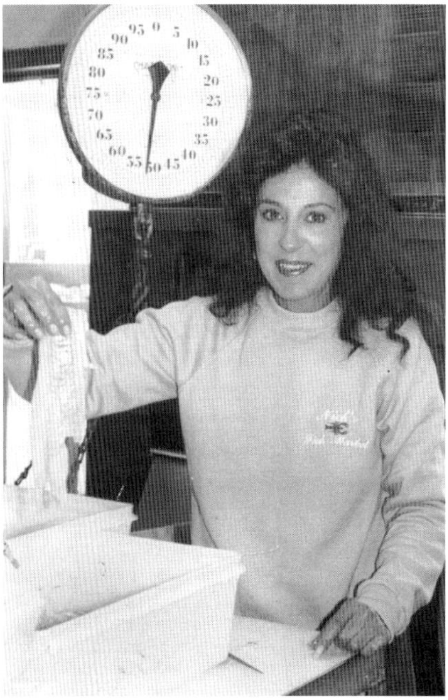

The Business of Fish
Four decades ago, Nicholas and Joan Castigliego did something that nobody in Nick's family had done before; they opened a fish market. Nick comes from a long line of fish purveyors, going all the way back to the old country. But opening a store was not the traditional business model: they worked out of trucks, moving from one neighborhood to another, depending on the day. Nick hadn't necessarily planned on going into the family business anyway—he was actually on the police force in the early 1970s, working as a patrolman. In 1973, they took over a storefront from "Foot" Squatrito on Bradford Street, and four years later, they built on the corner of Wood and Bradford Streets, their current location. In the intervening years, they have become one of a handful of go-to places when it's time to buy ingredients for the Christmas Eve "seven fishes" or July Fourth stuffies. (Courtesy of Nick Castigliego.)

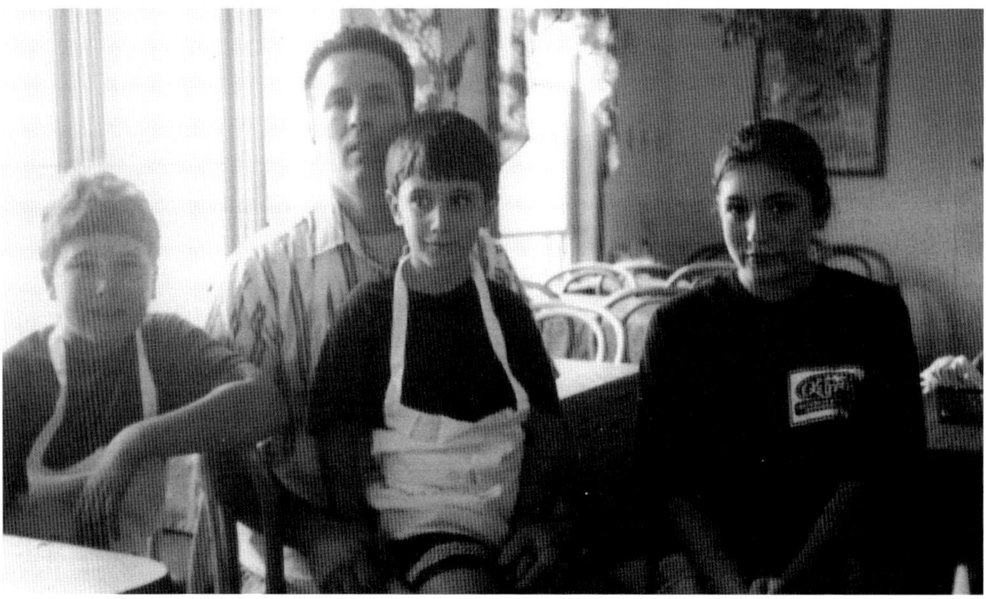

Food, Family, and Location, Location, Location
For 60 years, Quito's has been a fixture on the harborside, and its reputation is growing beyond Bristol's borders. Peter Quito's shellfish market began selling Friday fish and chips, prepared by his wife, Joanne, in 1954. It's long been a great place for takeout, but it wasn't until the early 1990s that Al (center), Joanne and Peter's son, made the move to a sit-down restaurant. Since then, Quito's has grown to include more than 30 tables, inside and out. It is still very much a family business, with the third generation, including, from left, sons Peter and Michael, and daughter Alyssa, who manages the front-of-house, carrying on the tradition. Al, who once hoped to play professional baseball before he was sidelined by an injury, never planned to go into the restaurant business, but Bristol is certainly glad he did.

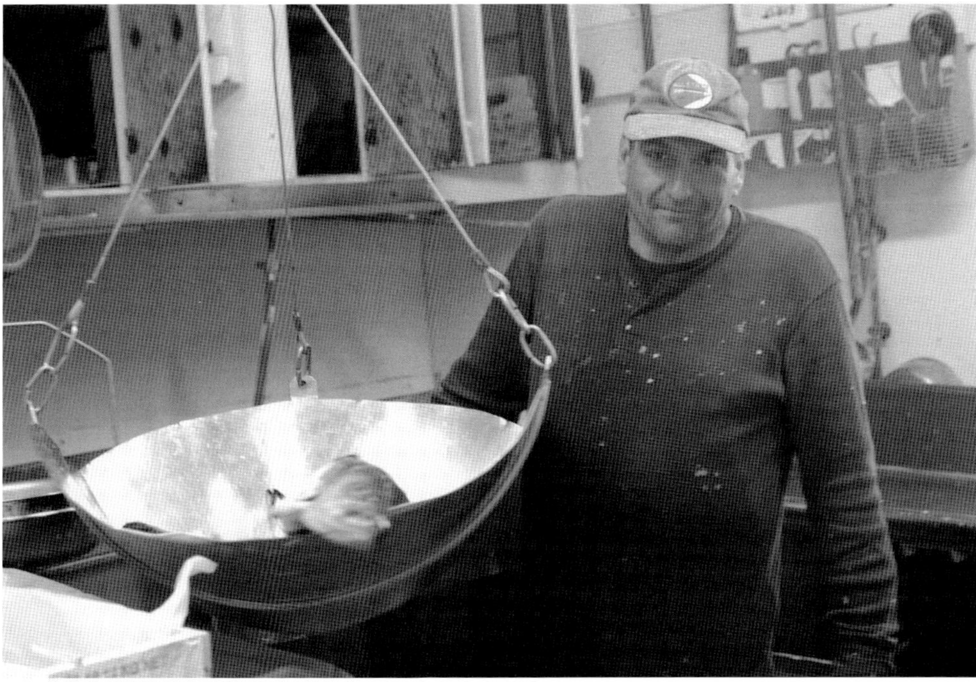

Shopping for Fish, Old-School Style
If an old-timer complains that nobody does anything the way he used to anymore, take him to Roma Street to see Angelo Pirri's fish market. Ask Angelo how he got into the business and he'll give a straight answer: "I was born in it." Pirri learned from his late father, Frank (pictured at right), who learned from his father, Angelo, and so on. There aren't any special seasonings or condiments, any prepared dishes, or any fish that weren't in the ocean yesterday or the day before at most. What customers will find is a handful of boxes, a scale, and a knife. They show up, see what he's got, and if they want it, Pirri will filet it for them in seconds. The fish goes in a plastic bag, the plastic bag goes in a paper bag, and that's it. The paper bag, or the customer's change, might have a scale or two on it, but this is Bristol, and fish doesn't come in sticks. (Both, courtesy of Angelo Pirri.)

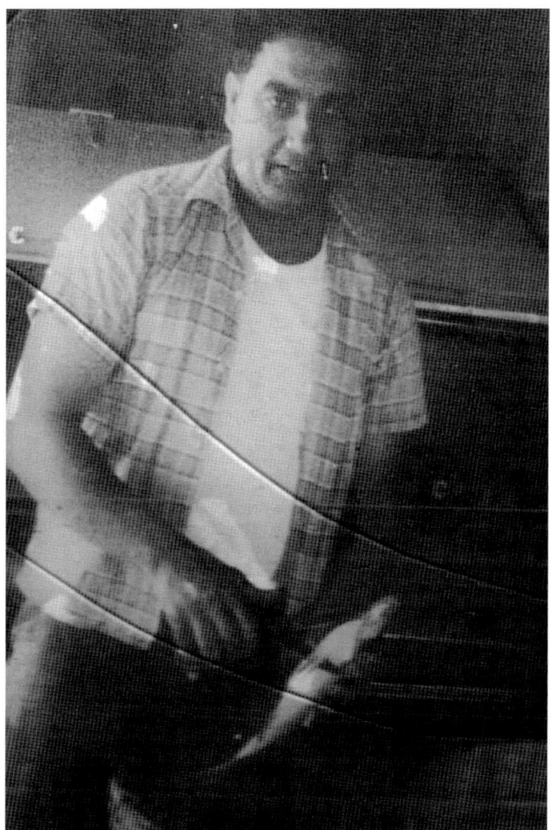

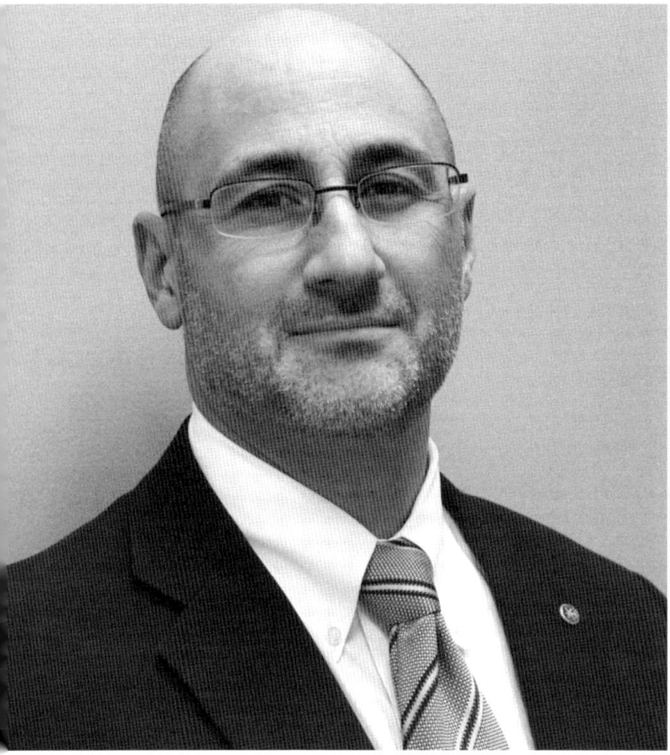

A Hands-On Kind of Guy

There aren't too many people in Bristol who have had their hands on more people than Dr. Mark Alano. A board-certified chiropractor who graduated with honors from the renowned Palmer College of Chiropractic in Davenport, Iowa, Alano is one of less than 300 doctors in the United States trained in the NUCCA technique, a highly specialized and gentle adjusting technique. Alano is also the only doctor in the state of Rhode Island to hold a FICPA: a Fellowship of the International Chiropractic Pediatric Association. Recently named by his peers as one of *Rhode Island Monthly*'s "Top Docs," Alano is always happy to respectfully debate politics during an adjustment, if that's the patient's thing. (Courtesy of Mark Alano.)

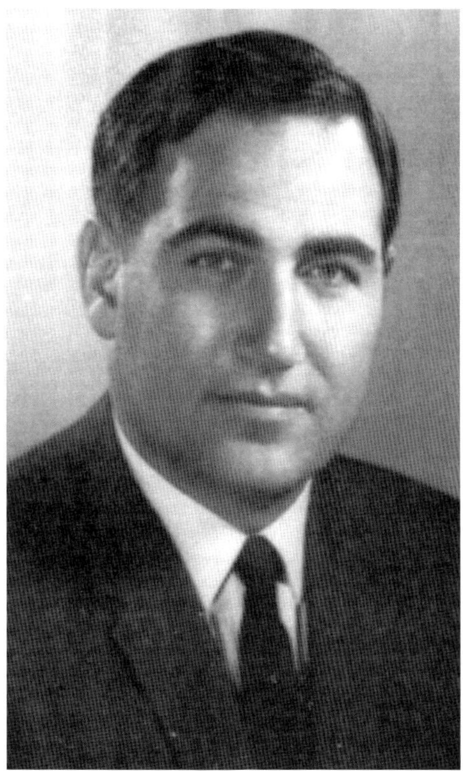

Hard Work, Solid Convictions

Raymond S. DeLeo (1923–2013) was an athlete, World War II veteran, diversified businessman, investor, developer, political leader, and family man. It took a lot of work to be all of those things, and according to his wife, Ann, he worked on one thing or another almost until the end. In his later years, the one thing this Bristol Athletic Hall of Fame inductee did find time to do was see his grandchildren's games and matches. "He missed a lot of his children's games when they were growing up," Ann says. "But he made up for it with his grandchildren." A lifelong resident of Bristol, DeLeo was made an honorary lifetime member of the Bristol Historical Society for his efforts in preserving many features of the Wardwell-Bosworth House in the construction of the current Bristol Post Office, which was built on the site of the demolished Russell Warren masterpiece. He was instrumental in laying the groundwork for the establishment of the Benjamin Church Manor elderly housing complex and more recently fought to preserve the Colt and Andrews buildings as public elementary schools. (Courtesy of Ann DeLeo.)

A Beauty, Inside and Out

Alayne White's tagline as Bristol's "inner-beauty advocate and self-proclaimed spa goddess" is not hyperbole. She is, quite literally, all that and more. Since opening in 2002, Alayne White Spas have become a gold standard for day spas, and Alayne is the heart and soul—and brains—behind every client experience. A 25-year veteran of the beauty business, White is not only passionate about exceptional client care and premium products and services, she has created a company that simultaneously supports women's careers and encourages family and life balance. White practices what she preaches throughout Bristol, giving freely to nonprofit events and fundraisers and supporting fellow small-business owners. Recently named one of Rhode Island's "2014 Women to Watch," White says, "After 25 years working with women, I still wake up every day excited and joyous that I get to do what I love . . . with an honest and positive outlook on both outer and inner beauty for women of all shapes and sizes." (Courtesy of Alayne White.)

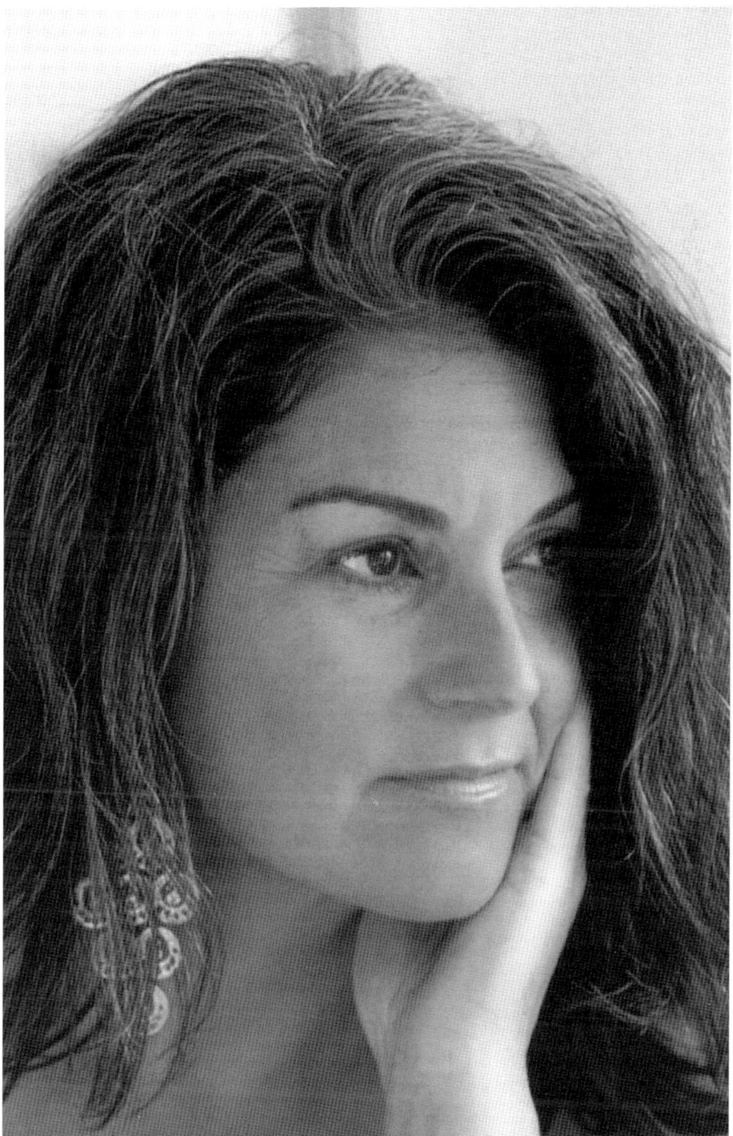

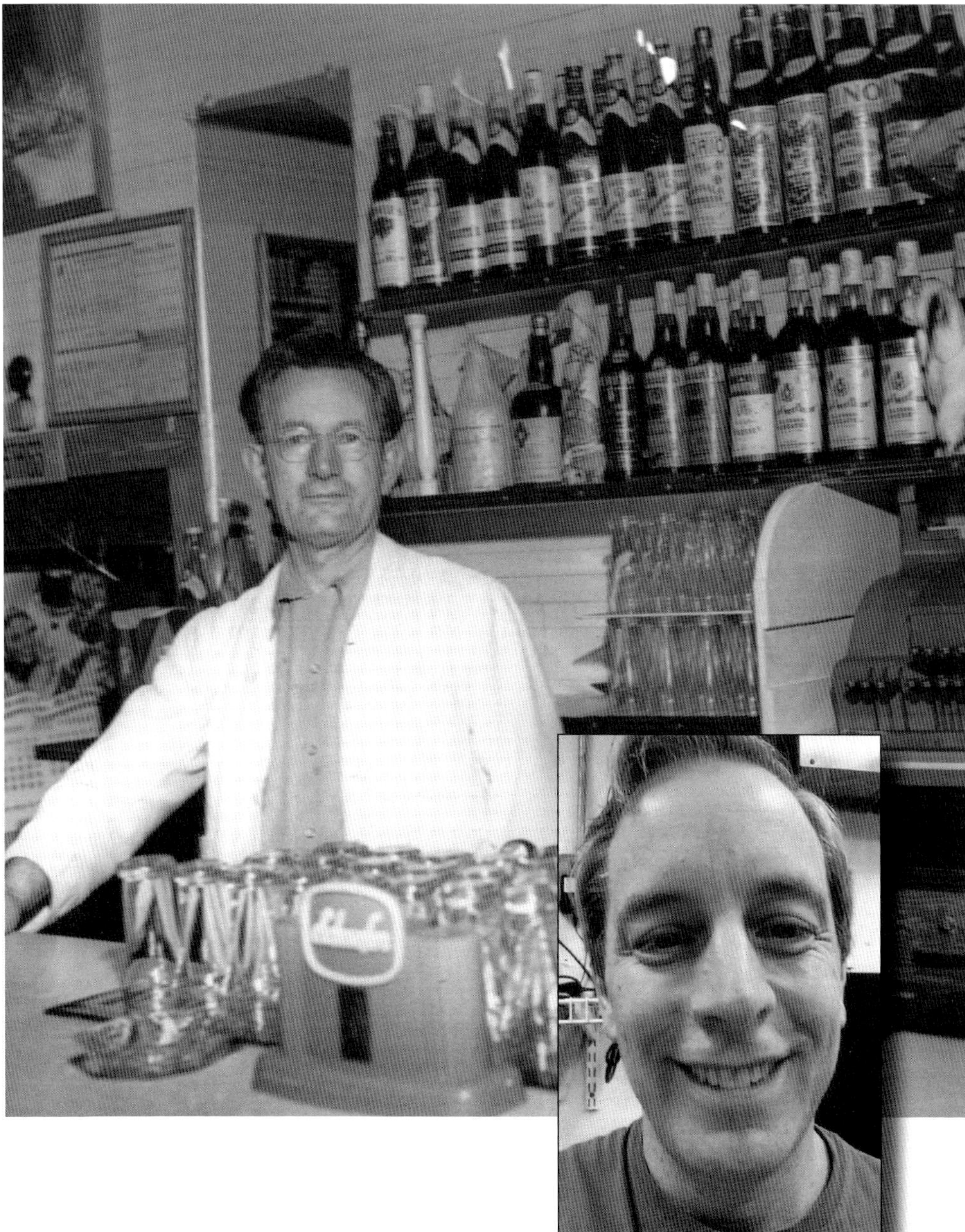

Legendary Leo's

Panteleone Mancieri, also known as "Leo," was a 50 year-old no-nonsense saloon manager who decided he wanted to work for himself. So, in 1948, he opened Leo's. It started as a small Italian eatery on State Street, and it served good, honest, homestyle Italian food. In 2000, Leo's grandson Paul Mancieri relocated to 365 Hope Street, on the corner of Church Street. Mancieri expanded not only the seating capacity but also the menu options, featuring authentic Italian and American cuisine while focusing on high-quality food and a friendly atmosphere. With 25 years in the business, Paul is proud to be the third-generation proprietor of Leo's Ristorante, and he can be found in the kitchen preparing meals himself as well as in the dining room conversing with new and regular customers. (Both, courtesy of Paul Mancieri.)

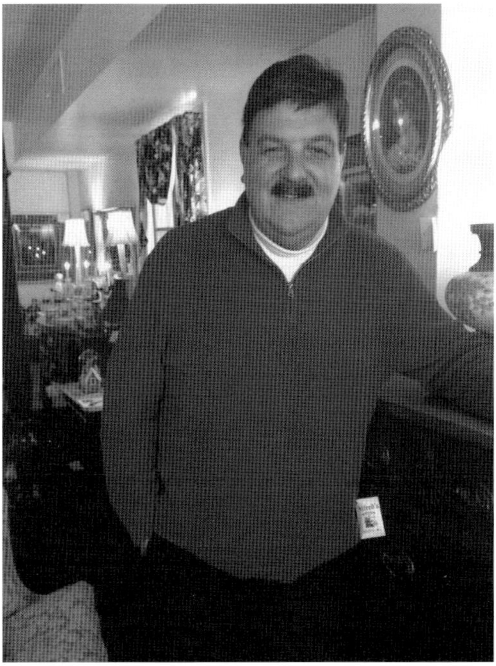

The Tastemaker

The son of Azorean immigrants, Alfred Brazil has worked since the age of 12, first as a stock boy at Maryann's Gift Shop, formerly on the corner of Wood and State Streets, and doing odd landscaping and maintenance jobs at the home of Robert W. Nelson, who lived in the Talbot House, a grand Greek Revival at 647 Hope Street. "I told Mr. Nelson that I was going to live here someday," Brazil recalls. "I don't think he believed me, a little Portuguese kid. But he was a wonderful man." Between the Nelson home and the gift shop, Brazil quickly developed a love of antiques. Still a teenager, he opened his first antique store on the corner of Wood and Union Streets, moving to his present Hope Street location a few years later in 1974. He was just 22 years old. Six years later, in 1980, he purchased the Talbot House from Nelson. Like his flagship Bristol store, it's a showplace of tasteful antiques and decorative arts.

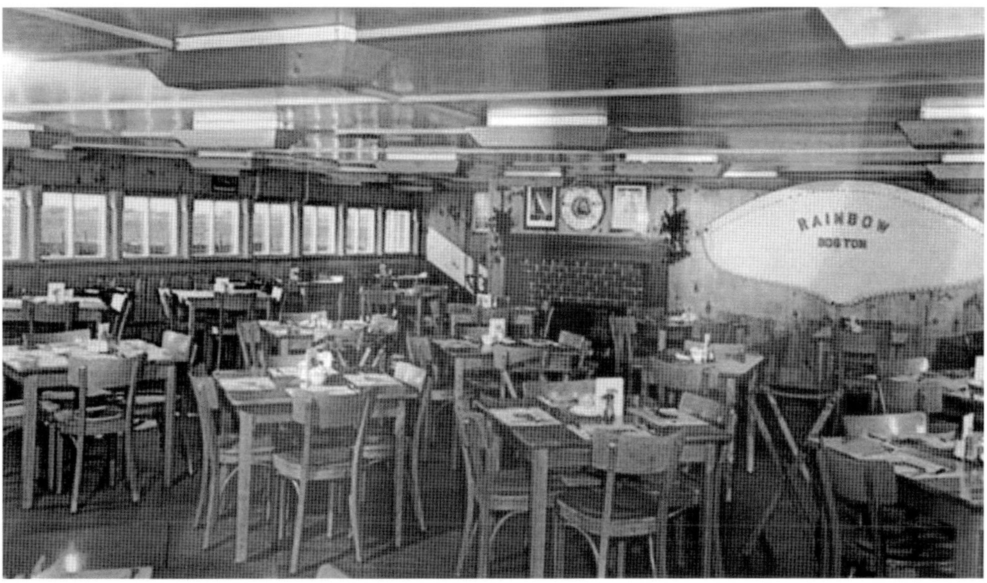

Standing the Test of Time

In this most fickle of industries, the Lobster Pot has provided locals with the finest traditional New England classics—that's Bristol comfort food—and seafood with a contemporary twist for nearly 90 years. The Lobster Pot's location, directly on the water, provides a spectacular view of the bay, but the location has also made for some epic storm damage. Still, the Lobster Pot endures. Owner Jeff Hirsch is only the third in this business that began as a fish market, bar, and gas station. Ultimately, the restaurant was added, the fish and gas went by the boards, and a local landmark was born. For Hirsch, the best part is all the stories people tell about family memories and special events at his establishment. "I feel very honored to be the steward of this very special and long-standing part of Bristol," Hirsch says.

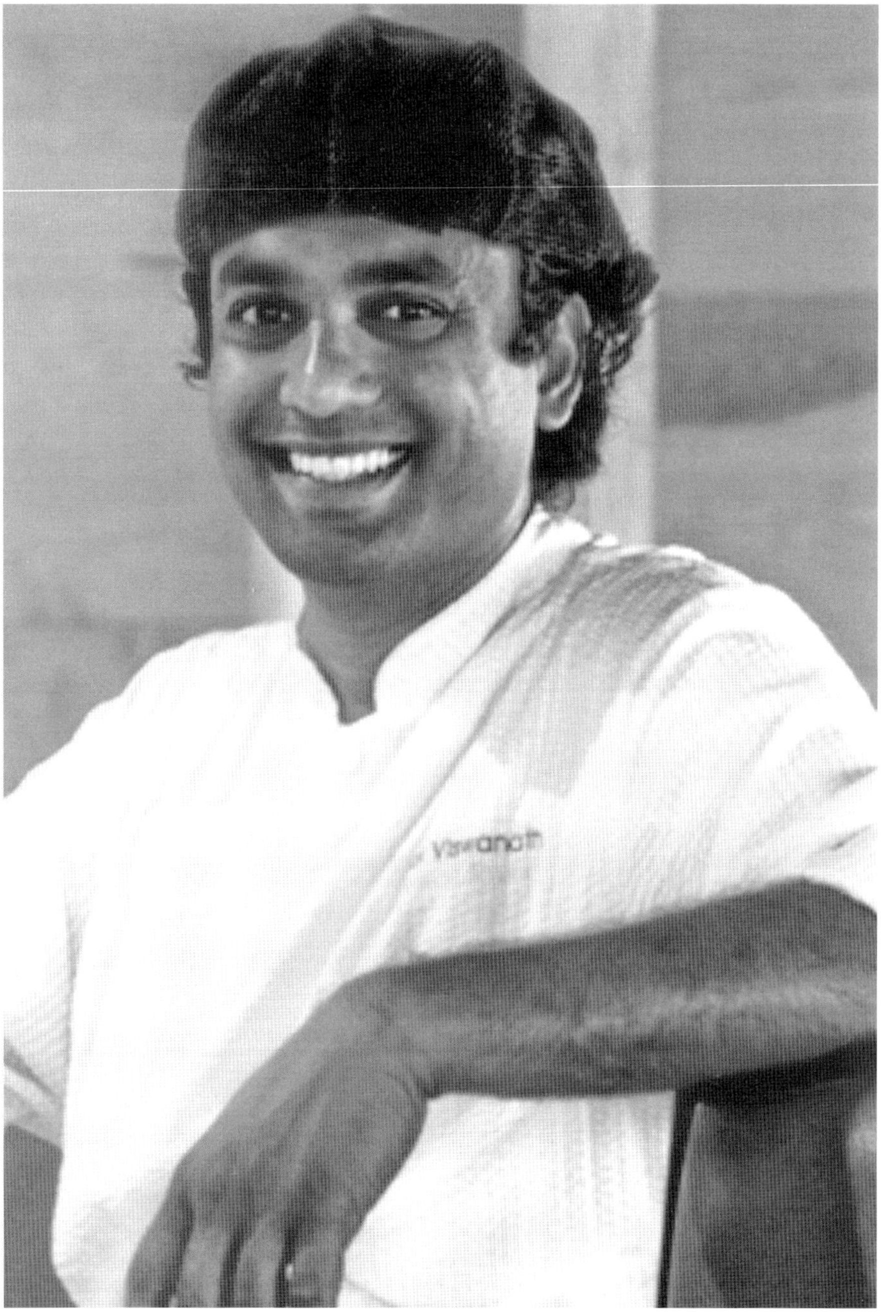

Putting Bristol on the Food Map

Sai Viswanath, the DeWolf Tavern's incredibly talented chef, has refined his craft in such renowned restaurants as Mumbai's Indigo (voted one of the world's best 60 restaurants by *Conde Nast*) and New York City's Union Square Café. With an unmistakable but deftly handled Indian influence, Viswanath's kitchen produces singularly unique and original dishes that keep residents and visitors coming back time and again. Viswanath was a semifinalist for a James Beard Foundation Award in 2008, 2009, 2010, and 2012. (Courtesy of Sai Viswanath.)

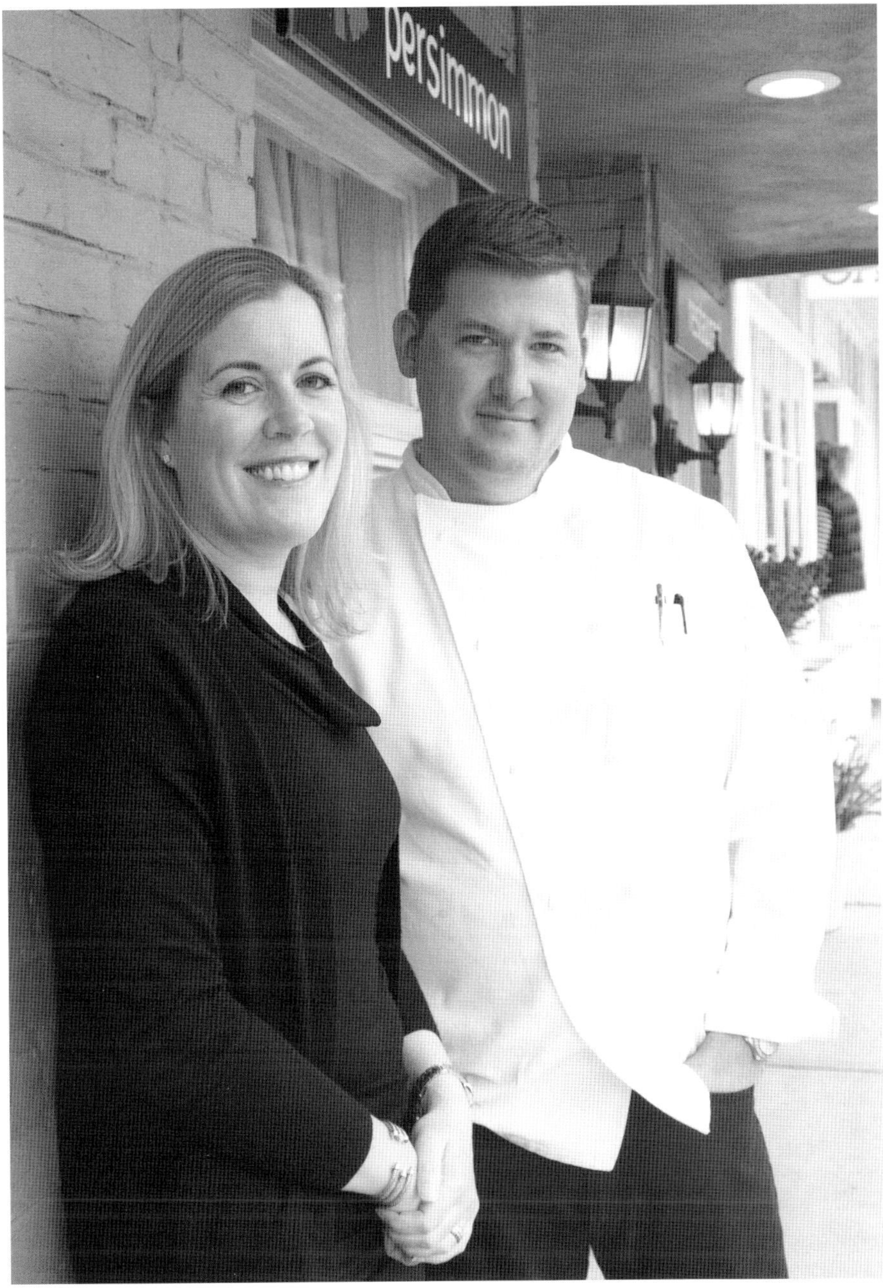

As Good as It Gets

Enthusiasm, innovation, and a fierce commitment to sourcing the best local ingredients make up the raw materials for an amazing meal. Add Champe Speidel's personal culinary vision and wife Lisa's expert front-of-house service and the result is Persimmon, a truly one-of-a-kind dining experience in a town where, 25 years ago, people couldn't go out to dinner without getting tomato sauce on their shirts. Chef Champe Speidel and his wife, Lisa, opened Persimmon in the spring of 2005, garnering regional and national praise and, like their neighbor to the west, perennial nods from the James Beard Foundation. (Photograph by Angel Tavares, courtesy of Lisa Speidel.)

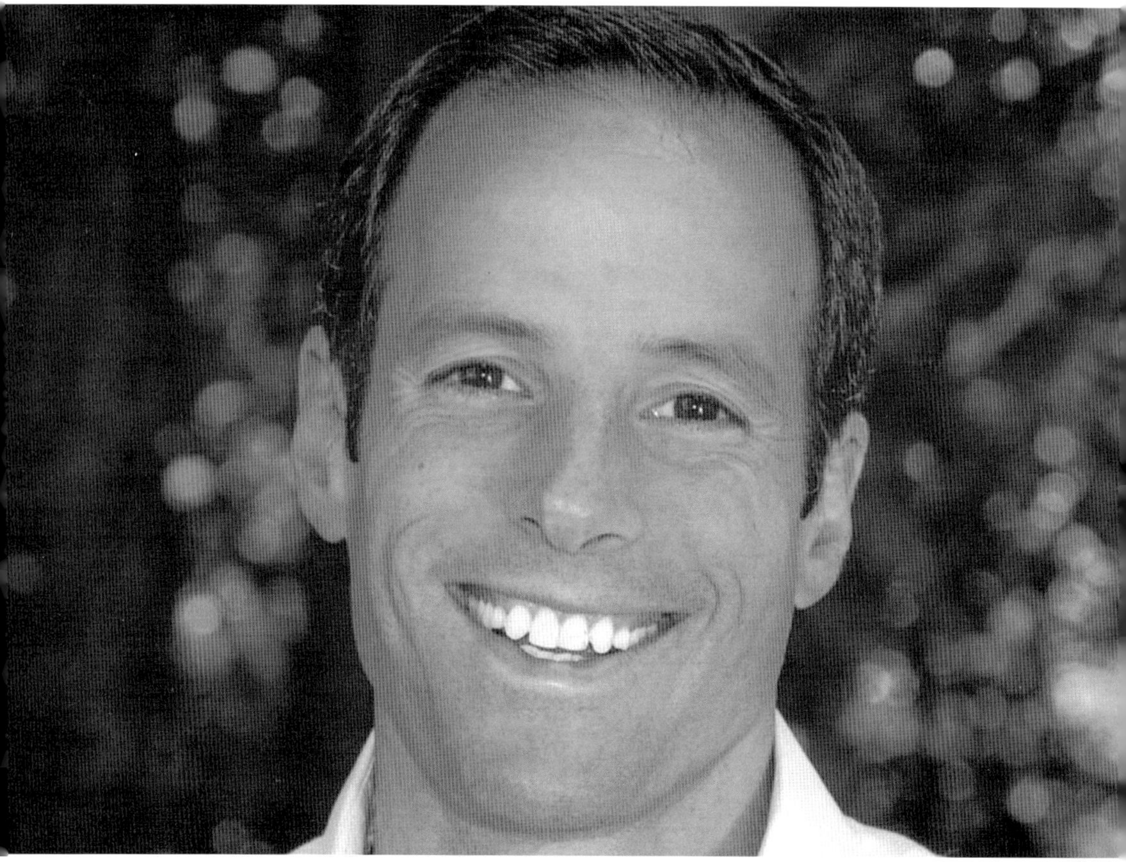

Right Here, Right Now

Former broadcast meteorologist Fred Campagna isn't afraid to try new things, and nothing illustrates that more clearly than his unprecedented jump from television to social media. His new venture, Right Weather, is accurate smartphone- or tablet-based forecasting when and where it is needed. It was a calculated move, only considered after Campagna realized that his share of Twitter and Facebook followers exceeded his network's market share—by a lot. Campagna has long been a favorite in the local market among people who reject unwarranted weather-related hysteria, an observation borne out by an impressive record of accuracy certified by Weatherate, an independent forecast verification service. So far, Campagna's new challenge seems to be working out. And thanks to webcams, his loyal following still gets the pleasure of watching the excitement of a real weather event and Fred's rolling-up-the-sleeves ritual. (Courtesy of Fred Campagna.)

CHAPTER THREE

Community and Service

One of the benefits of a town like Bristol is its strong sense of place. Most people who live in Bristol love Bristol, and many who leave eventually return. The loyalty that a cohesive, enduring, non-transient community engenders from its people, many of whom have been here for many generations, is evident. Bristolians are overwhelmingly committed to local volunteerism. They are community-oriented; they are house-proud; and they are truly vested in their home and are willing to work have to leave it a better place than it was when they arrived. On the following pages are a handful of local characters as well as some people who have made a difference and enriched Bristol, past and present, whether through philanthropy, preservation, conservation, spirituality, education, or public service.

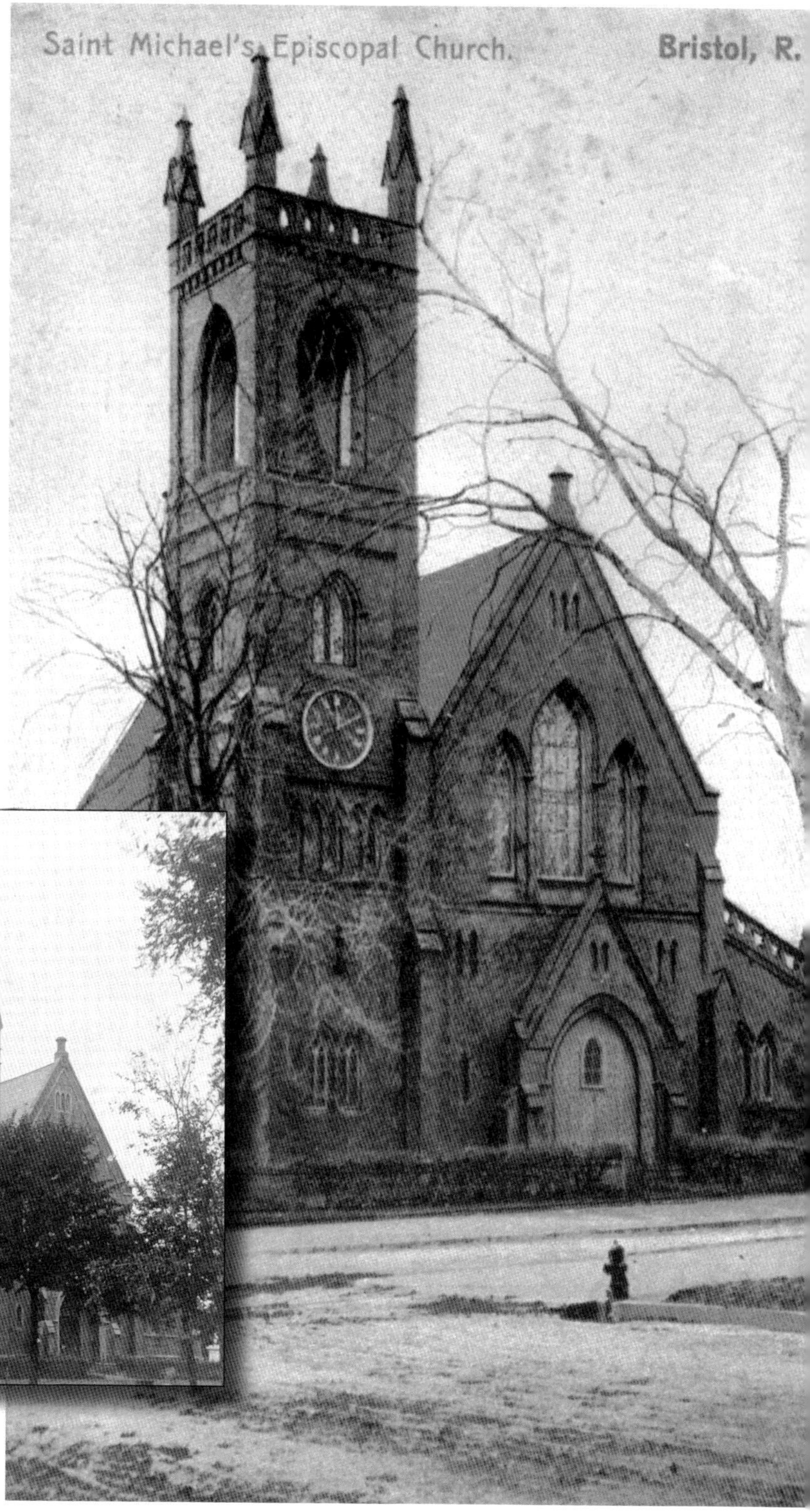

We can Rebuild It
St. Michael's Church was organized in 1718 by laypersons in Bristol, and it has occupied the corner of Hope and Church Streets since 1720. The current church is the fourth building on this site, completed in 1861. Below is the spire design originally intended. At right is the belfry that replaced it after a roof collapse. (Both, courtesy of St. Michael's Church.)

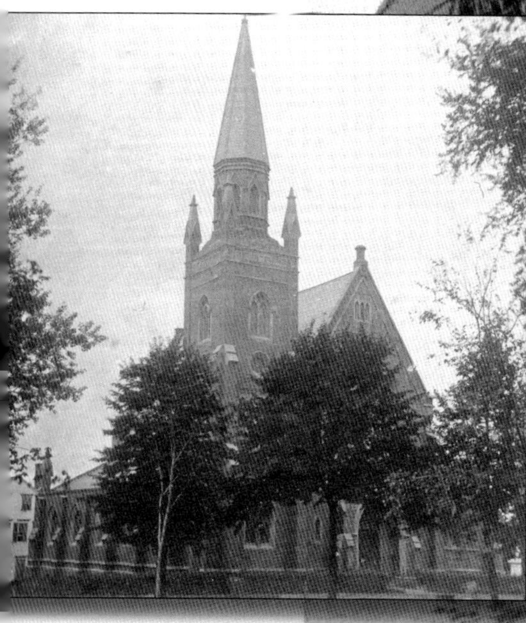

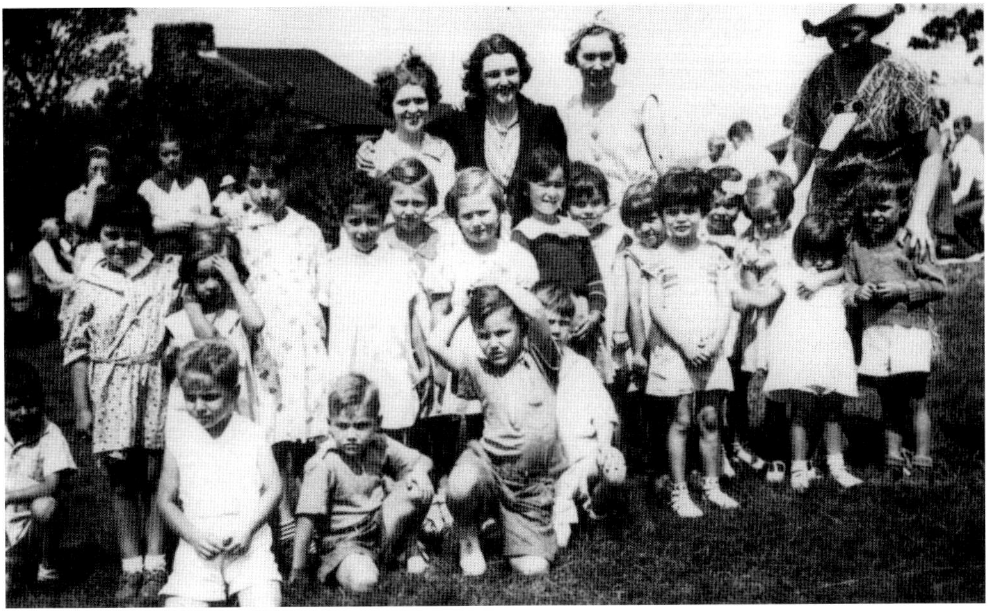

From Summer Picnics . . .
Sunday school children enjoy the balmy weather at a pre-war summer gathering. (Courtesy of St. Michael's Church.)

. . . to Nativity Plays
The Miracle Play was performed at Christmas in 1938. From left to right are Chester Burgess (wise man), Allan Newman (wise man), Muriel Bullock (Mary), Mildred Coggeshall (Elizabeth), Calbraith Perry (Joseph), and Vernon Gray (wise man). (Courtesy of St. Michael's Church.)

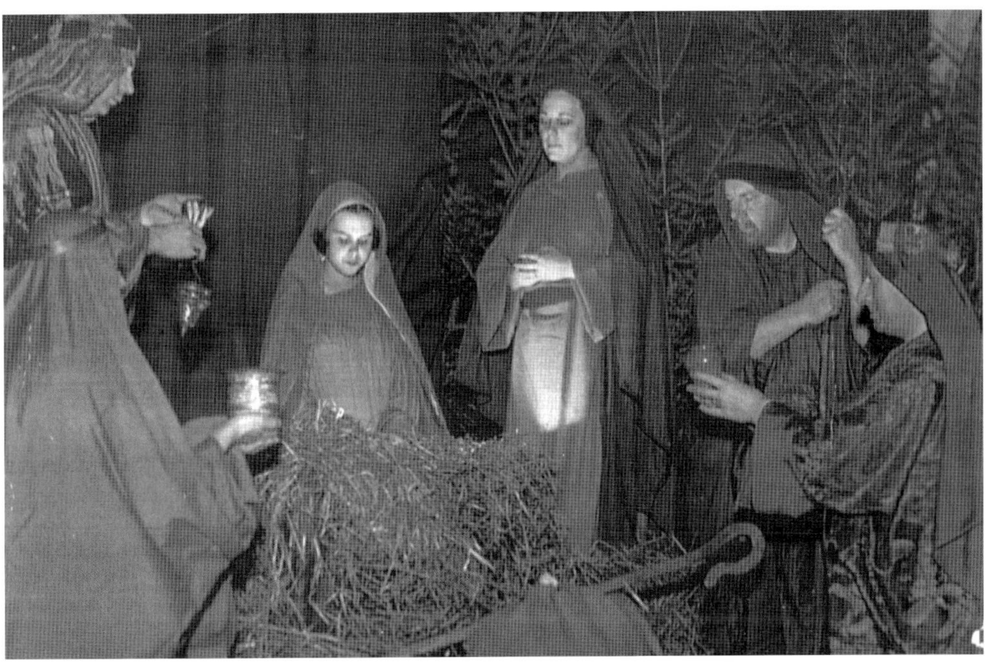

First Father

The Reverend John Usher succeeded James Orem, the first rector of St. Michael's Church. Usher established a vestry to serve as the governing body of the church, which raised the money to purchase a church bell. Usher was the rector of St. Michael's until 1775, when he died, leaving his son, John Usher Jr., in the unenviable position of holding the church together during the Revolutionary War. John Usher Jr. was finally ordained after the war, in 1791, and continued as rector of the church until his death in 1803. (Courtesy of St. Michael's Church.)

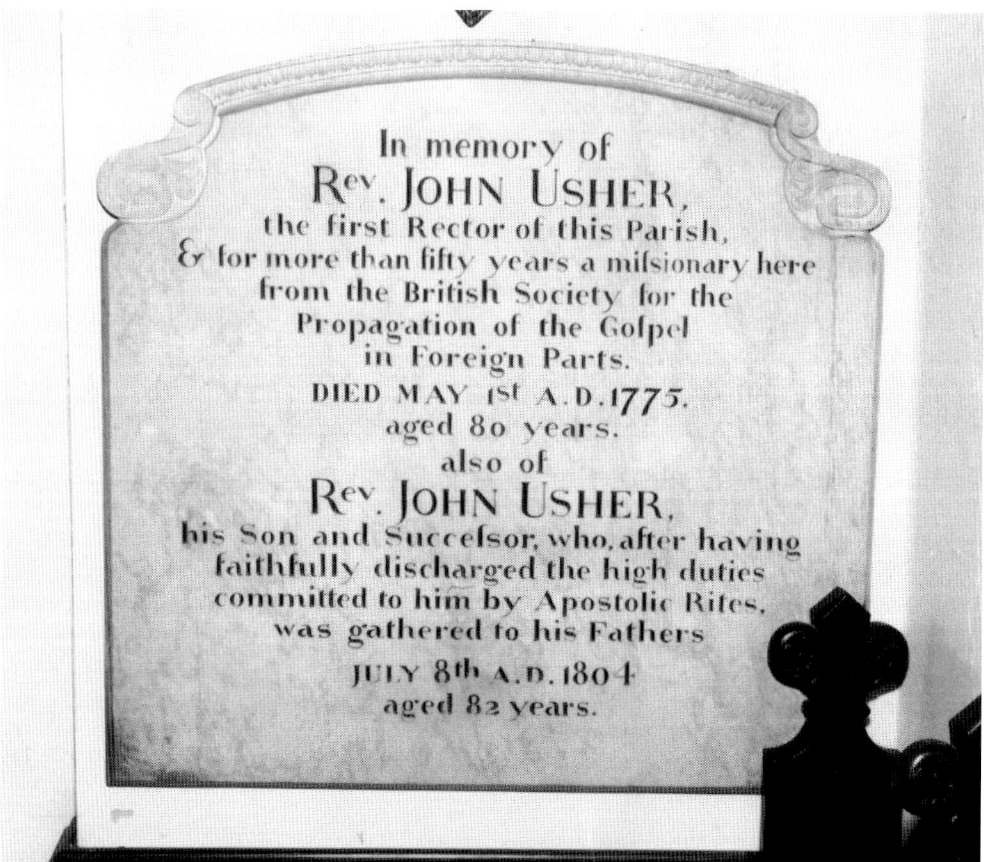

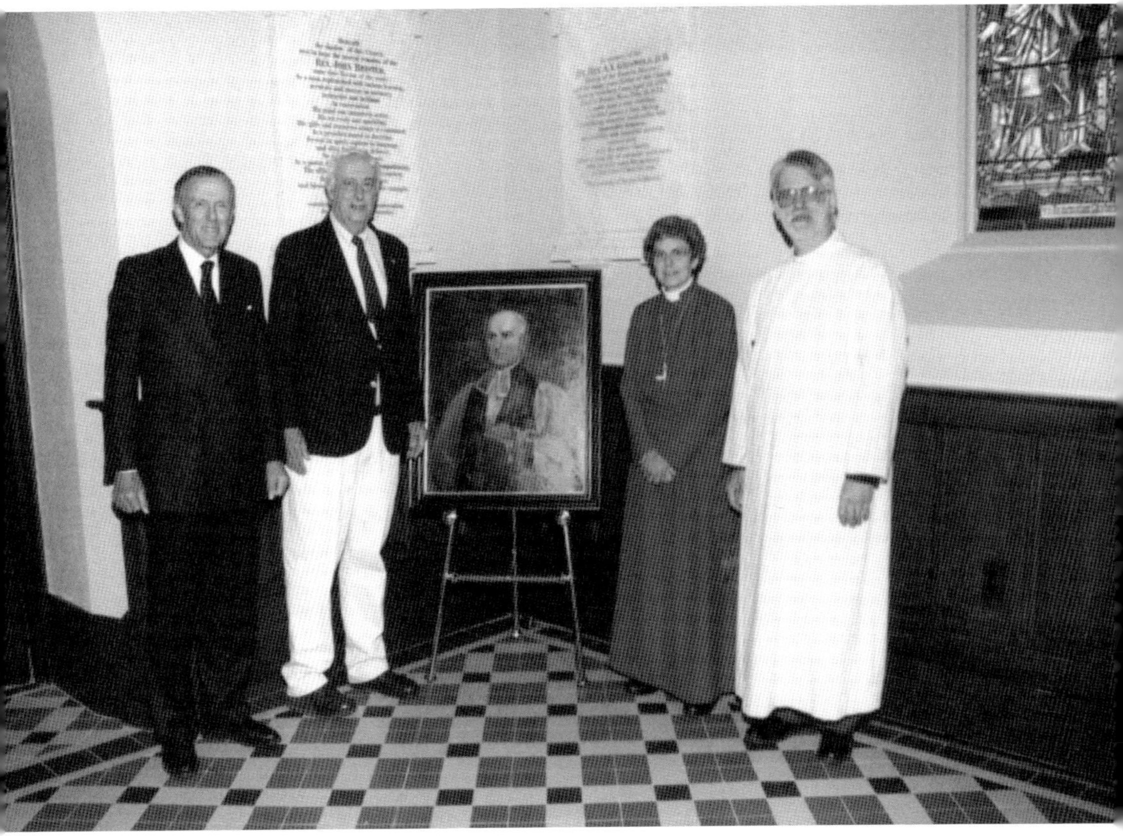

Revival Leader
The Reverend Alexander Viets Griswold left a Connecticut parish to become rector of St. Michael's in 1804. In 1810, he was also elected the first and only bishop of the Eastern Diocese, which included all of New England except Connecticut. Consecrated in 1811, he continued to serve as parish rector at St. Michael's until 1830. Shown here with a portrait of Griswold, honoring his induction in the Rhode Island Heritage Hall of Fame, are (from left to right) town councilman Halsey Herreshoff, Nathanael Herreshoff, Bishop Jerrilyn Wolf, and Rev. John VanSiclen. (Courtesy of St. Michael's Church.)

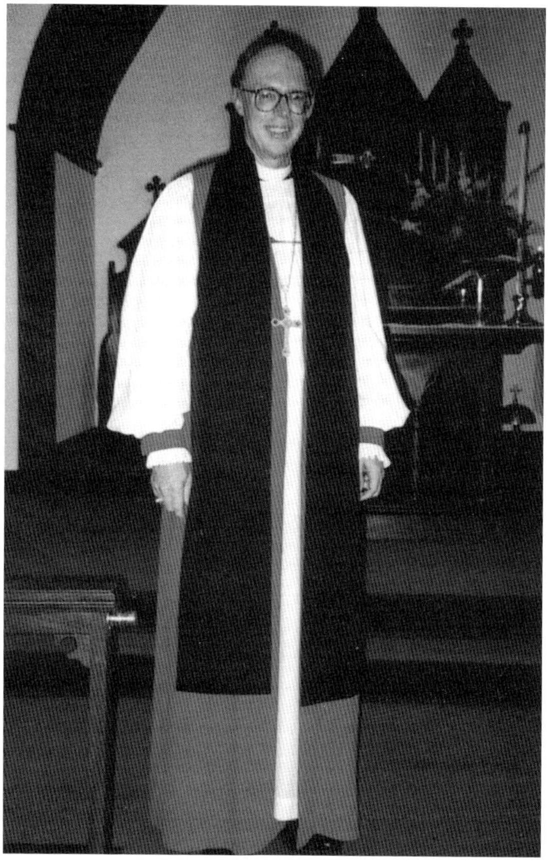

A Birthday Celebration 275 Years in the Making The Reverend Clifton Daniels (left) took over as rector of St. Michael's in 1984 and served until 1996. During that time, the church celebrated its 275th anniversary with a year's worth of activities. Canon Delbert W. Tildesley, a well-loved rector of St. Michael's from 1954 to 1982, was on hand (below). (Both, courtesy of St. Michael's Church.)

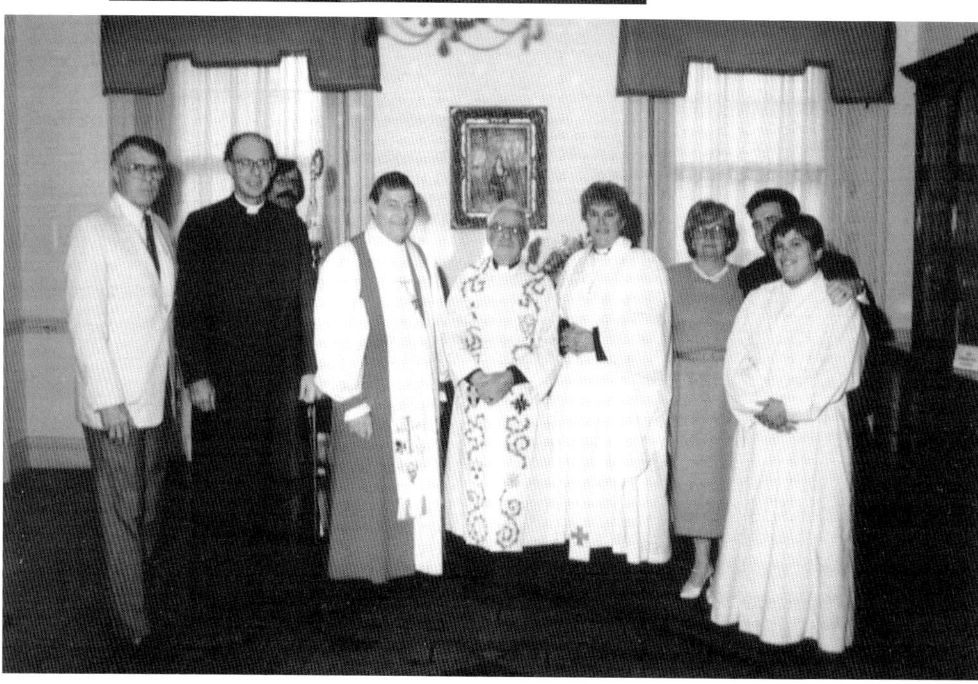

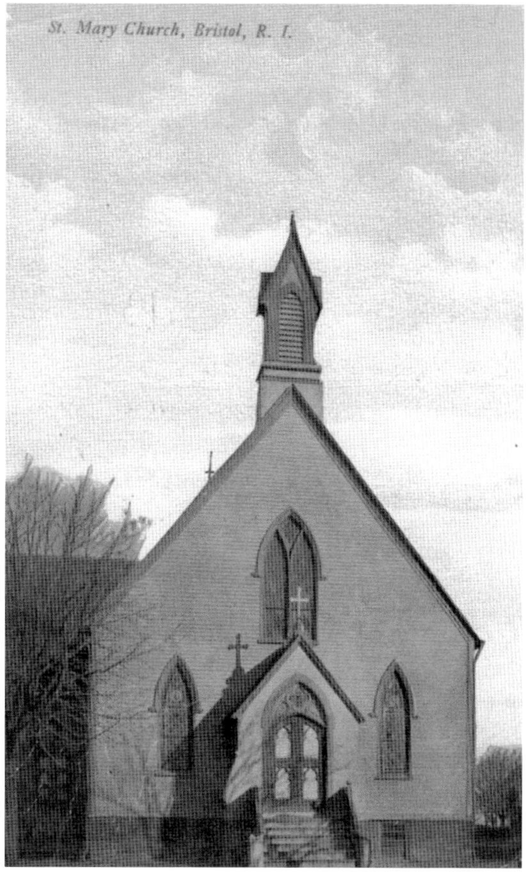

Old and New at St. Mary's

Around the end of the 19th century, it was evident that St. Mary's needed to grow along with the parish, which was expanding as new Catholics emigrated from Europe. Ground was broken in the fall of 1910, and in the spring of 1911, construction began.

The massive upper part of the brick-and-steel structure, in the perpendicular Norman Gothic style, was only a shell; the interior architectural embellishments and furnishings were not completed until 1927.

Meanwhile, the old church was relocated to the parking lot adjacent to Goglia's market.

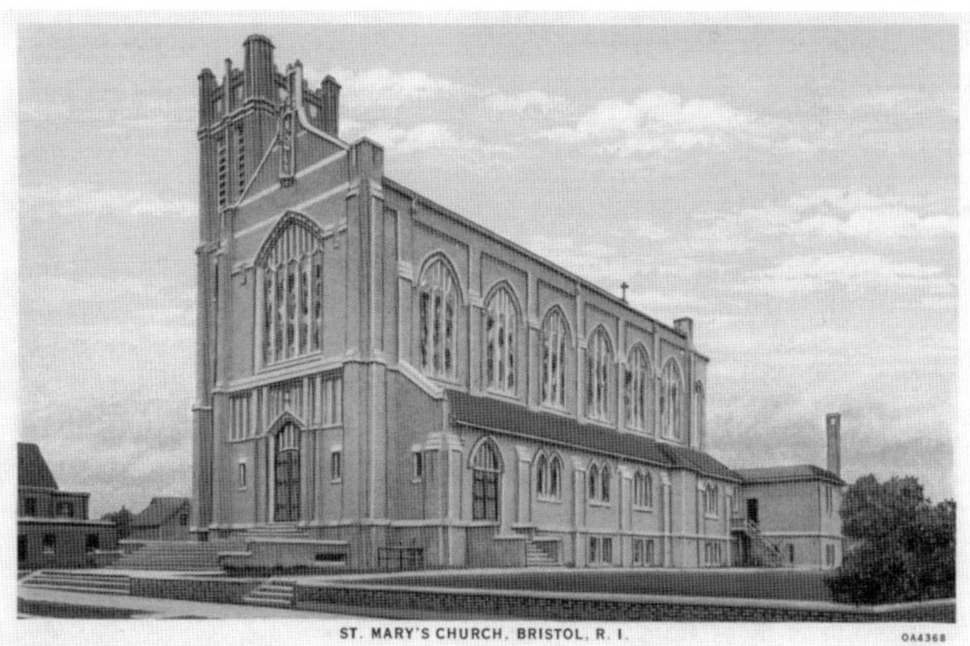

Father of the Fourth

The Reverend Henry Wight came to the Congregational church in 1785, a time of hope and promise. A new church building had just been completed, the new nation was free, and Bristol was a center of patriotic energy. Reverend Wight was a veteran of the Revolutionary War, so he led the way in establishing what are now known as "Patriotic Exercises" way back in 1785. These Patriotic Exercises focused on remembering, honoring, and celebrating all that the Revolutionary War veterans had done in establishing the nation. Ever since, on the Fourth of July, Patriotic Exercises are held to honor the work of those who founded the nation. Reverend Wight himself was the patriotic speaker at the Patriotic Exercises for more than 40 years. (Courtesy Cathy and Garry Holmstrom.)

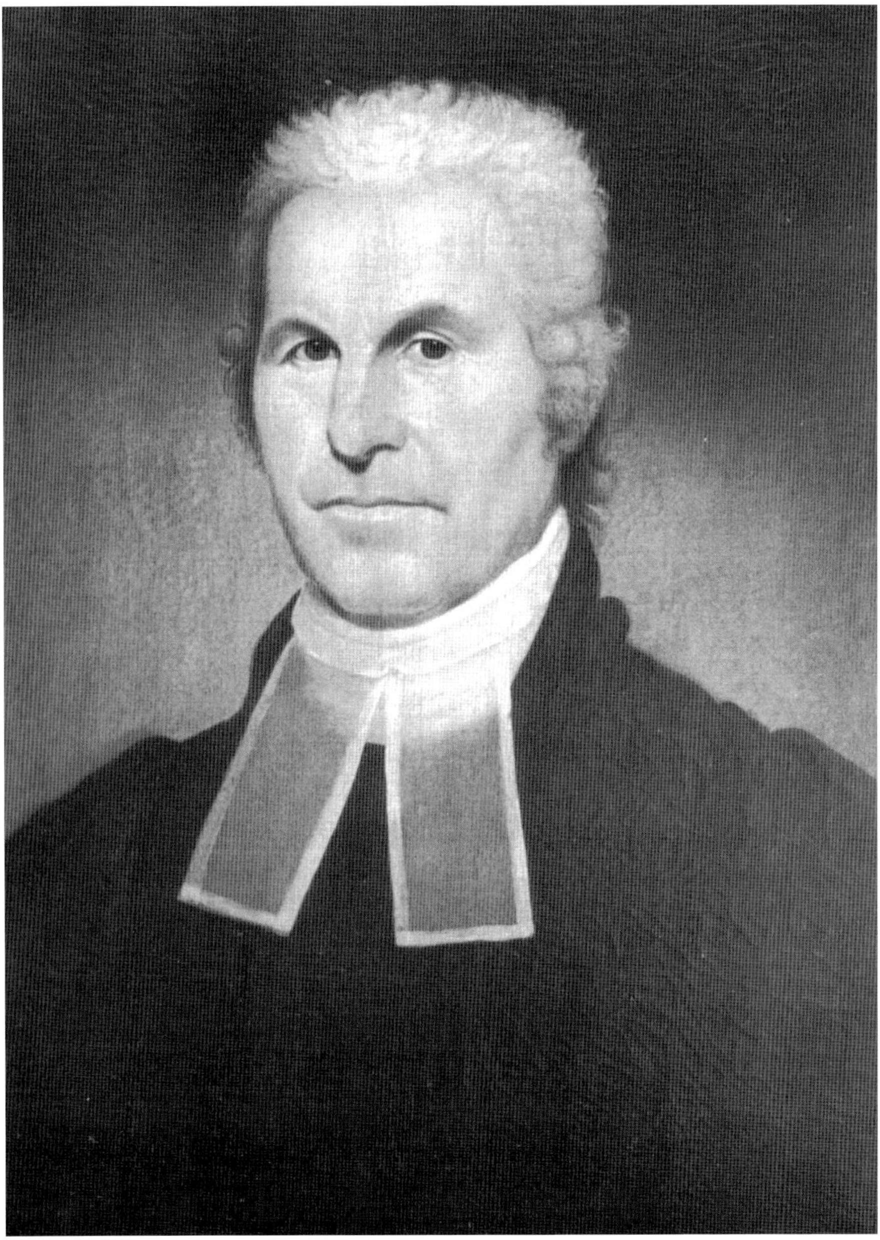

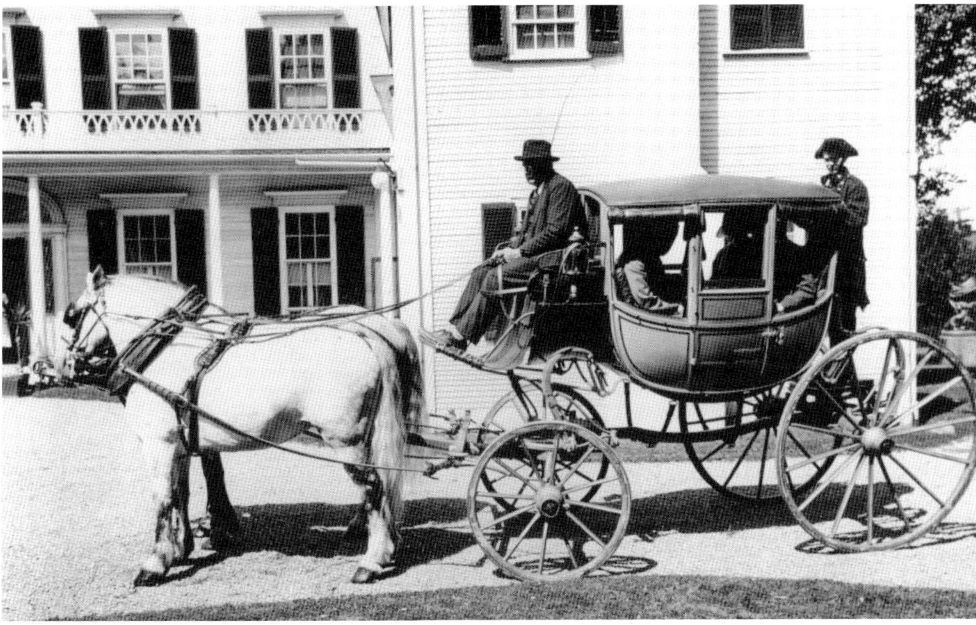

Driving Senator Jim

The Linden Place Museum collection includes this fabulous coach, a rare extant example of the horse-drawn vehicles used by the wealthy and powerful in the 1820s. This coach belonged to James DeWolf, who at the time was the second-wealthiest man in America. DeWolf used the coach to travel from Bristol to Washington, DC, where he represented Rhode Island in the US Senate. Industrialist Samuel P. Colt, who was a nephew of both Senator DeWolf and the Samuel Colt of firearms fame, rode the Linden Place coach in Bristol's Fourth of July Parade at least one of the four times he served as chief marshal in the 1870s and 1880s. (Both, courtesy of Linden Place.)

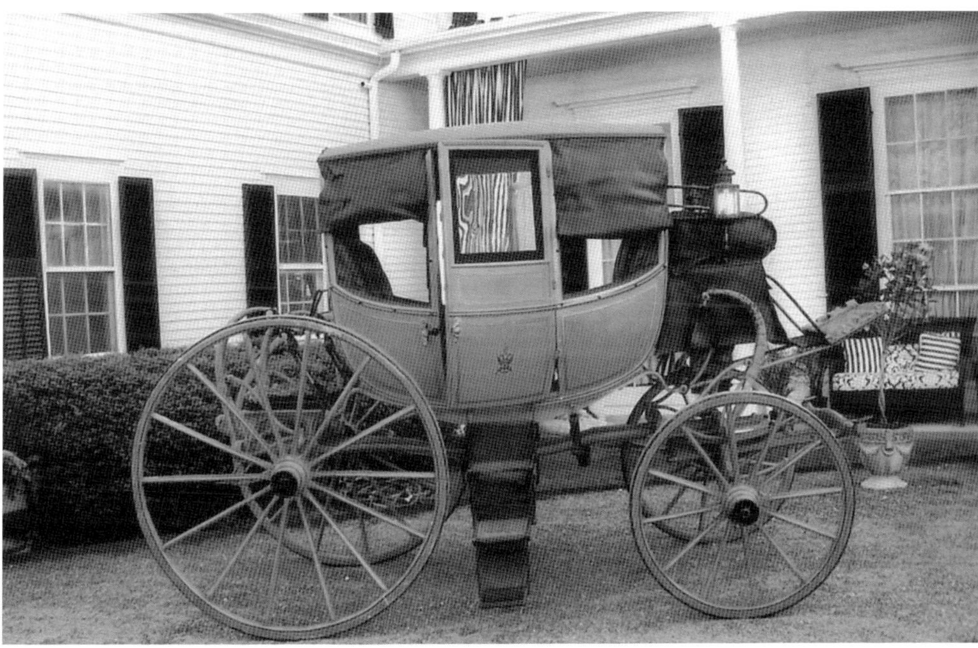

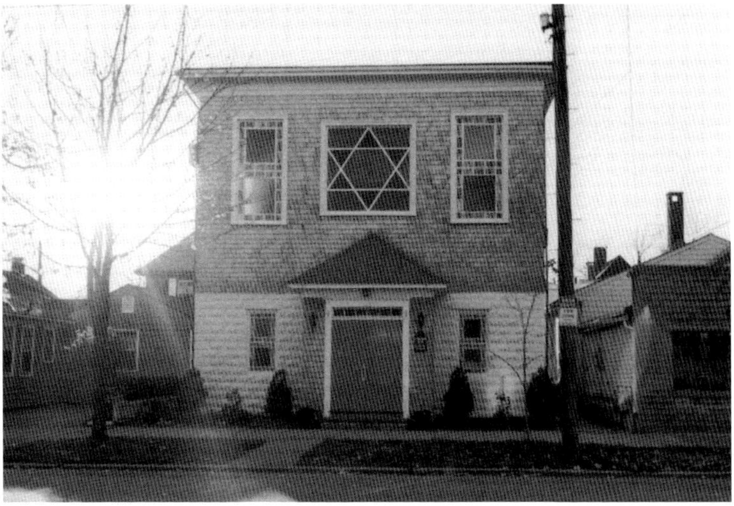

1900: Bristol Welcomes a New Community
Chevra Agudas Achim, the United Brothers Synagogue, was chartered in 1900, making it the second oldest synagogue in Rhode Island after Newport's Truro. The congregation's founders were Eastern European Orthodox Jews who immigrated to Bristol, drawn by the promise of jobs in the India rubber plant. Initially, the congregation did not have a permanent home. It held services at a few different locations in downtown Bristol until its present home was constructed in 1916. From the exterior, it is a well-kept if nondescript shingled building. Inside, it is a lovely space, Lilliputian in scale but rich with detail. It was not long before the older generation of Bristol's newest community of immigrants returned to the professions they left behind in the old country. So the town gained an older generation of tradespeople, grocers, and merchants who helped shape Bristol's business community at the dawn of the 20th century. (Both, courtesy of United Brothers Synagogue.)

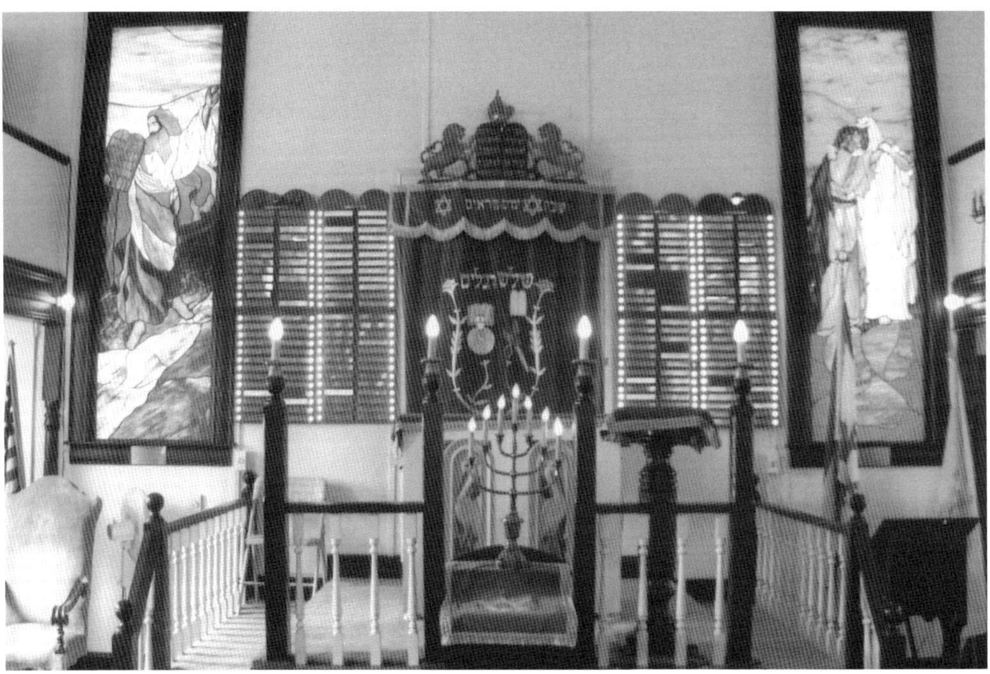

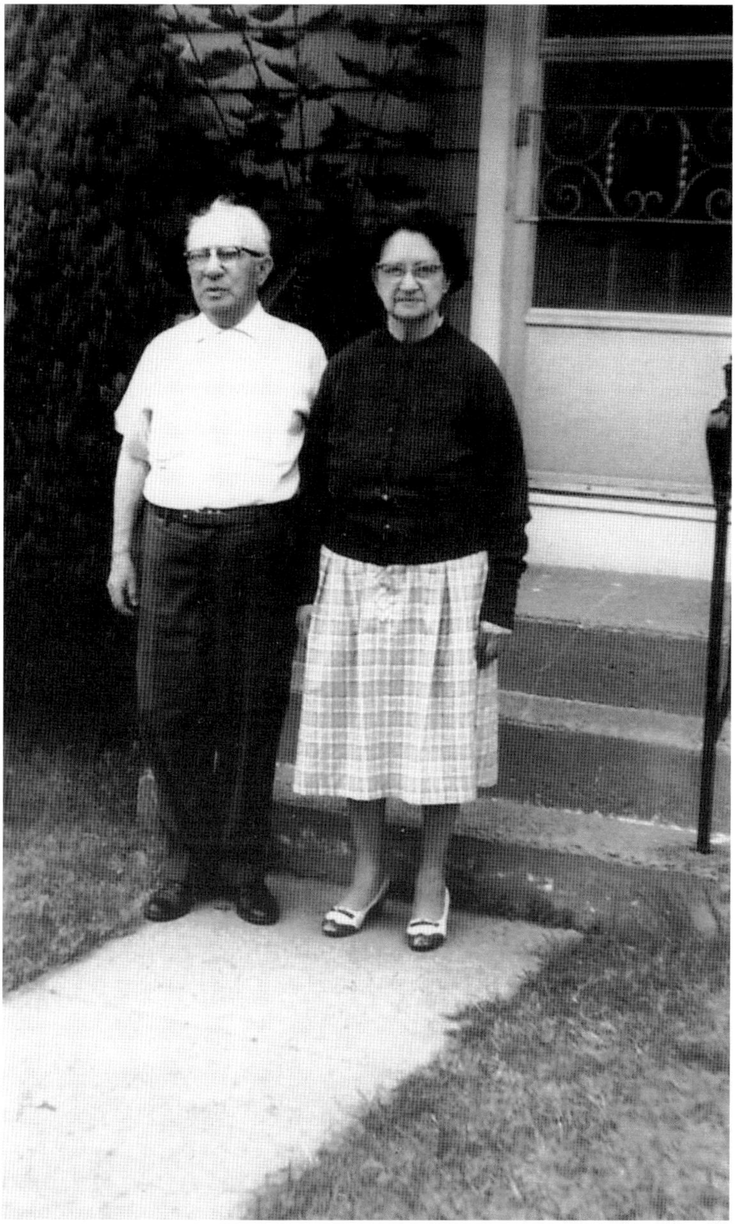

A New Merchant Class Emerges

Several early members of the congregation were prominent members of Bristol's merchant class. The State and Hope Streets location currently occupied by Citizens Bank used to house a shoe store and department store owned by the Eisenstadt family. The State Street building that is the current location of Jesse James Antiques used to be the site of a variety store owned by United Brothers Synagogue charter member and first president Louis Molasky. His descendants still own the building. Gussie and Philip Shushman, pictured, owned and operated Philip's Dry Goods at 574 Wood Street. Suzman's clothing store was another business owned by members of the congregation. It was located on the west side of Hope Street between State and Bradford Streets until relatively recently. (Courtesy of United Brothers Synagogue.)

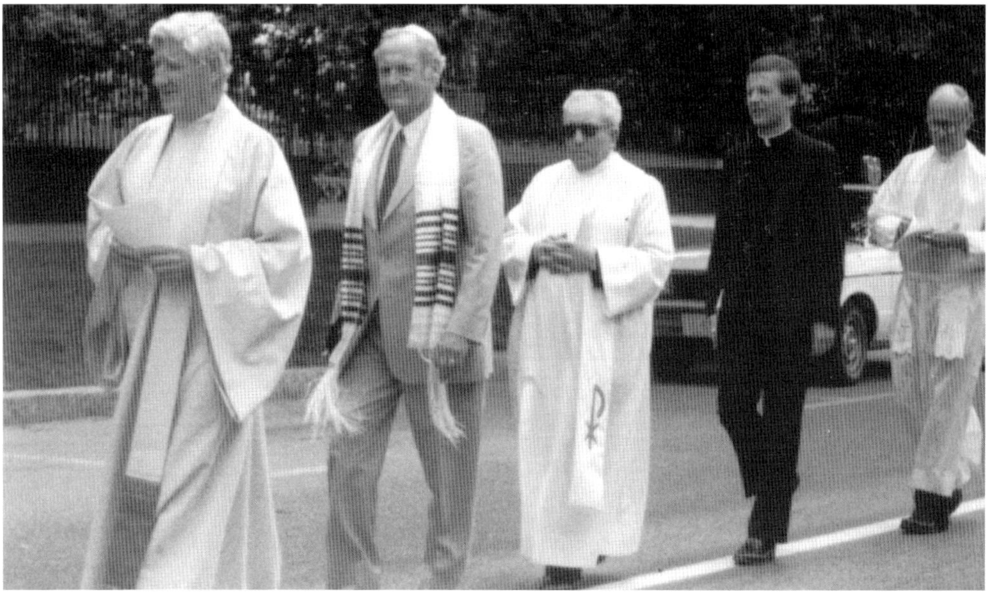

Decline and Rebirth
The United Brothers congregation grew until the 1960s, when it contracted to the point where services were canceled. It was through the stewardship of Dora, Lena, and David Leviten, who maintained the building, and the commitment of community leaders like Alton (above, second in line) and Gloria Brody, Nancy Hillman, and Maynard Suzman that the United Brothers Synagogue was able to enjoy a rebirth in the mid-1970s. (Courtesy of United Brothers Synagogue.)

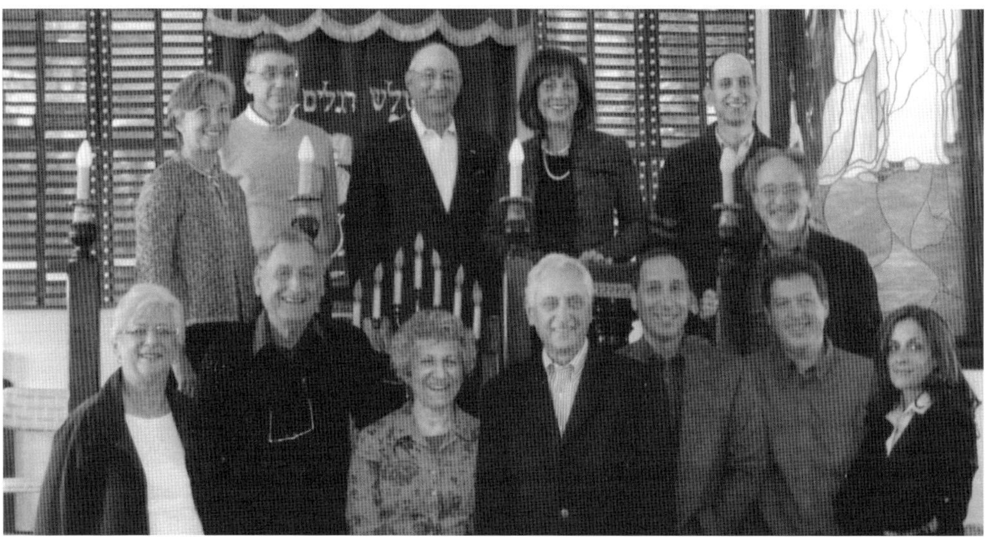

Looking to the Future
Today, the United Brothers congregation consists of some 50 families, totaling a little over 80 individual members. The synagogue recently celebrated its 110th birthday. More than 120 people attended, including descendants of seven of the original founders. The family of one of the founders, Joseph Benjamin and his wife, Emma, held a reunion at the event (above), with some of the Benjamins meeting each other for the first time. (Courtesy of United Brothers Synagogue.)

Stealing Home
Forced to sneak away under cover of darkness from the only home she had ever known clearly made a lasting impression of Theodora DeWolf Colt. Born in Bristol, she lived at Linden Place until she was forced to flee with her family when father George went bankrupt and took Bristol down with him. She spent much of her childhood living on the family sugar plantation, but she never forgot her beautiful home. She married Christopher Colt, the brother of Samuel Colt of gun fame, and had two children, LeBaron and Samuel, the latter of whom grew up to repurchase Linden Place for his mother. She died there in 1901, and Samuel built the Colt Memorial School next door in her honor. (Both, courtesy of Linden Place.)

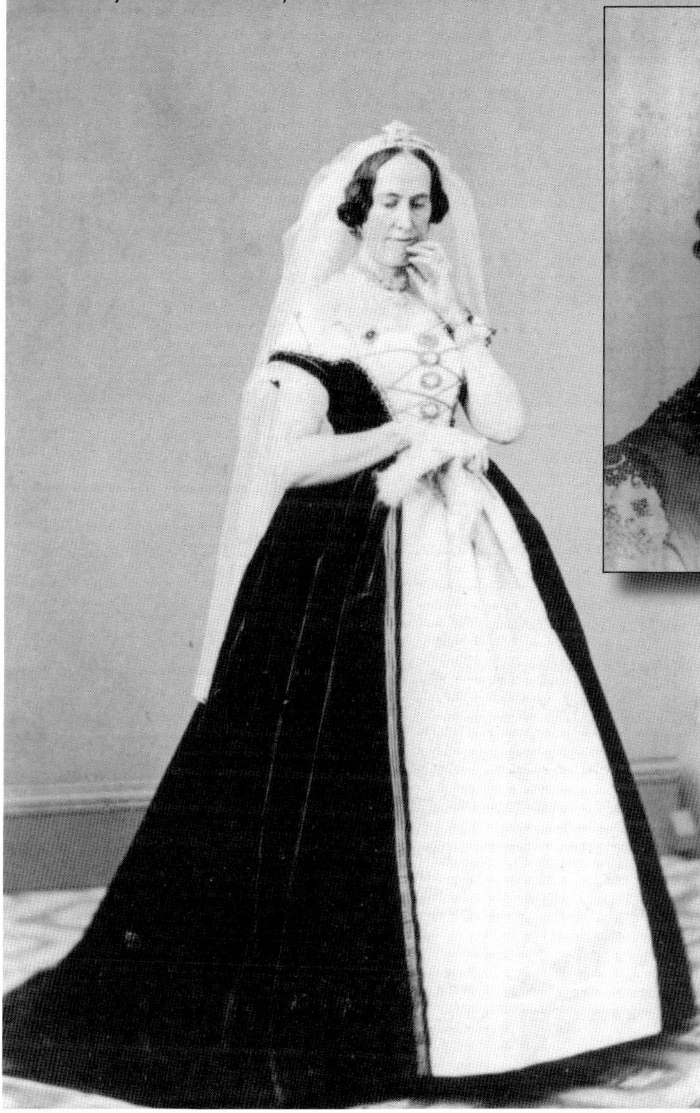

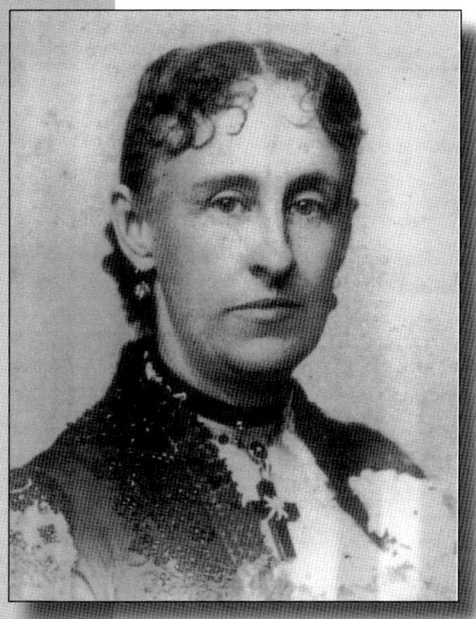

A Fatal Crash?

Though it is hard to say with certainty, these undated photographs may well depict the aftermath of the accident that would end the life of LeBaron Colt, son of LeBaron Bradford and nephew of Samuel Colt. The younger LeBaron died a week after a Colt Farm car crash in 1916 claimed the life of a friend. While this scene may look like a college prank, it almost certainly was not. (All, courtesy of Linden Place.)

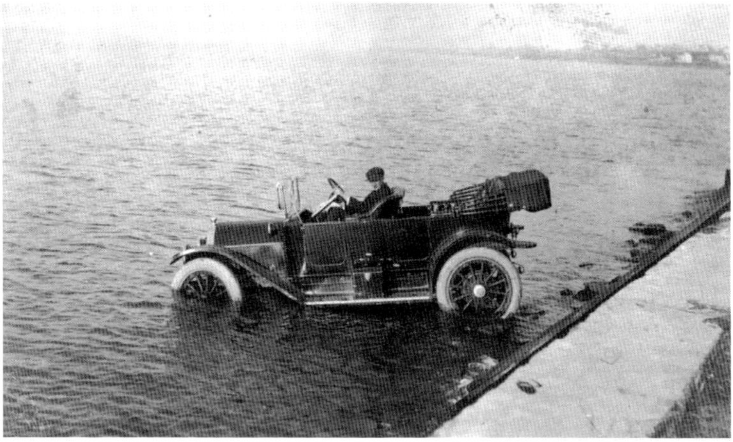

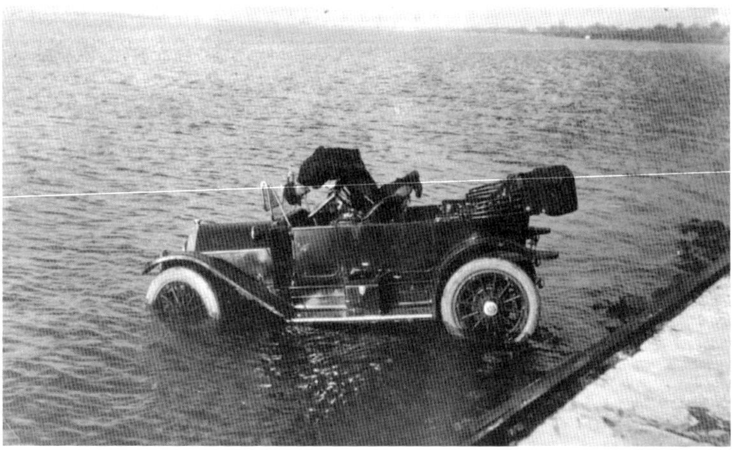

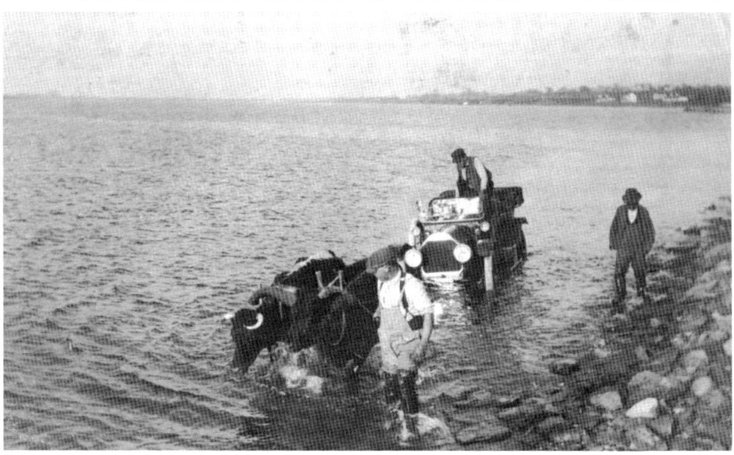

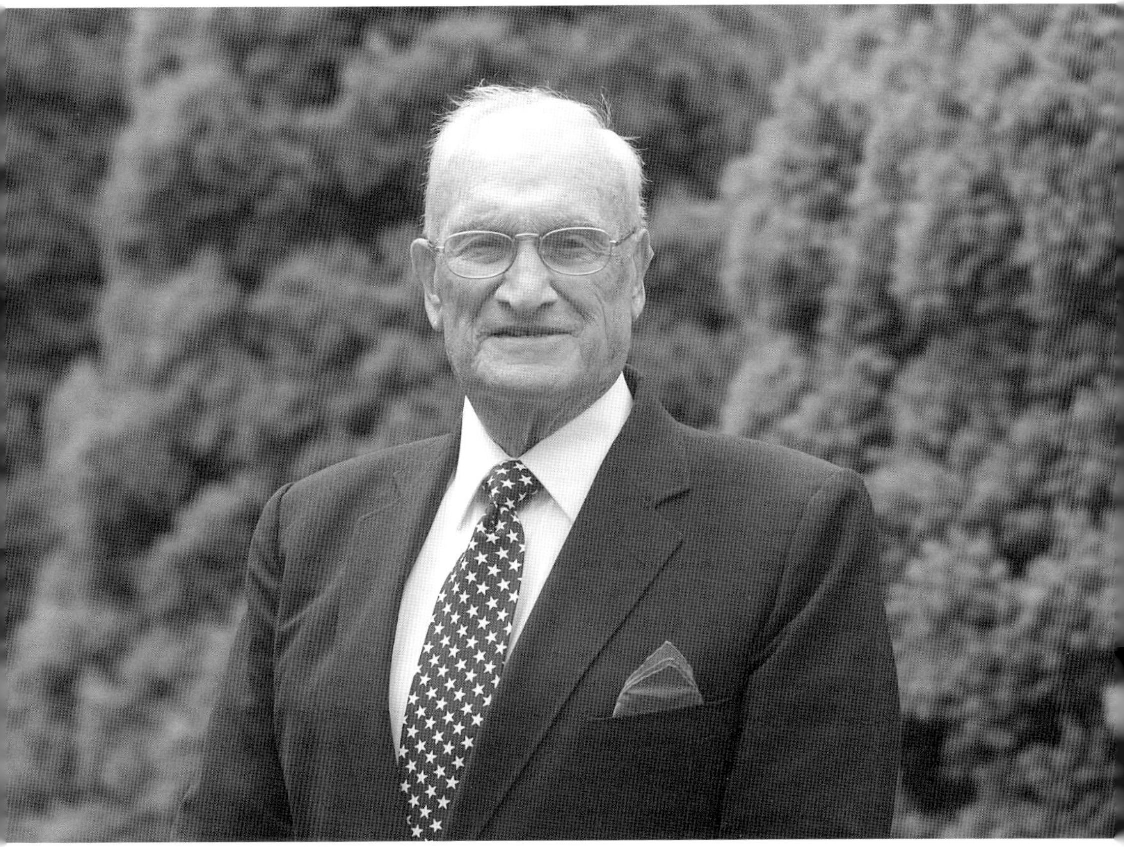

Hector, Sir

It takes a special person to be a role mode for a kid. So what kind of a person does it take to be one for literally hundreds of kids? That would be Hector Massa. A three-sport, All-State athlete at Colt Memorial High School, Massa was the highly regarded athletic director at the old Bristol YMCA, director of Camp Hess Day Camp on Hog Island, and the Roger Williams University athletic director. Massa retired from Roger Williams in 1988. While he has had an impact on several generations of young Bristolians, they have also had an impact on him. "I've worked with people all my life," Massa says, "and I have enjoyed life, and enjoyed the people. Names I forget, faces I don't. I've remembered them all."

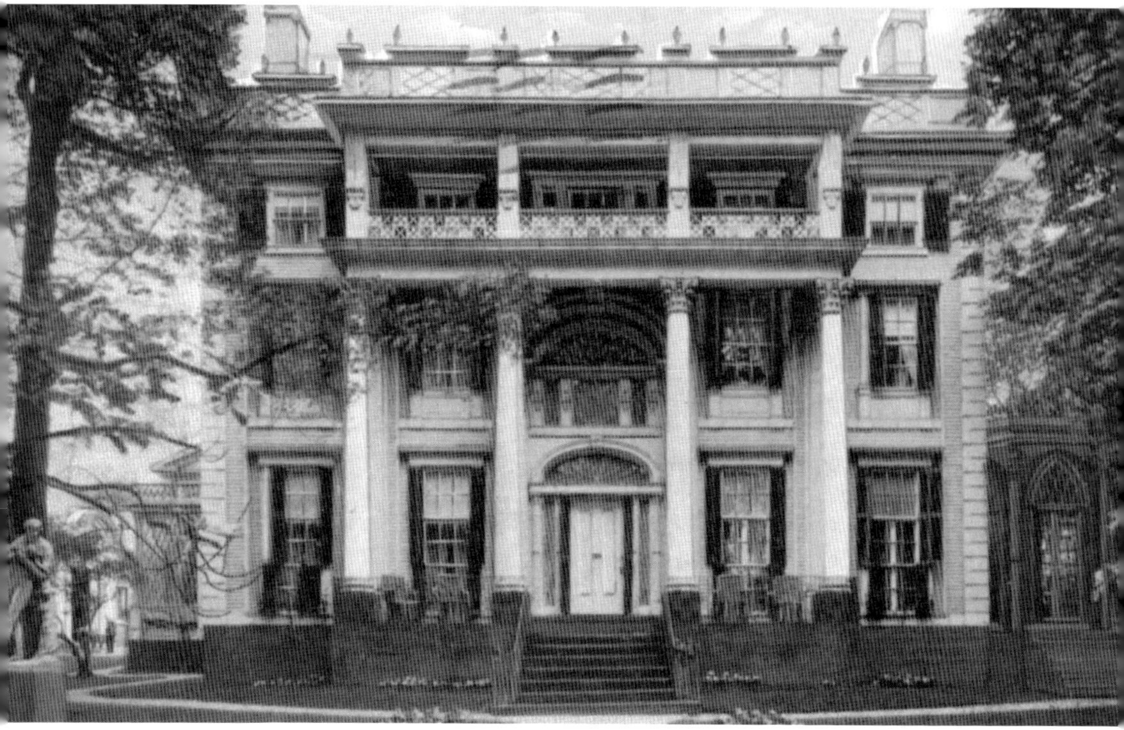

Bristol's Crown Jewel

Whether motivated by admiration or jealousy, George DeWolf hired Russell Warren, the same architect who created his uncle James's mansion, to build a masterpiece in the center of downtown Bristol. Warren was paid $60,000—a king's ransom at the time—and directed to make something more magnificent than James's home, the Mount. Completed in 1810, "Linden Place" features two-story Corinthian columns, two enormous Palladian windows, and a grand, three-story spiral staircase capped with a grand skylight. Linden Place was home to five generations of the DeWolf and Colt families until it was purchased (with the help of a state bond) by the nonprofit Friends of Linden Place from heir Elizabeth Colt Stansfield for $1.5 million. (Both, courtesy of Linden Place.)

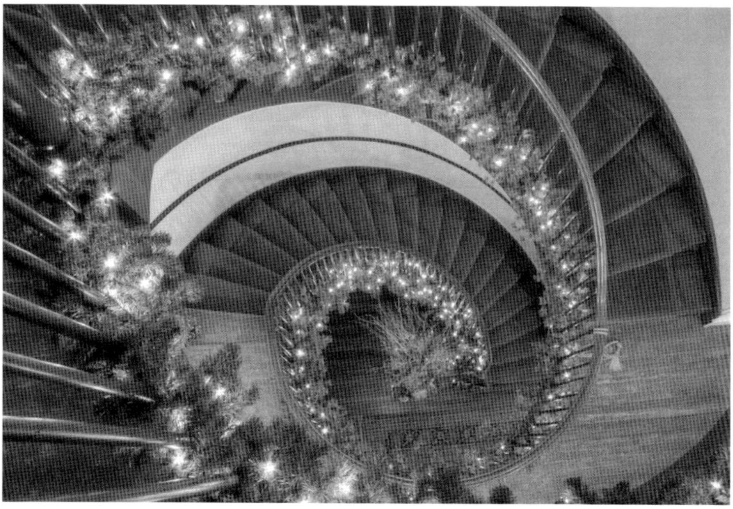

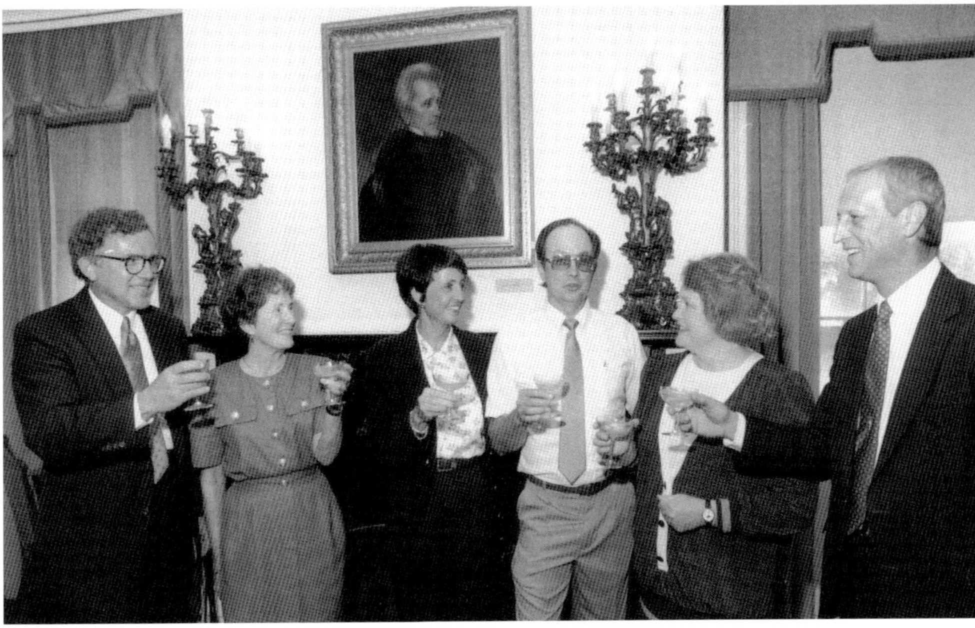

Toasting History

The Friends of Linden Place was formed in the late 1980s in an effort to raise funds to purchase Russell Warren's masterpiece and preserve it for future generations. Here, Friends raising a glass to the property's successful acquisition include, from left to right, an unidentified Fleet Trust officer, Gertie Pardee, Dorothy Emes (the daughter of heir Elizabeth Colt Stansfield), Sam Colt, Mary Millard, and Bill Davis. Below, one of the earliest Friends fundraisers, Colonel Colt's Casino, featured classic cars and classic faces, including, from left to right, Ed Weston, Bonnie Warren, Betty Weston, and Lou Cirillo. (Both, courtesy of Linden Place.)

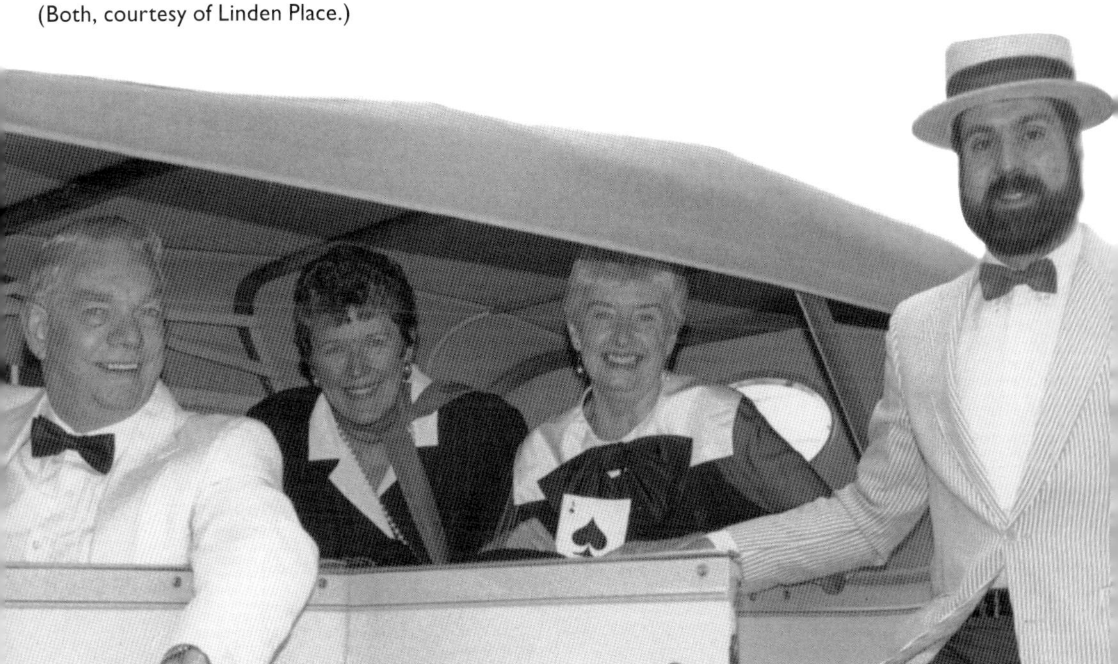

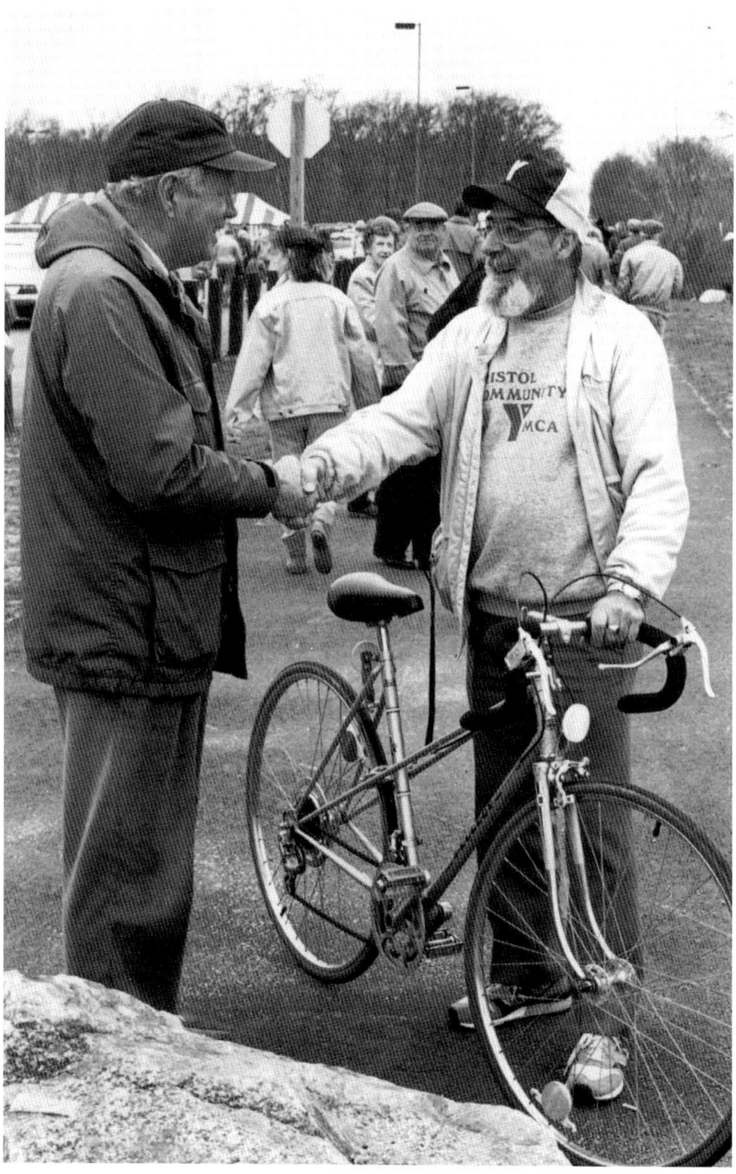

Lasting Legacies

Thomas Byrnes (right) led a long life of community service as town administrator, the District 91 representative to the Rhode Island General Assembly, and executive director of the Bristol YMCA in addition to his 30 years spent with the US Postal Service. But it was his efforts with Friends of the Bike Path, a two-decade effort to see a former rail line transformed to a Bristol-to-Providence bike route, that has secured Byrnes's legacy in Bristol.

Along with Thomas Byrnes, George Sisson (left) led the fight to construct a bike path along the state-owned rail bed between Providence and Bristol. In addition, as delegate from Bristol to the 1986 state constitutional convention, Sisson introduced amendments securing public rights of passage to the waterfront. He also led a group of citizens in an effort to restore the historic 1816 Bristol County Courthouse and Statehouse for public use, receiving both the Jefferson Award for Public Service and the Antoinette Downing Award for Historic Preservation through his efforts. (Courtesy of Michael T. Byrnes.)

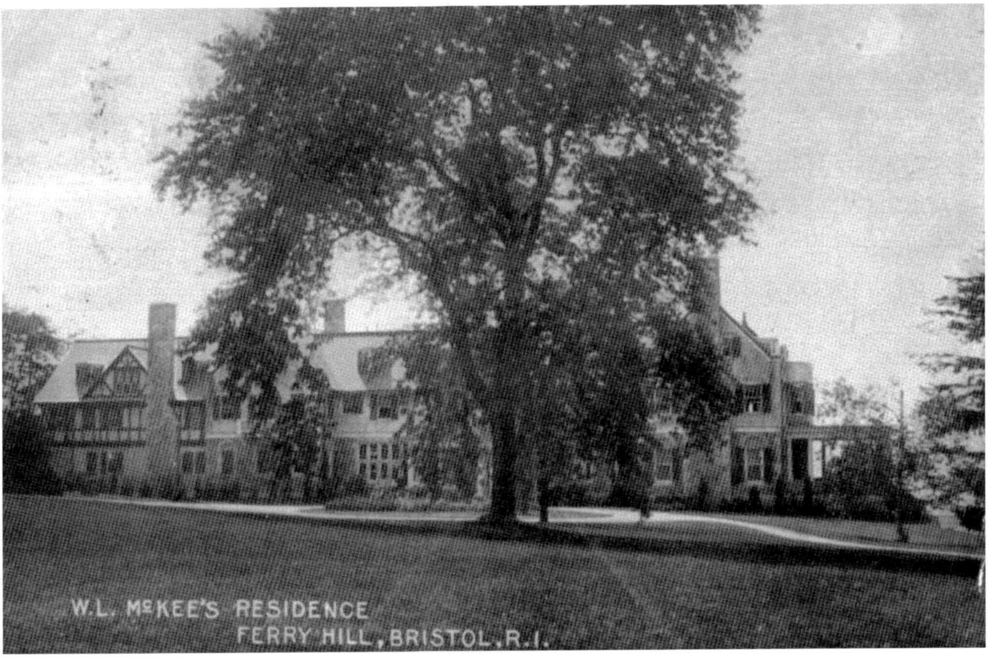

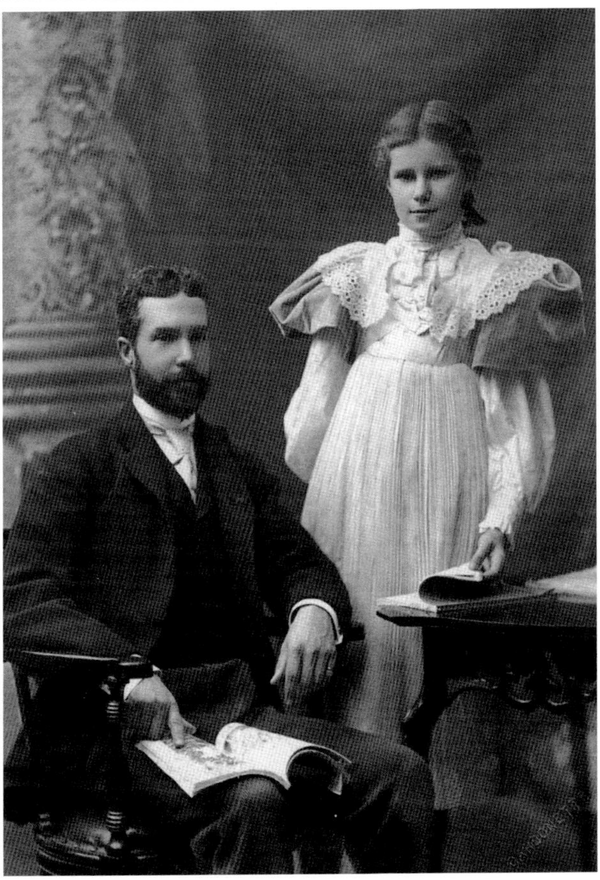

A Gracious Estate, Open to All
Up-and-coming coal baron Augustus Van Wickle met Bessie Pardee, herself a daughter of a coal fortune, in the early 1880s. They married in 1882, and their daughter, Marjorie, was born in 1883. Eleven years later, while summering in Narragansett, Augustus bought a 72-foot steam yacht from the Herreshoff Manufacturing Company and named his yacht *Marjorie* after his beloved young daughter. Looking for suitable land near which he could moor his new toy, Augustus found the piece of property of which Blithewold now sits.

The original Blithewold mansion burned to the ground in June 1906. Bessie and her second husband, William McKee, replaced it with an even larger home that was ready for occupancy by the summer of 1908. (Both, courtesy of Blithewood.)

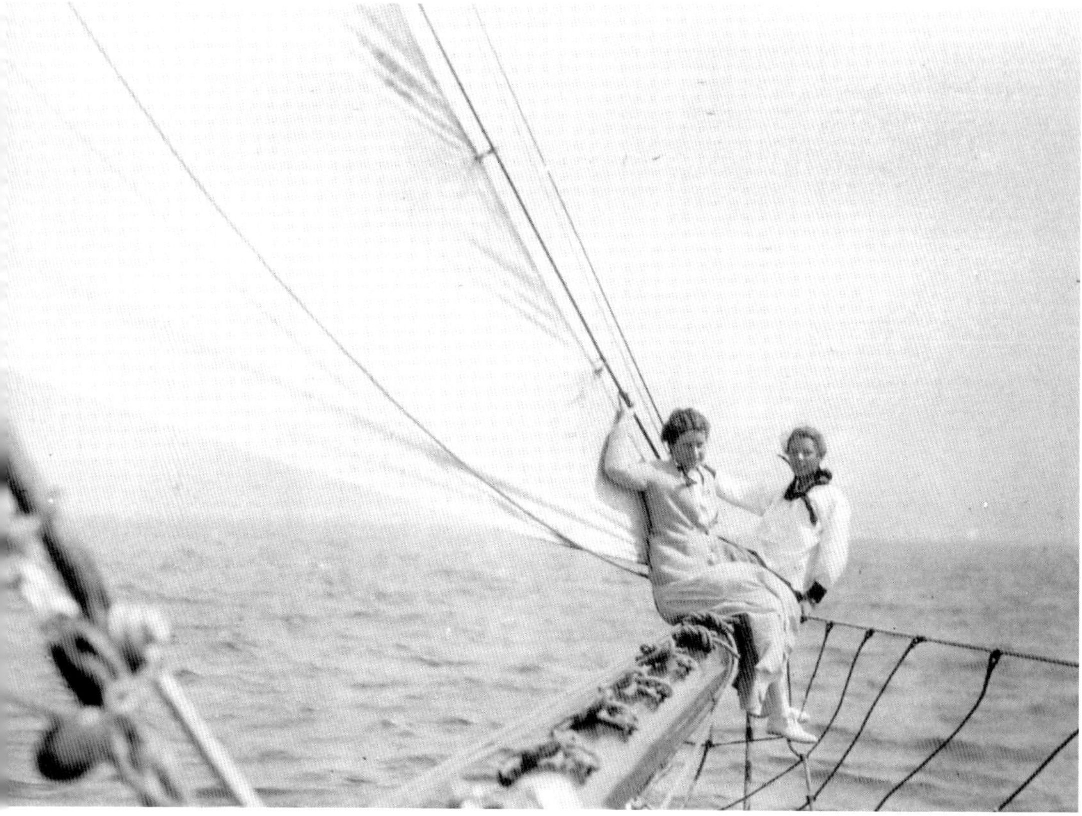

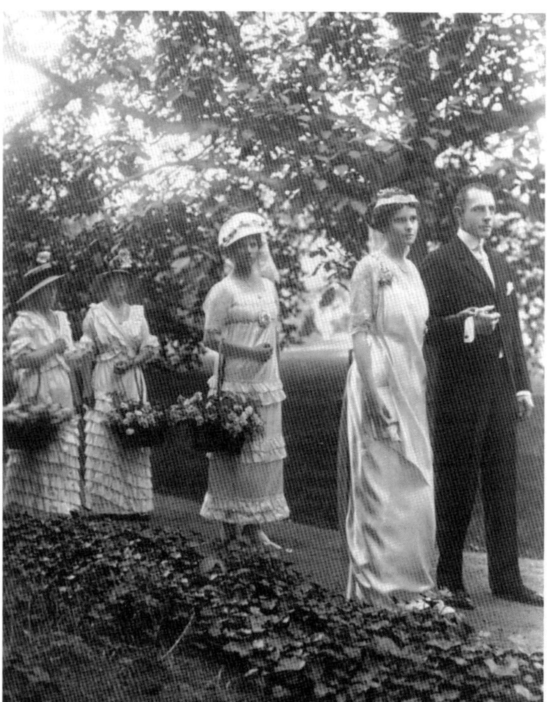

A Second Generation

In 1914, Marjorie married George Armstrong Lyon. The Lyons never had children but enjoyed frequent travel.

The family fortune took a sizable hit in the 1929 stock market crash, forcing the McKees to sell off much of the land to the south of the residence along with their Boston real estate.

Bessie died in 1936, and Marjorie purchased her younger sister Augustine's share of the estate (both are pictured above, sailing). Blithewold remained very dear to Marjorie throughout her life, much of which she spent improving and expanding her collection of specimen trees and other plants. (Both, courtesy of Blithewood.)

70

A Long Life, Well Lived

Marjorie, an avid and skilled painter, died in 1976 at the age of 93, and it was her wish that Blithewold be preserved for the public in perpetuity. That wish was in jeopardy in 1998 when a series of financial missteps threatened to force Blithewold's closure, but the efforts and dedication of a small group of mostly Bristol and Barrington residents quickly raised the needed funds. Today, Blithewold is operating in the black. (Courtesy of Blithewood.)

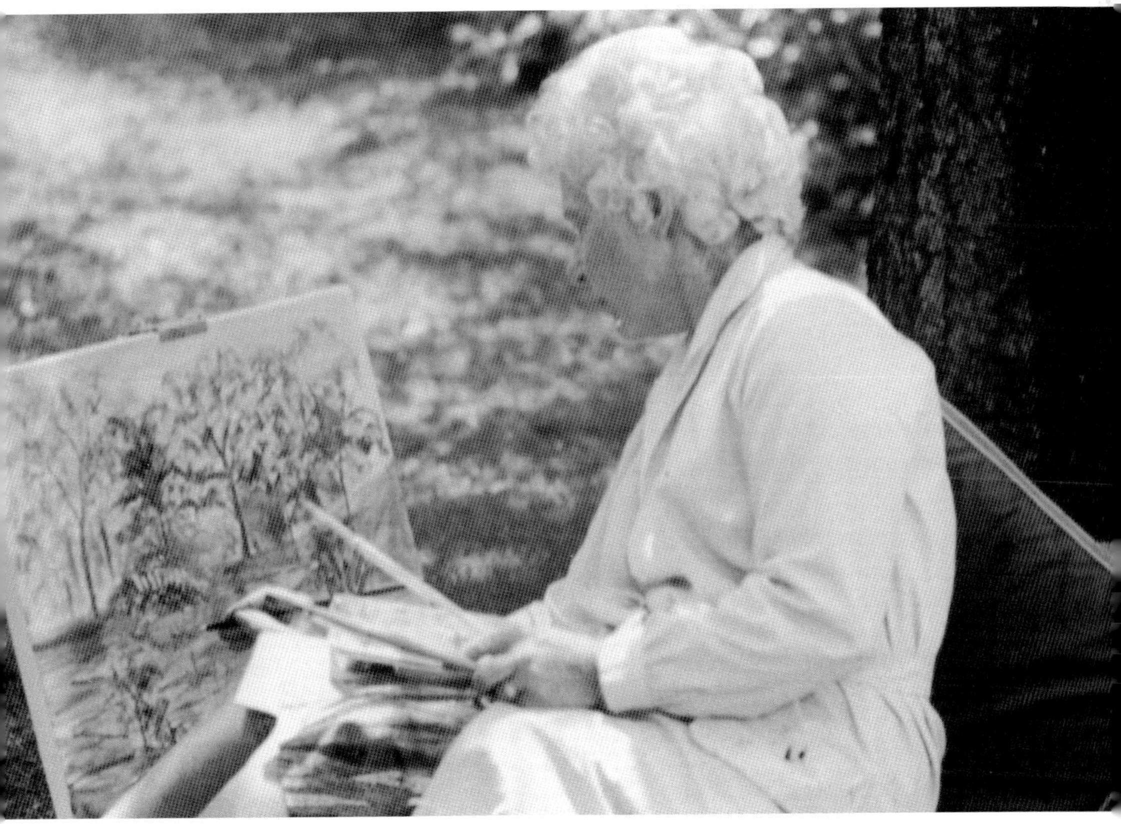

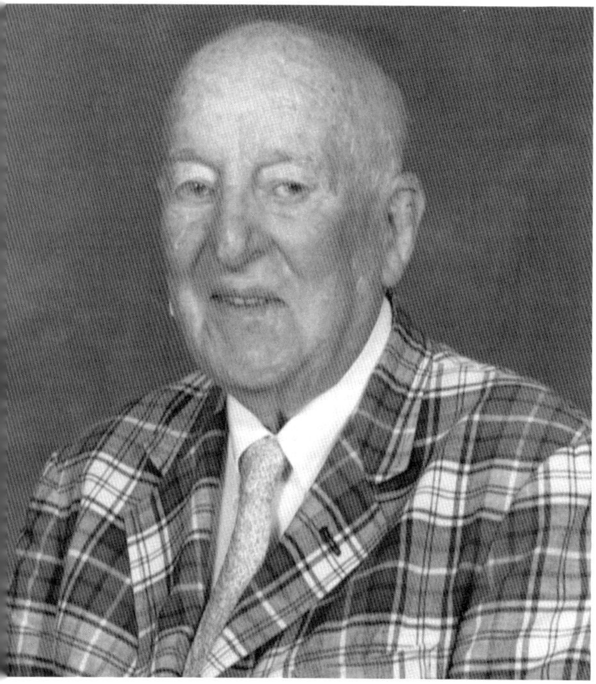

A Lifesaving Endowment

A US Army veteran serving in World War II, Lt. Col. Harold R. "Banny" Bannister (1915–2009) was present at the invasion of Leyte and later Luzon and participated in the then-famous race to Manila to capture that city. Honorably discharged from active duty in 1946, he then served in various assignments and retired as lieutenant colonel in 1968. An outstanding tennis player, Bannister coached the Durfee High School and Southeastern Massachusetts University tennis teams for many years. He was also an avid skier and traveler who skied in all of the major areas of the United States, South America, and Europe. He was also a trustee of the LeBaron Colt Ambulance Corps in Bristol and established an endowment to the town of Bristol to maintain an ambulance in memory of his late wife, Mary Street Bannister, whom he married late in life. (Courtesy of Jeff Hirsch.)

Lady about Town

Louise DeWolf (1898–1986) was a gentlewoman who never married and was always cheerful, despite her estrangement from her only sister, Katherine, after the latter's late-in-life wedding and honeymoon caused her to miss their mother's funeral. DeWolf did not own a car, nor did she need one, choosing instead to walk around town to collect the rents from the many properties she owned. Active in a number of organizations, including the Daughters of the American Revolution, the Rhode Island Historical Society, the Mayflower Society, and the Bristol Historical and Preservation Society, DeWolf also served as director of the Herreshoff Marine Museum. As a member of the board of the Juniper Hill Cemetery, she was instrumental in introducing perpetual care to the property. (Courtesy of Mark Perry.)

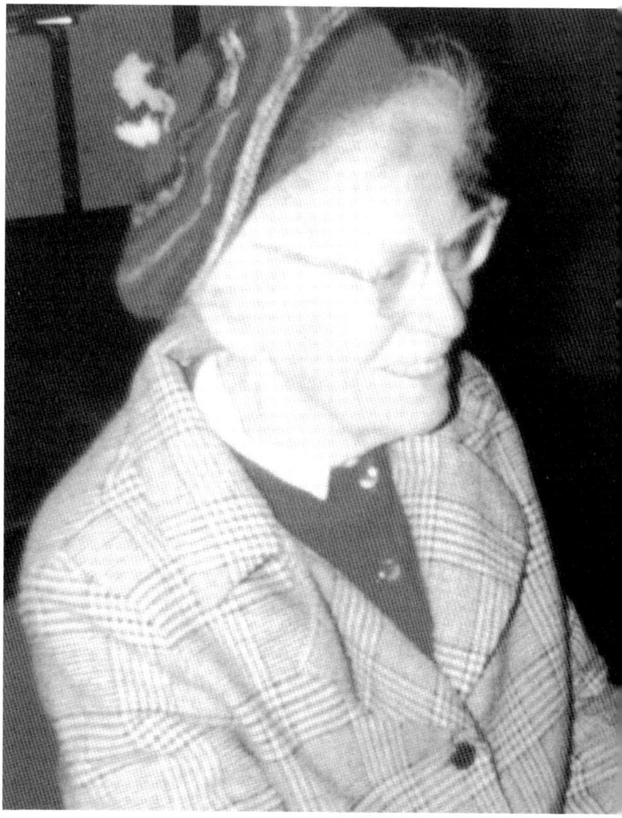

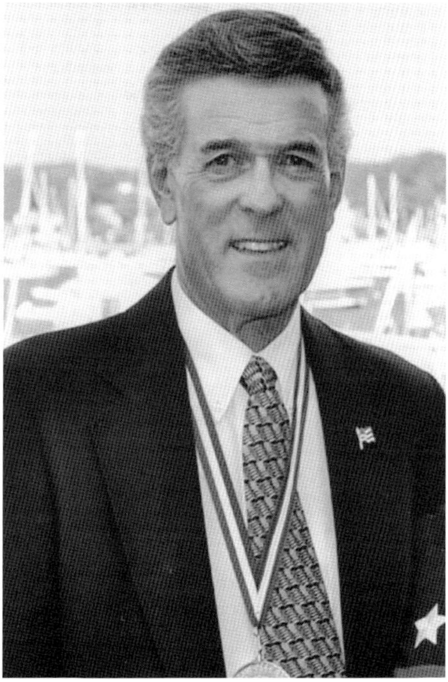

Bloom Where You are Planted
A graduate of the Colt Memorial High School, Edward Castro was an athletic and academic standout who excelled in a 40-year career with Raytheon. As a National Guardsman, YMCA counselor, Little League volunteer and baseball coach, and local historian, he has made countless contributions to Bristol over the years, and he was honored with selection as 2008 Bristol Fourth of July chief marshal. But it may be his amazing, prolific garden for which he is best known. Ed Castro can make his garden grow like almost nobody else, and he had shared that knowledge with local students, teaching children how to maintain their own gardens for more than 15 years. (Courtesy of Edward Castro.)

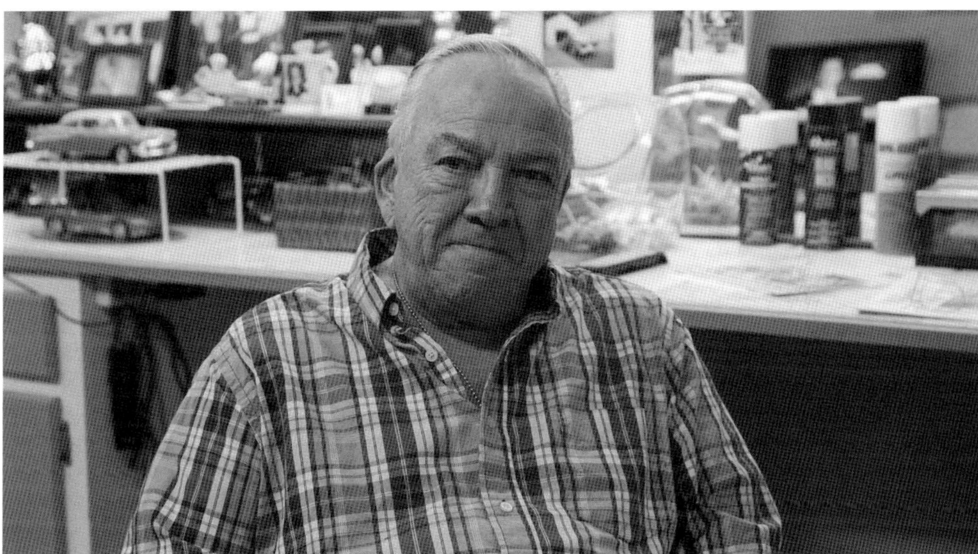

An Honest Cut
Like anywhere else, Bristol's locals know where to go for a proper men's haircut and a little straight talk. For decades, Joseph DiPalma has been providing just that out of a small High Street storefront. He estimates that he has given thousands of haircuts since he started in the trade. Like many people, DiPalma became a barber by following in the footsteps of his father and grandfather. Though he worked doing commercial construction for many years, he returned to scissors after hanging up his hammer. DiPalma cut his first head at the age of 12 as an apprentice in his father's shop, and initially, it wasn't entirely his choice. "My dad made me come to work for him," DiPalma says, "so I would stop chasing the ladies."

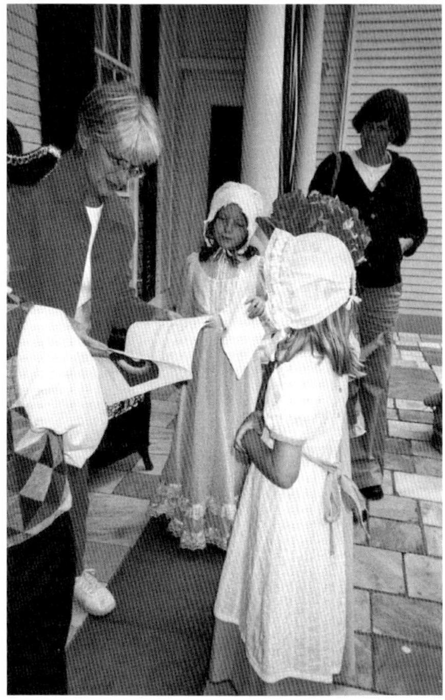

Teaching Them Well

Though Carol Bellmore Glanville officially launched the History Kids club in 2001 while teaching at the former Reynolds Arts Magnet School, the program had its genesis years earlier, when she dressed her own young son and daughter in period clothes and brought them with her while serving as a docent at Warren's Maxwell House. Since then, hundreds of children have participated in History Kids, some beginning as pre-kindergarten students, tagging along with older siblings and continuing through the fifth grade. In 2008, Glanville and her History Kids were recognized in *Best Practices For Teaching Social Studies: What Award-Winning Teachers Do* by Randi Stone. Now retired from her career in the classroom, it's hard to believe that it almost didn't happen. Her parents thought dental hygiene or secretarial school was a better option and that was what they were willing to pay for. So Glanville became a hygienist long enough to earn the money to get a bachelor's degree herself. Now that's dedication. (Both, courtesy of Carol Glanville.)

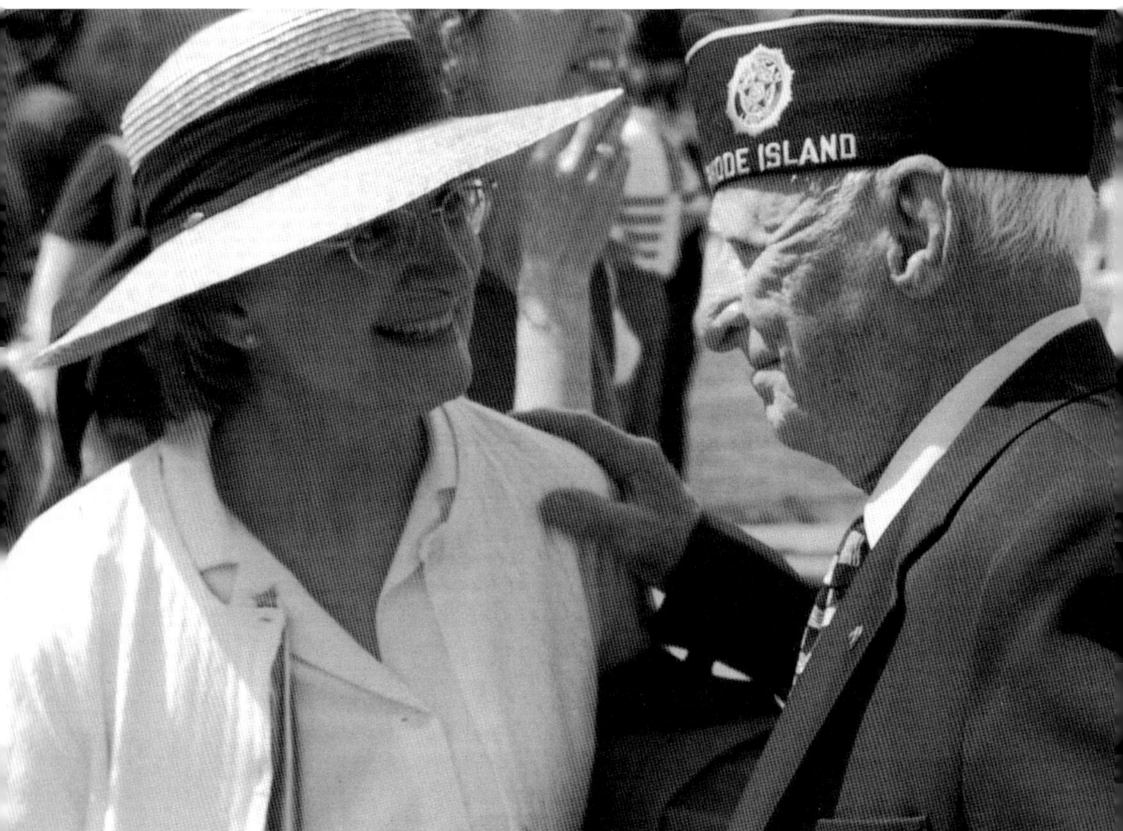

A Generous and Gentle Spirit

When Bristol lost Lombard Pozzi (1945–2013) at the far-too-young age of 67, it lost the person who was probably more than any other, responsible for the successful preservation of the town's architectural heritage. A historic preservation architect who spent most of his career in private practice, Pozzi has saved countless neglected structures throughout Rhode Island and particularly in Bristol and Warren. As Bristol's "architect-in-residence," some of the many buildings Lombard helped create or preserve include the Benjamin Church Home, Burnside Memorial Hall, Linden Place, Mount Hope Farm, the Bristol Statehouse, the Roger Williams University Performing Arts Center, Rogers Free Library, and the Peaberry Block. Pozzi routinely offered his architectural expertise to friends and strangers alike, making it impossible to quantify the number of buildings that have benefitted from one of his sketches or suggestions. (Courtesy of Lindsay Green.)

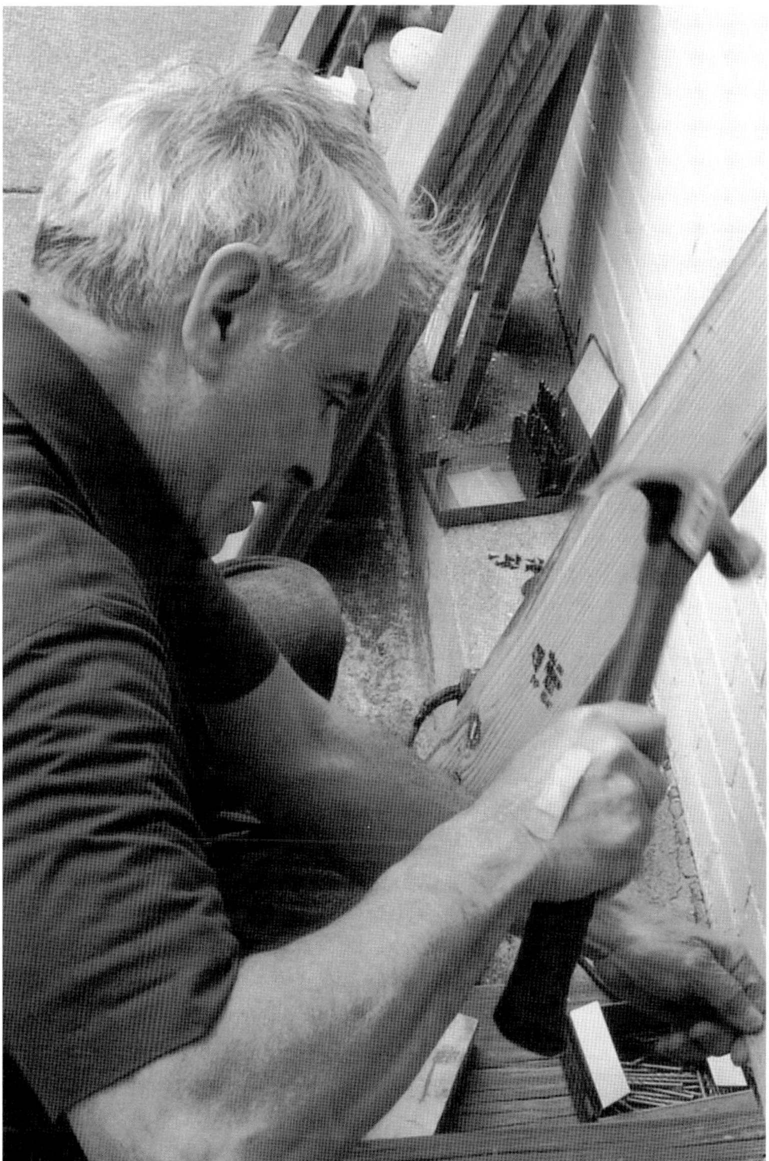

Energy to Spare

For years, Joan Roth used to work as a teacher in the public schools, and while the common term for "used to work" is "retired," it's impossible to suggest that Roth has retired from anything, whether directing her Bristol County Chorus, serving as docent extraordinaire at the Linden Place Mansion and Museum, or adopting new technologies and mastering social media. With an energy that belies the number on her driver's license (which she will no doubt be renewing for decades to come), this octogenarian force of nature has done far more than her share for her hometown. Bristol, and all its residents, are fortunate to have her in their corner. (Courtesy of Joan Roth.)

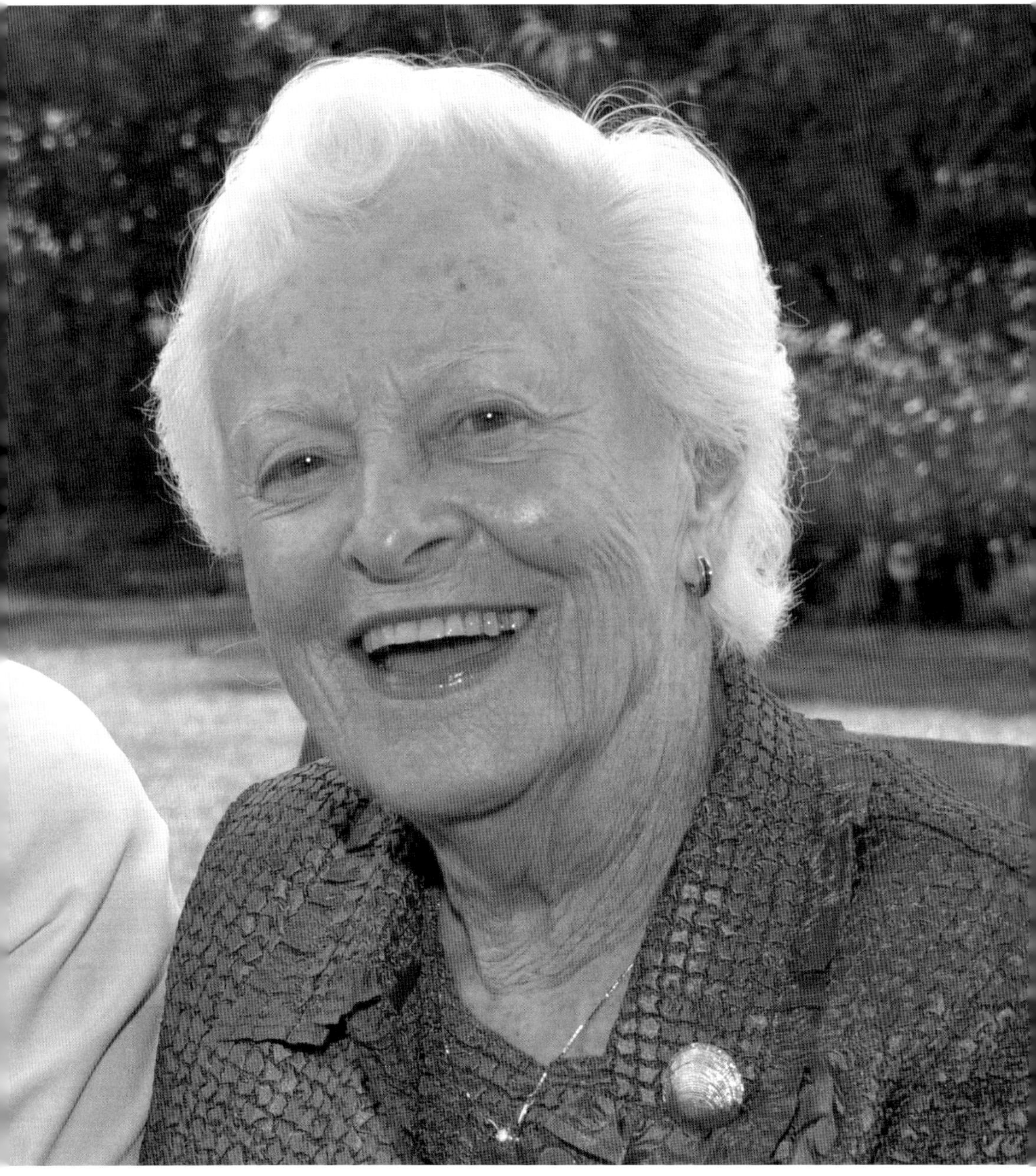

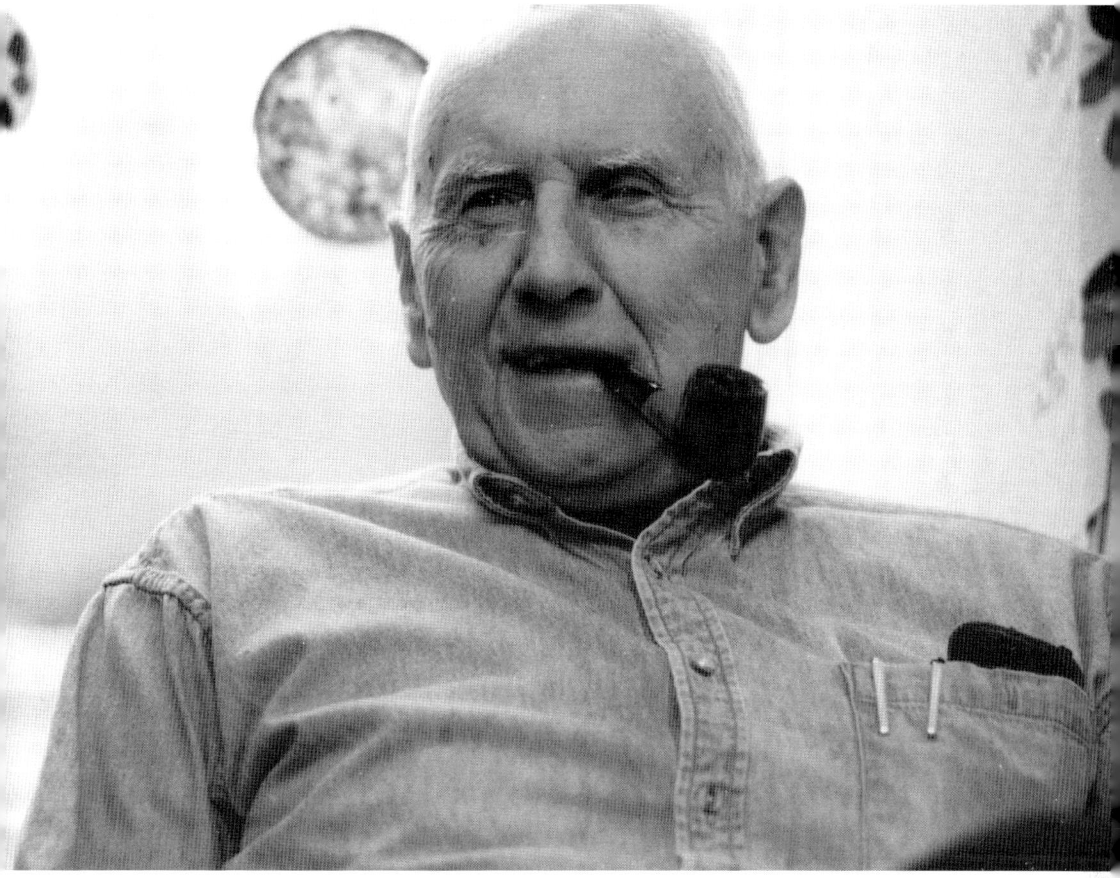

The Healer

The Reverend Aaron Usher grew up on a dairy farm in Bristol and received a degree from the Berkeley Divinity School at Yale in 1966. Ordained as a priest the following year, Usher conducted healing commissions beginning in 1988. He served several years as rector of various parishes and has conducted healing missions in 42 states as well as in Germany, France, Canada, Italy, the Soviet Union, Grenada, and Geneva. He received a proclamation from the governor of Rhode Island for his work on hunger awareness, and the City of Pawtucket declared September 15, 1985, "Aaron Usher Day." Usher also authored several books, including *Selma Diary*, *Fullness of Emptiness*, and *With Russia From Love.* (Both, courtesy of St. Michael's Church.)

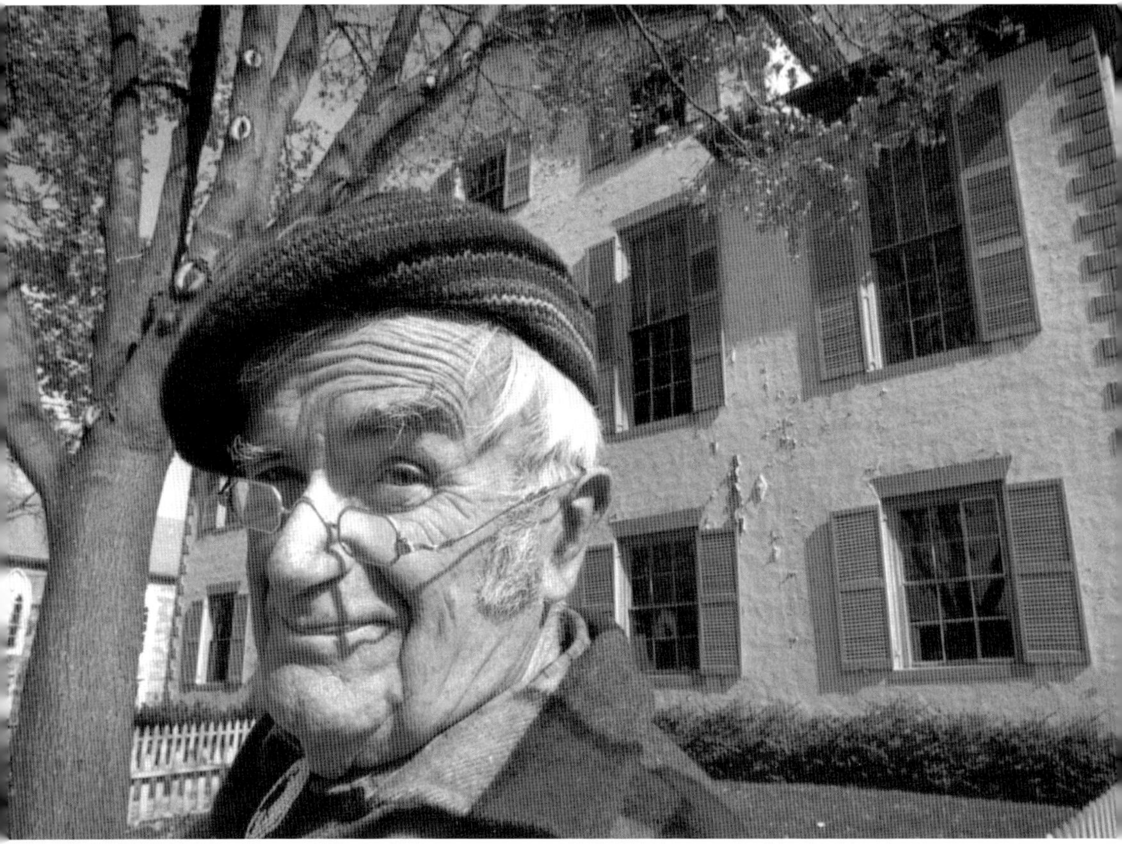

Even the Pope Believed in This Santa

For more than 60 years, Bristolian James D. "Jimmy" Rielly (1908–1991) was Rhode Island's top Santa, a career that began in 1928 at the age of 19 at an abandoned chicken coop where several underprivileged children had made their home. Rielly appeared as Santa Claus primarily at charitable organizations, orphanages, military bases, and medical facilities and never took any money for his appearances. He was featured in hundreds of newspapers and magazines and on national television shows, and he received

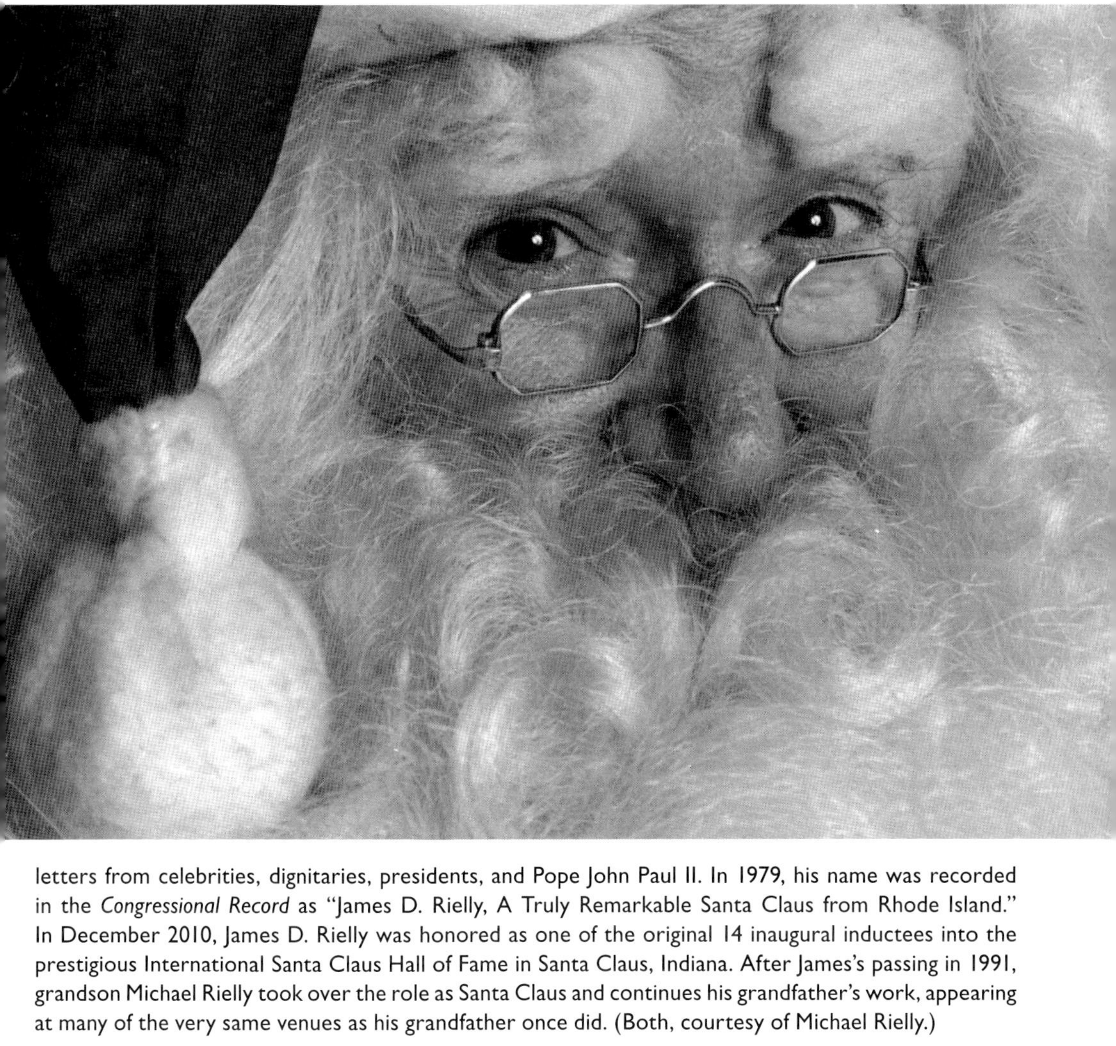

letters from celebrities, dignitaries, presidents, and Pope John Paul II. In 1979, his name was recorded in the *Congressional Record* as "James D. Rielly, A Truly Remarkable Santa Claus from Rhode Island." In December 2010, James D. Rielly was honored as one of the original 14 inaugural inductees into the prestigious International Santa Claus Hall of Fame in Santa Claus, Indiana. After James's passing in 1991, grandson Michael Rielly took over the role as Santa Claus and continues his grandfather's work, appearing at many of the very same venues as his grandfather once did. (Both, courtesy of Michael Rielly.)

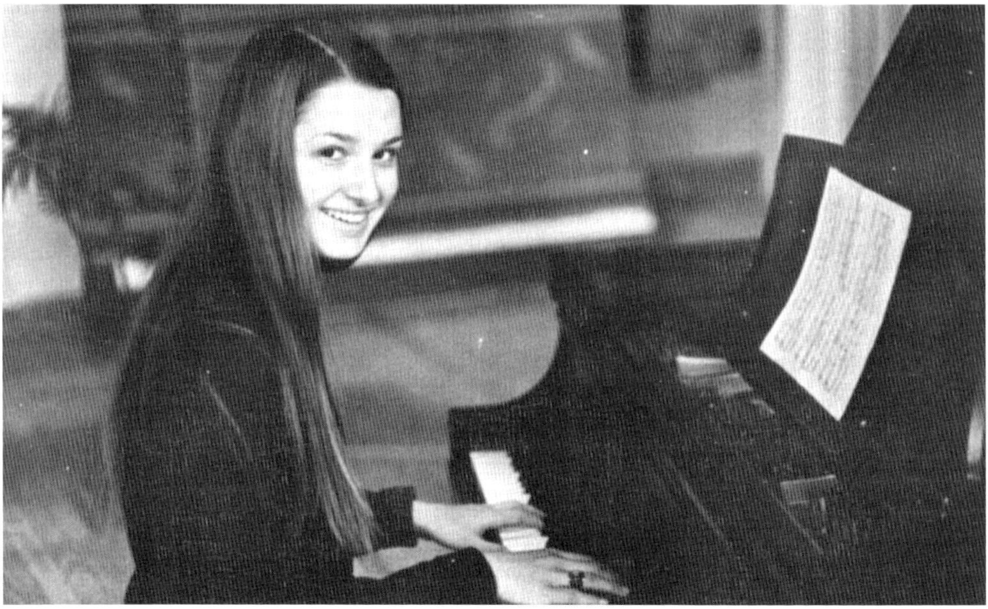

Beautiful Music
Candy Burnham Alessandro estimates that she has taught more than 1,000 students in her more than 37 years as a piano teacher, though she admits it is something she never stopped to think about. And what about getting kids to practice? It depends on the student. "It's not a problem with many of them, but with some you have to dig deep into your bag of tricks," she says. Studying music education at Rhode Island College after graduating from Bristol High School was an easy choice for Candy—she grew up in a musical family, with her piano teacher right down the street. Some of her former students are quite accomplished musicians, and she knows of at least one who has gone into music education herself. "I appreciate the fact that I may not have made all my students into musicians," she says. "But if I can at least get most of them to maintain an appreciation for music, I will have done my job." (Courtesy of Candace Burnham Alessandro.)

An Artful Love of Learning
The Sea Side Nursery School has served as a wonderful place for young children to learn, play, and grow for more than three decades. Recognizing the need for a school that more actively integrated the arts, Pamela and John Paul Fernandes opened Sea Side's doors in September 1983. Pamela is a professional singer, avid gardener, and herbalist; John Paul is an artist whose work has been featured at the Newport Art Museum, DuBlois Gallery, Imago Gallery, and Hope Gallery and shown by the Art League of Rhode Island. Together, they are giving generations of Bristolians their best possible start in life, regardless of ability to pay. Sea Side offers need-based financial scholarships, and no child has ever been turned away. (Courtesy of Pamela Fernandes.)

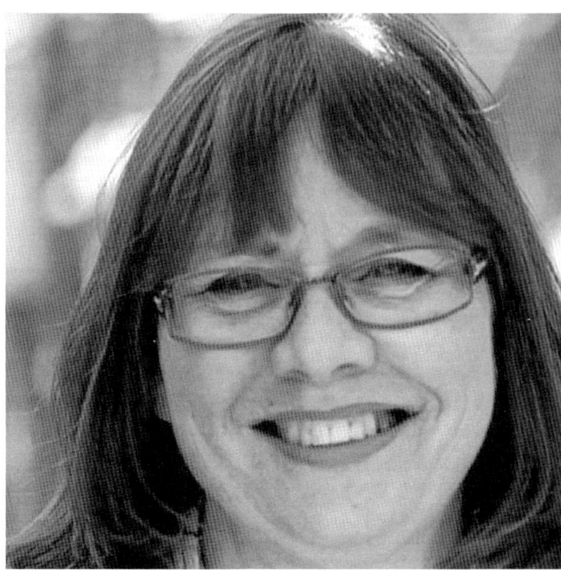

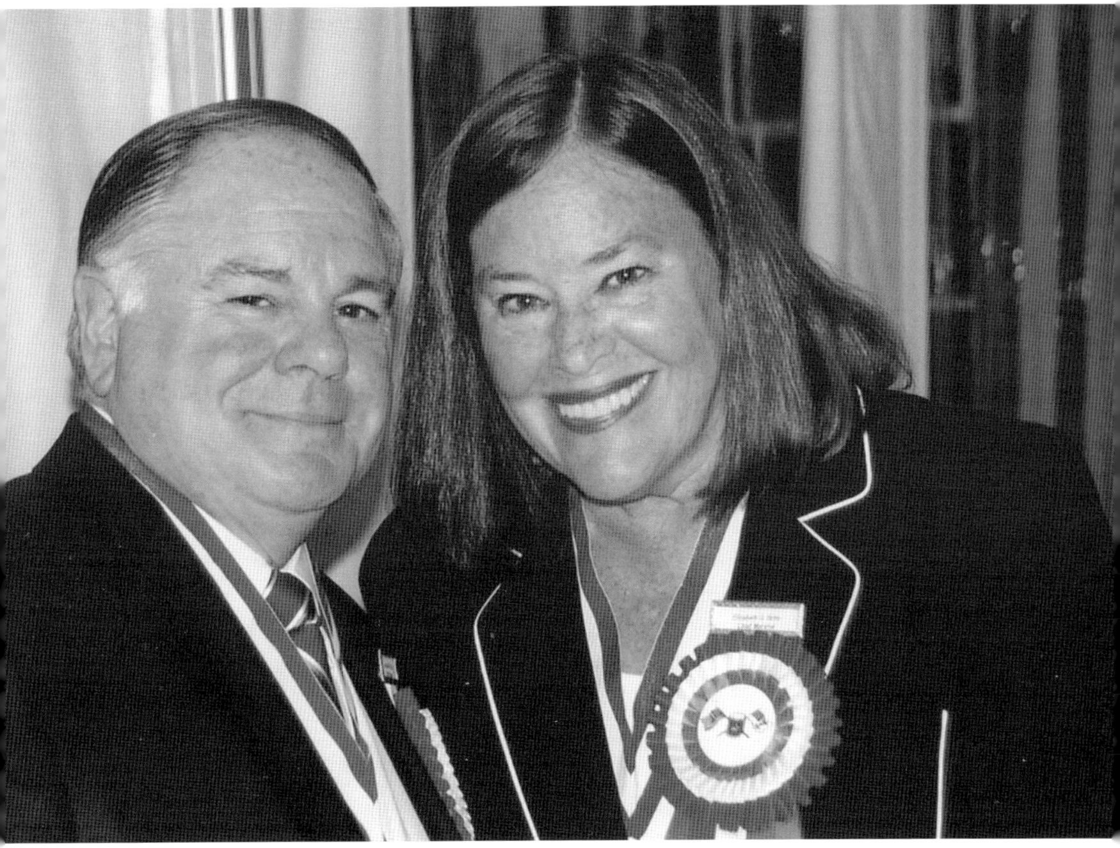

Teamwork
Joe and Betty Brito have been married for more than 30 years, and both together and individually, they have accomplished a lot. A former English teacher and department chair at Mount Hope High School, Betty now serves as the executive director of a national organization that impacts educational excellence in issues related to teaching, learning, and leading. Joe is the third generation in his family utility contacting company, launched by a grandfather who, at the time, could not read or write, but he certainly knew how to work. When they aren't working at their day jobs, Betty can usually be found volunteering for her church, the Rogers Free Library, or the animal shelter; for his part, Joe serves as a trustee for Roger Williams University, on the Mount Hope Farm Board of Directors, as vice commodore at the Bristol Yacht Club, and on the Bank Newport Board of Governors. And that's just the "Readers Digest" version. For both Britos, family is a priority. When asked what he considered to be his greatest achievement, Joe's answer came quickly: "I'm Betty Brito's husband." (Courtesy of Betty and Joe Brito.)

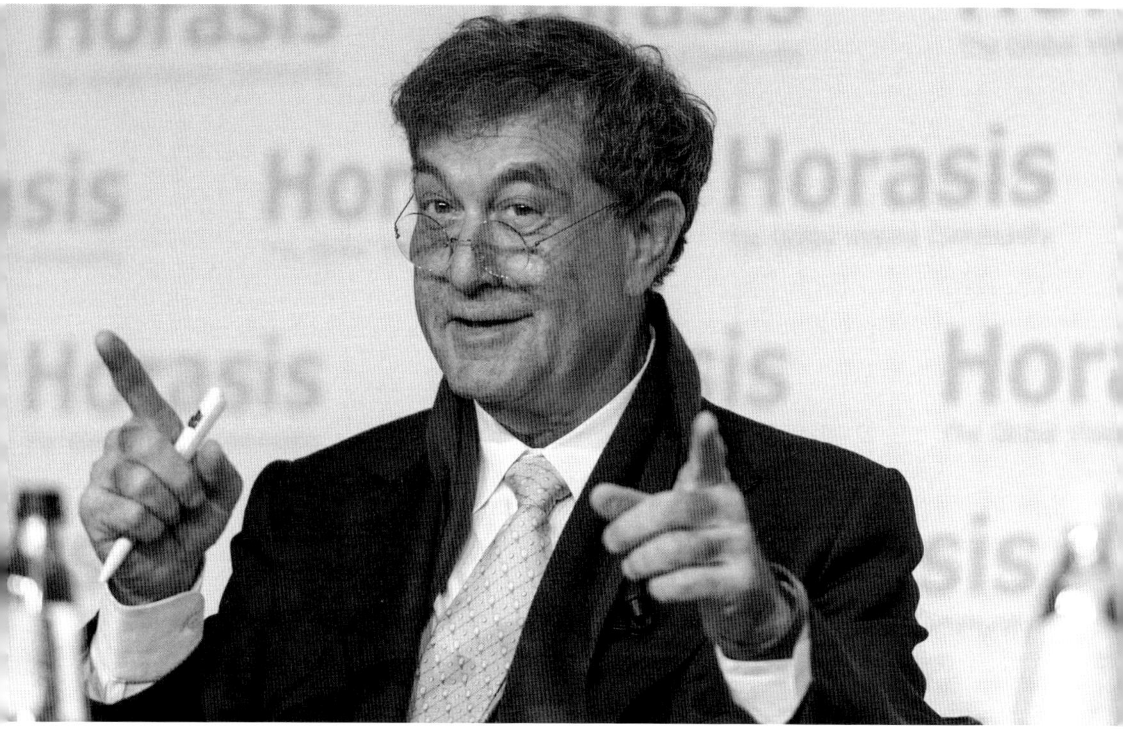

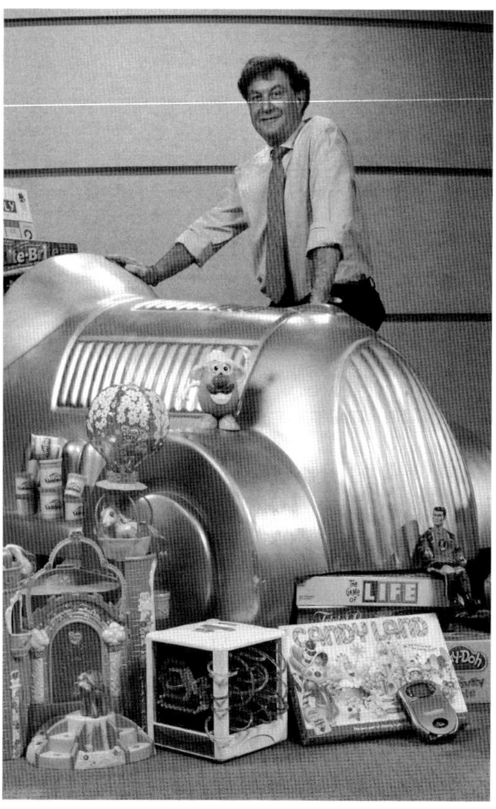

Philanthropy, a World Away from Child's Play
As chief executive officer, Alan Hassenfeld, currently Hasbro's Executive Committee chairman, made his multi-billion-dollar international toy company one of the most recognized and respected in the world. During and since that time, he has been involved in literally hundreds of charitable and social causes. His enthusiasm and spirit has touched the lives of millions of people and impacted communities across the world, whether fighting for the human rights of manufacturing workers in Asia or coexistence in the Middle East. Alan's charitable work includes children's issues, social responsibility, political reform, and social entrepreneurship; his family foundation serves as a catalyst for positive change and collaboration. He has been honored many times by organizations from universities to political and religious communities to corporate institutes for successfully parlaying his position at Hasbro to positively affect the lives of people across the world. (Both, courtesy of Alan Hassenfeld.)

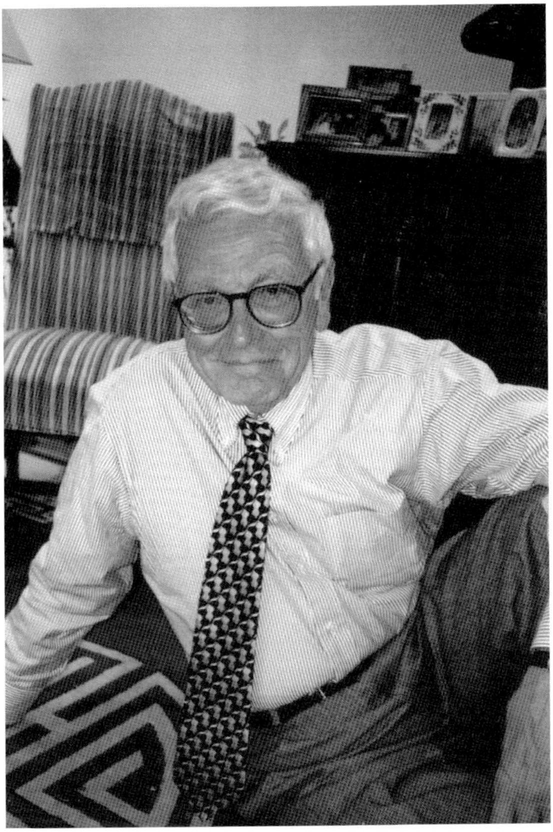

A Love of French and the Arts

Bob Arruda has spent much of his life on the same block in downtown Bristol, but his studies, work, and passion have brought him around the world. Well versed in languages including French, Spanish, Portuguese, and Russian, Arruda received a bachelor of science degree from the Georgetown School of Foreign Service and spent many years working and studying in Europe, bringing his experiences back to Rhode Island and his many students here. Much of his career has been spent teaching languages at Rhode Island universities including Brown, Providence College, Rhode Island College, and Salve Regina, and his many degrees include a master's from Brown and a doctorate from Middlebury College in Vermont. One of the original members of the Bristol Art Museum, Arruda has also served with Mosaico, Mount Hope Farm, and the Rogers Free Library. He and his wife, Linda, proprietor of Paper, Packaging, and Panache, still live on his home block. (Both, courtesy Bob and Linda Arruda.)

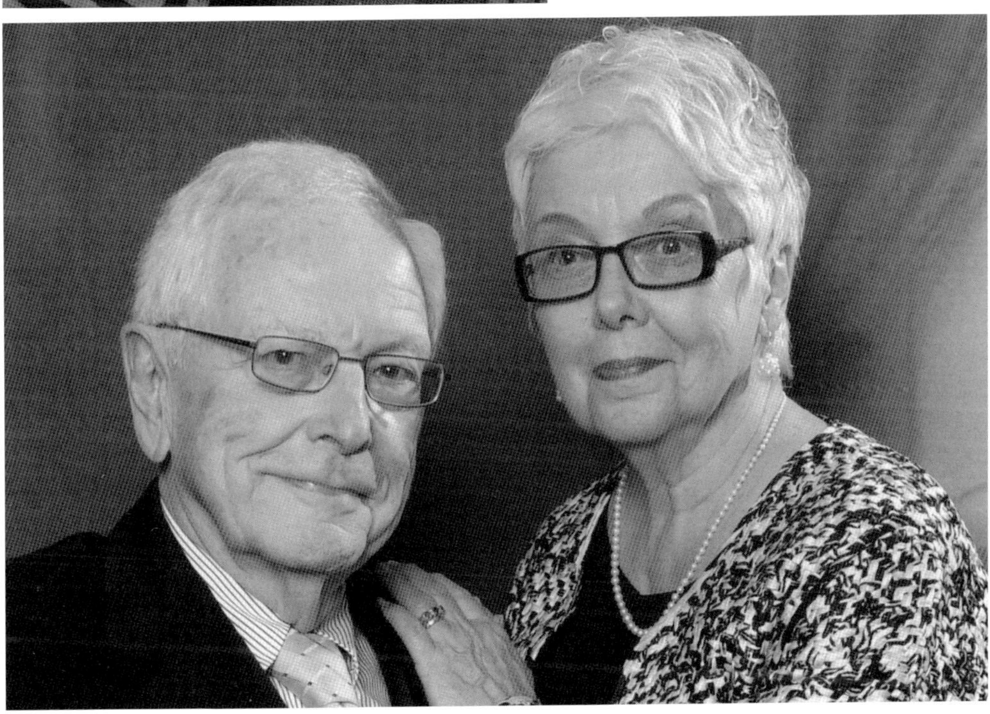

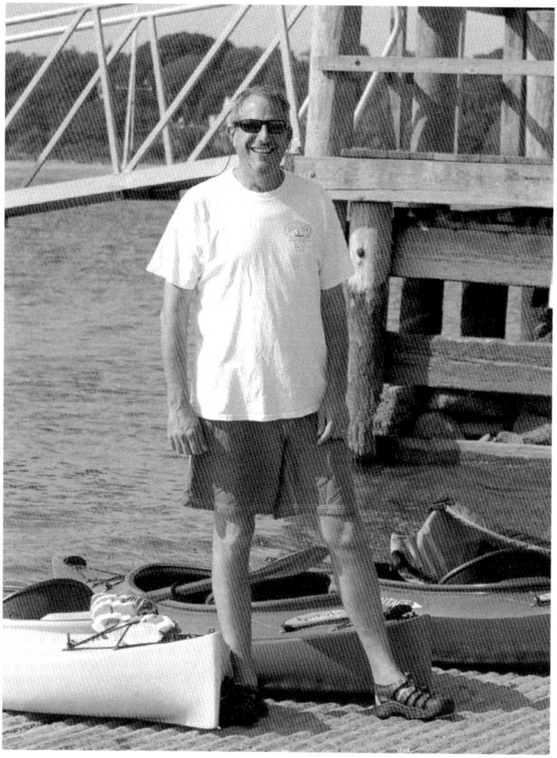

Master of Ceremonies

While the idea of an IBM business executive with pitch-perfect timing and stand-up comedy skills may paint an antithetical picture, that's exactly what Bristol has in Tony Morettini. An East Providence native, Morettini is a happy addition whose talents have been pressed into service on many occasions as the master of ceremonies for local fundraisers as well as the merchants' association holiday raffle, where he (dressed as Jack Frost for the latter) holds crowds of hundreds rapt. Morettini has a serious side, too, giving of his time and efforts for such groups as Save Bristol Harbor and Voices for Bristol. Often seen cruising town in his Mini Cooper, he was part of an honor guard that traveled the 2013 parade route with chief marshal Lou Cirillo, another Mini aficionado.

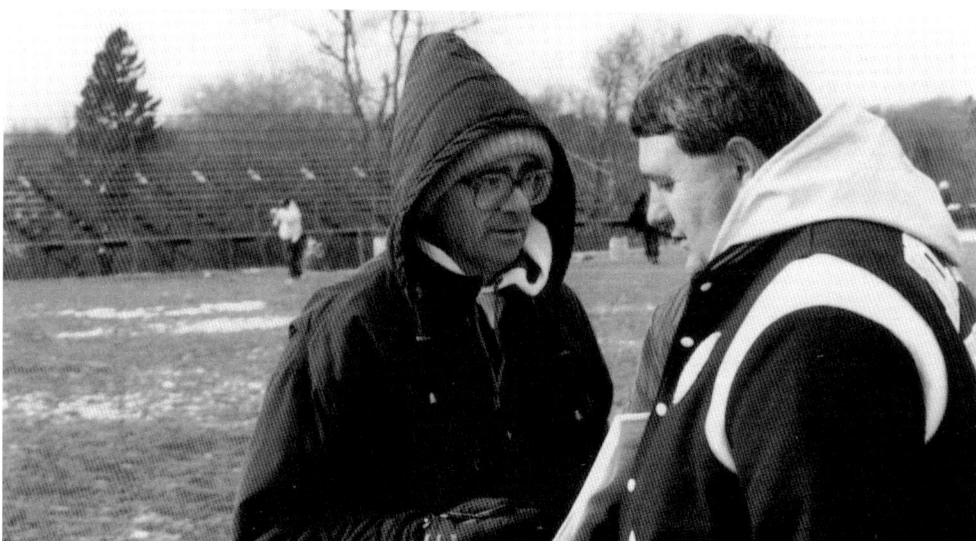

A Favorite Coach

Bristol lost Thomas Vendituoli (1952–2005) far too soon. A formidable athlete in his playing years, Vendituoli was inducted into the Bristol High School Athletic Hall of Fame and the Providence Gridiron Club Hall of Fame and received the Cronin Award as Rhode Island Football Coach of the Year in 1995. As a teacher, athletic director, and head football coach at Mount Hope High School, "Mr. Ven" was respected and beloved by his students. He is seen here being interviewed by East Bay Newspapers sports reporter Manny Correia. (Courtesy of Manny Correia.)

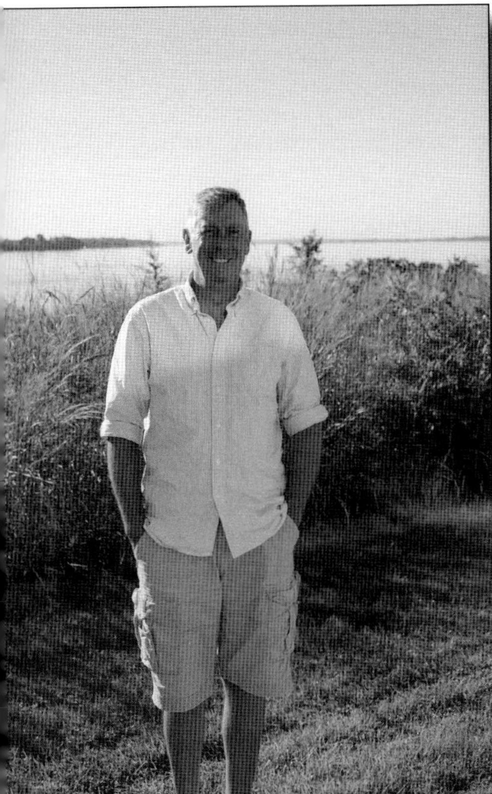

Environmental Artist

Emerson once said, "Love of beauty is taste. The creation of beauty is art." Since moving to Bristol in 1995, Stan Dimock's tasteful love of beauty has turned Bristol's shoreline into a work of art. From the moment he arrived in town, he fell in love with the harbor, which literally changed the direction of his life. Named Save the Bay's Volunteer of the Year in 1998, he was offered the staff position of volunteer coordinator, and under his direction, the program grew to over 1,000 active volunteers. Dimock has since stepped down but remains a volunteer with several conservation organizations, most notably his own "freelance" downtown and waterfront cleanups, on which he spends several hours each week picking up trash on streets and sidewalks and tending public gardens. "Arising every morning is like awakening to Shangri-la," Dimock says. "I'm living the life I want to lead, involving myself in activities that excite my soul, and hopefully making a difference in the world every day." (Both, courtesy of Stan Dimock.)

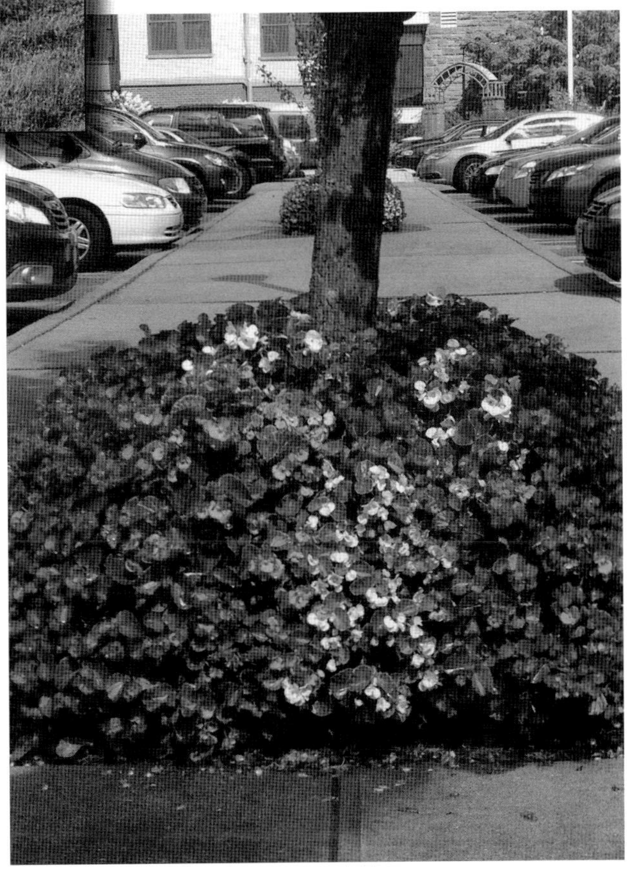

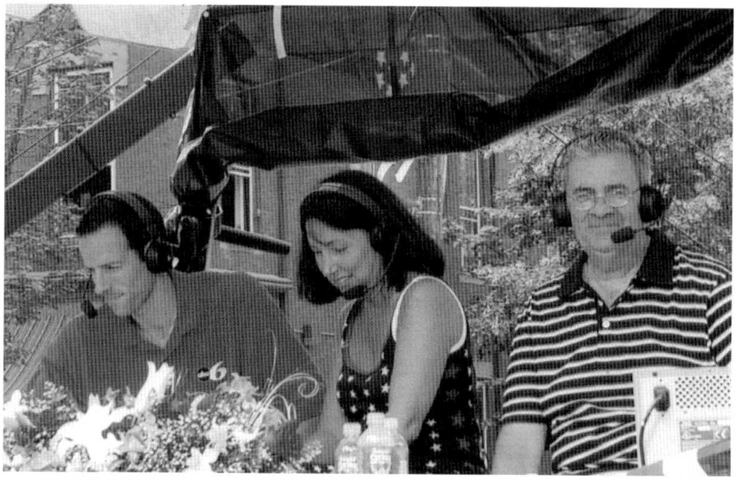

Master Storyteller

Reporter and sportswriter Manuel "Manny" Correia claims to be retired, but the regular appearance of his byline and photographs (and mastery of social media) suggests that he's a long way from putting down his pen or his camera. With five decades of service at both East Bay Newspapers and the *Providence Journal*, it is hard to imagine that there is a local sports hero Correia hasn't covered. The 2007 chief marshal of Bristol's Fourth of July celebration, Correia has been inducted into both the Rhode Island Press Association Journalism Hall of Fame and the Rhode Island Interscholastic League High School Athletic Hall of Fame and received the latter's Athletic Administrators Association Media Award in 2005 as the state's top high school sportswriter. One of Correia's feature stories, on Warren native baseball legend and hall-of-famer Lizzie Murphy, has been documented in the National Baseball Hall of Fame Museum in Cooperstown, New York. (Both, courtesy of Manuel Correia.)

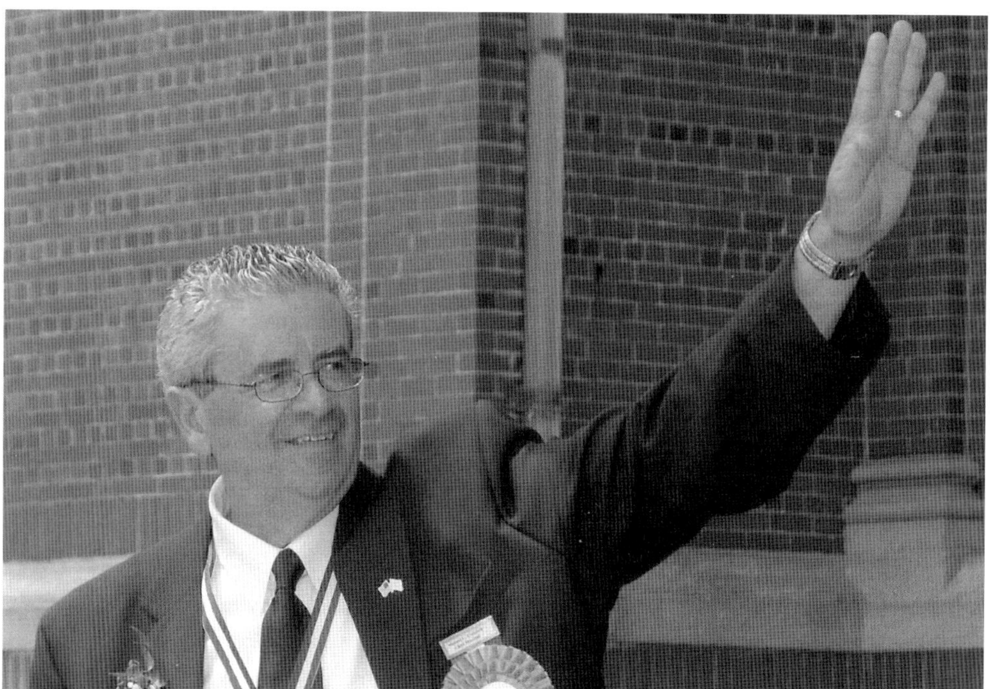

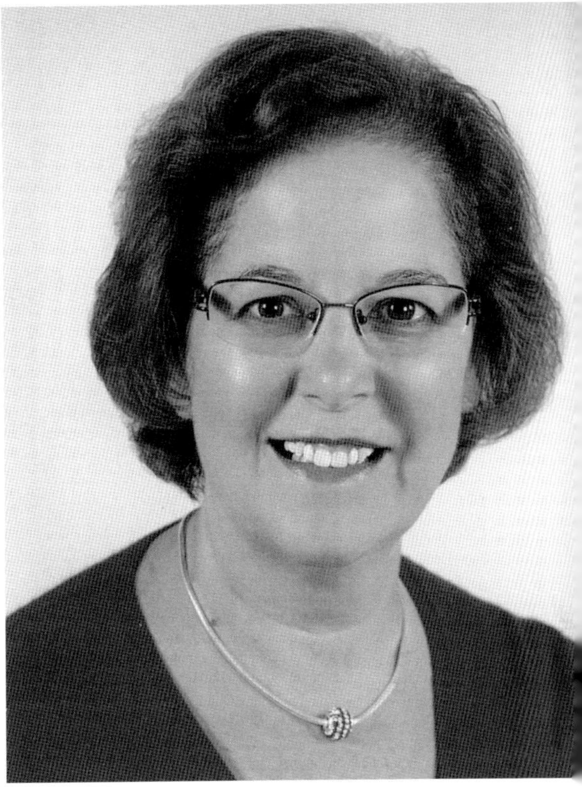

Making Things Happen

When Bristol native Diana Campbell returned to town after living in Hopkinton, Massachusetts, she immediately sought ways to participate, joining the Pastime Theater Foundation, the recreation board, and the local education foundation. Noticing that the town had become split between longtime residents and newcomers, she wanted to do something to bridge the divide. So, in 2006, she founded Voices for Bristol's Future, a forum for all Bristol residents to discuss priorities for Bristol's future. More than 150 people participated in the inaugural event, which had the happy effect of re-energizing several organizations. Currently, Campbell is the executive director of Mosaico, which was founded in 1992 by a group of residents from the Wood Street neighborhood who wanted to preserve the site of the former Kaiser aluminum factory. She manages all of Mosaico's programs, including scholarships for adults, Sense of Pride, mentoring for at-risk students, and other community development efforts, while also serving on the Bristol-Warren regional school committee. (Courtesy of Diana Campbell.)

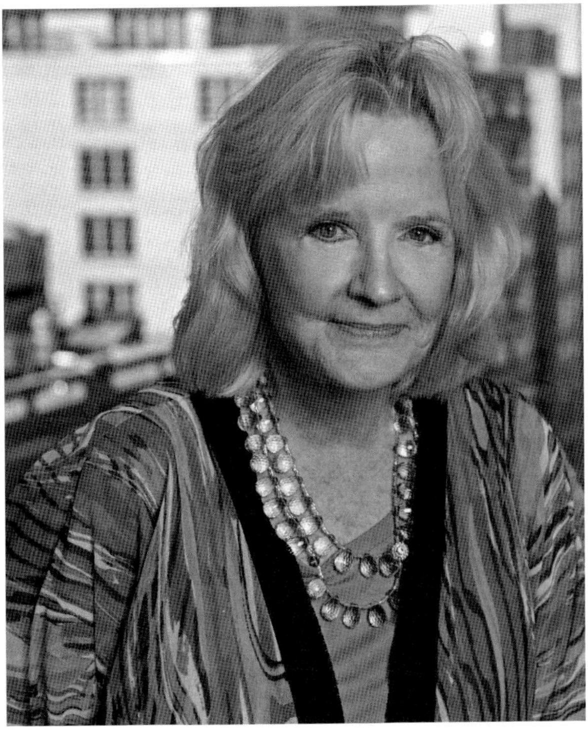

Intelligent Opposition

Gina Macdonald is a business development executive by day, a concerned citizen of Bristol always. Whether losing a zoning board appointment over her opposition to the construction of an eyesore or organizing the opposition to the original Rogers Free Library design, Macdonald is not afraid to lose popularity contests while following what she believes is the appropriate course of action. And the record shows her course is often the best one. She also organized Save Our Schools and worked to get two grants to fund opposition to the school committee's decision to abandon several downtown schools while building a new elementary school on the grounds of the high school. (Courtesy of Gina Macdonald.)

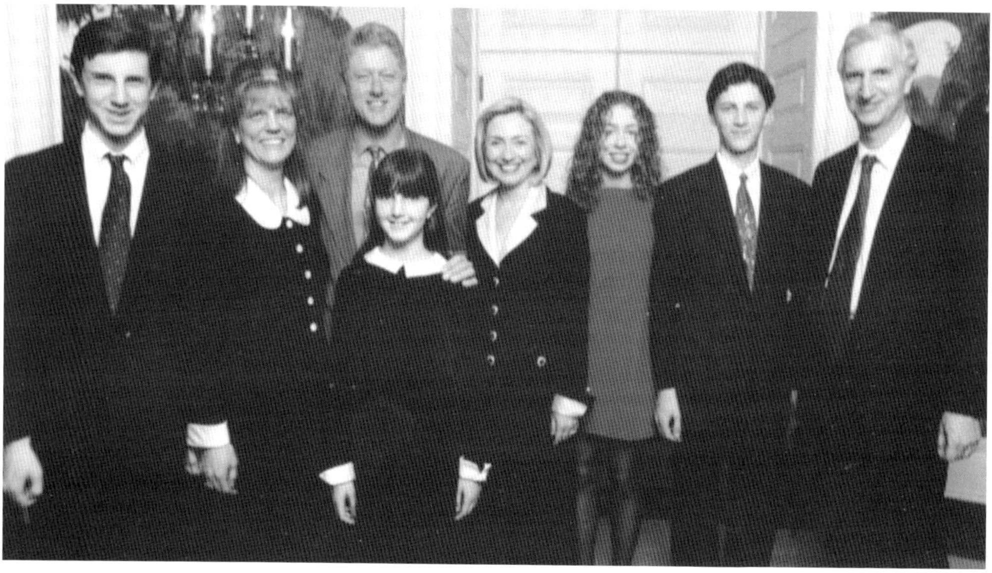

Globally and Locally
The husband-and-wife duo of Suzanne and Ira Magaziner has made a life of public service—she while staying close to home and he while traveling to the farthest reaches of the globe. Volunteering tirelessly for causes ranging from Save Bristol Harbor to Trinity Rep to Sophia Academy, Suzanne's dedication to conservation, education, and the arts has had a lasting impact on her wider community. As vice chairman and chief executive officer of the Clinton Health Access Initiative, Ira has had the opportunity to engage in lifesaving efforts throughout Africa, Asia, and the Caribbean to treat people with AIDS, reduce mortality from malaria, reduce maternal and infant mortality, accelerate the deployment of vaccines, educate doctors, nurses, midwives, and community health workers, and strengthen health systems. (Courtesy of Suzanne and Ira Magaziner.)

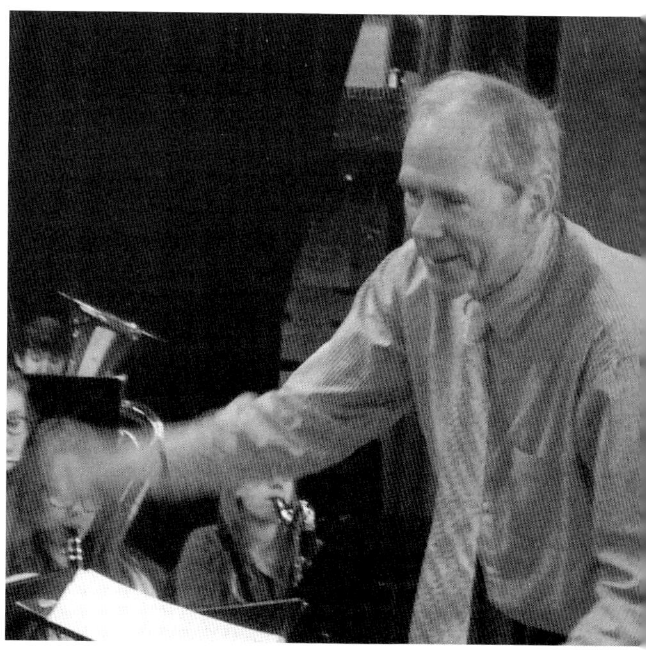

Music Man
Music teacher Robert Arsenault arrived in Bristol in 1988 with his wife, Denise, and five children and accepted posts at Colt Andrews and Guiteras Schools and Bristol High School. He made an immediate impact, doubling the marching band inside of three years and creating a jazz band and combo. As performing arts department chair, Bob expanded the music department to include a highly acclaimed four-year guitar program and innovative digital audio recording classes. In 2009, he founded the Community String Project, a nonprofit dedicated to providing local students with affordable string lessons and instruments. (Courtesy of Bob Arsenault.)

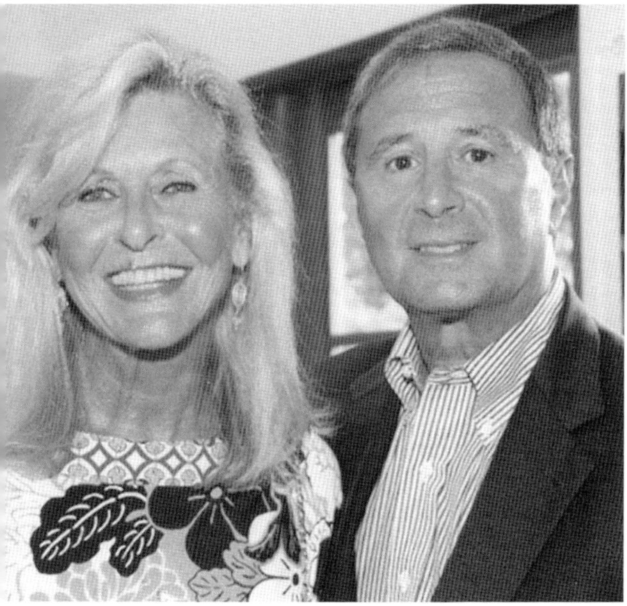

The "Save" Person
Joan Abrams, a professor of communications at Simmons College and formerly a public relations executive, became known locally as the "save" person for her skill in helping turn around distressed nonprofits and her passion for supporting causes of all kinds, but especially in humanities and historic preservation. Most notably, she has served as president of Festival of Ballet in Rhode Island and Save the Bay. Abrams has also given her time and talents to Blithewold, the Community Prep School, and the Rhode Island Council for the Humanities. She is pictured here with her husband, attorney Richard Abrams. (Courtesy of Joan Abrams.)

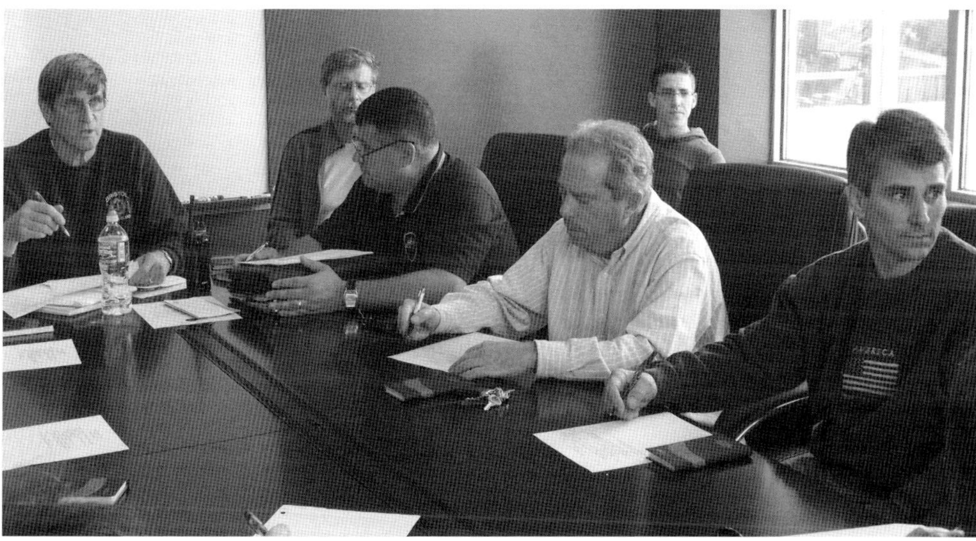

First Responder
David Barboza has already put in a lifetime of public service, and he still has a lot of life left to give. With more than 40 years associated with the Bristol Fire Department and several years serving on the town council, he's looking forward to continuing in public service in some capacity, and serving as chief marshal of the 2014 July Fourth celebration. A 1972 graduate of Bristol High School (and winner of most school spirit), David's memberships include the Bristol Rotary Club, Knights of Columbus, and the Elks Club; he helps produce Concerts on the Common and Last Night with the Rhode Island Philharmonic and spends every Sunday distributing Holy Communion to the homebound on behalf of St. Mary's Church. In this 2012 photograph, David (center) is seen discussing Hurricane Sandy emergency plans with fire chief Bob Martin, police chief Josue Canario, and fellow councilman Ken Marshall. (Courtesy of East Bay Newspapers.)

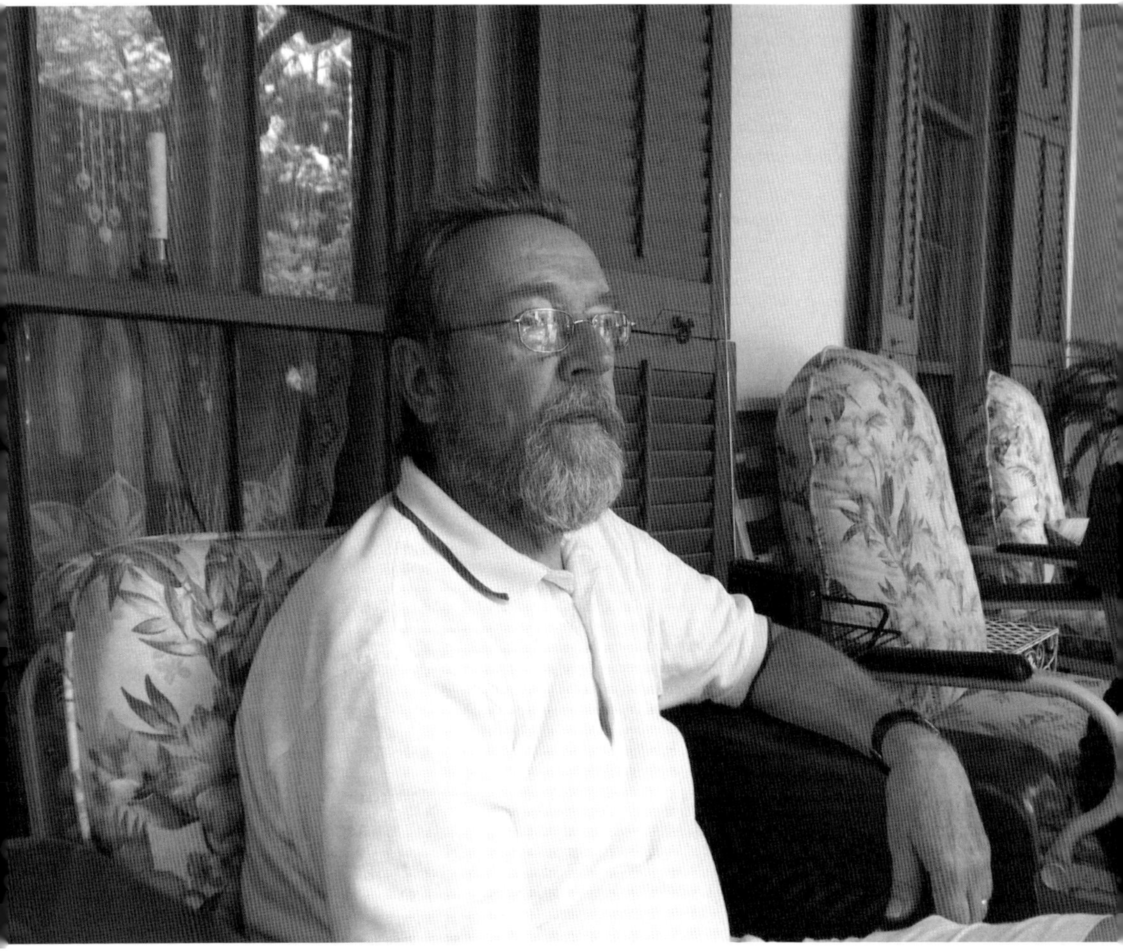

Gardener, Aeronautical Engineer

A lot of years have passed since the efforts of Gary Watros and his team of engineers brought the Apollo 13 astronauts home safely. As the first male member of the Bristol Garden Club, Watros proved he is as skilled with seeds as he is with systems, though the intricate framework he has constructed for his backyard bean crop (50 pounds in 2013 alone) belies his background. In the fall, with his gardens put to bed for the winter, and his sights set on the spring bulb crop, Watros can focus on his artfully decorated home on Earth; he's done his time in space. (Courtesy of Gary Watros.)

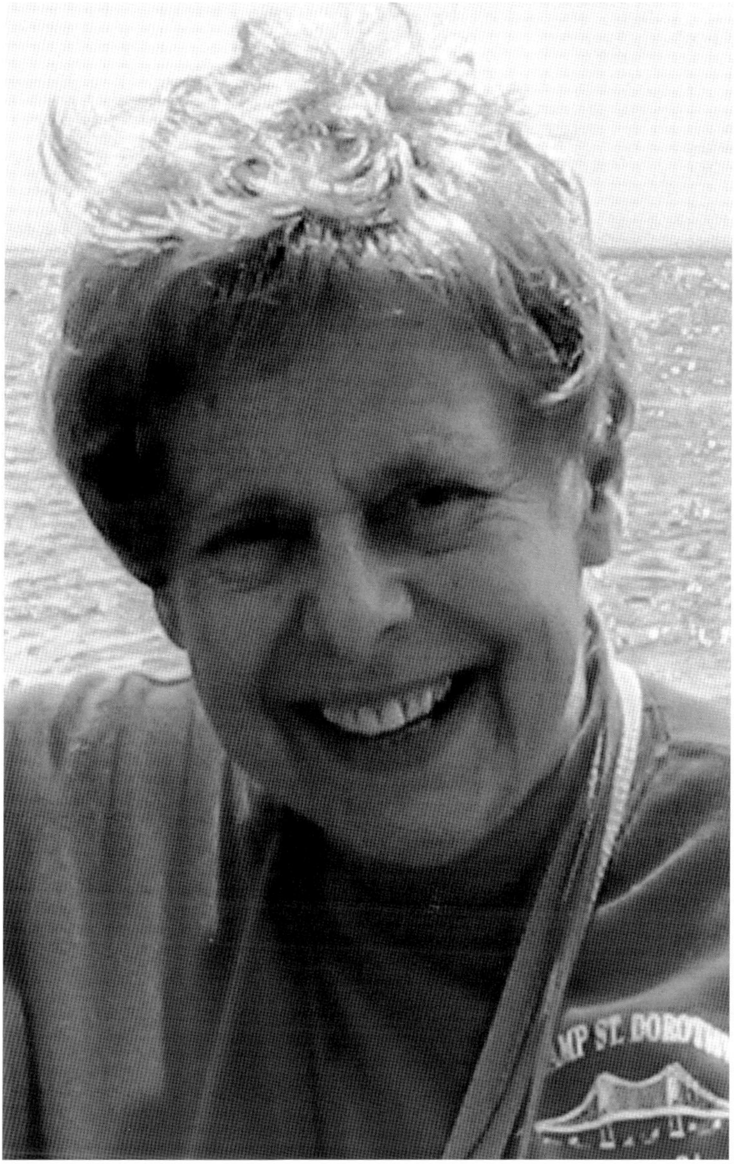

God and Family

Sr. Mary Sardinha didn't intend to become a nun. Her love of God has always been strong, but so has her love of family, and back in the day, once one took the vow, one never went home. But when all six of her brothers returned safely from war, she felt she needed to make a gesture. So she stared bargaining with God (something she knows she shouldn't do). She asked for signs, and she got every one of them. So she asked for unlikely signs and got them too. Eventually, Sister Sardinha told God that if she heard this one particular song, within the following 30 minutes, she would devote herself to His service. To make sure she would not hear it, she spent the next half hour walking the beach between Low Lane and Blithewold without a radio. In the last minutes, she walked up toward Ferry Road just in time to see a pickup truck pass, full of men, singing her song. But God never punished her for bargaining with him. He's given "Sister Sards," as she is known, a life rich with joy, travel, and adventure. "It has been," she says, "a perpetual act of Thanksgiving to God." (Courtesy of Sister Mary Sardinha.)

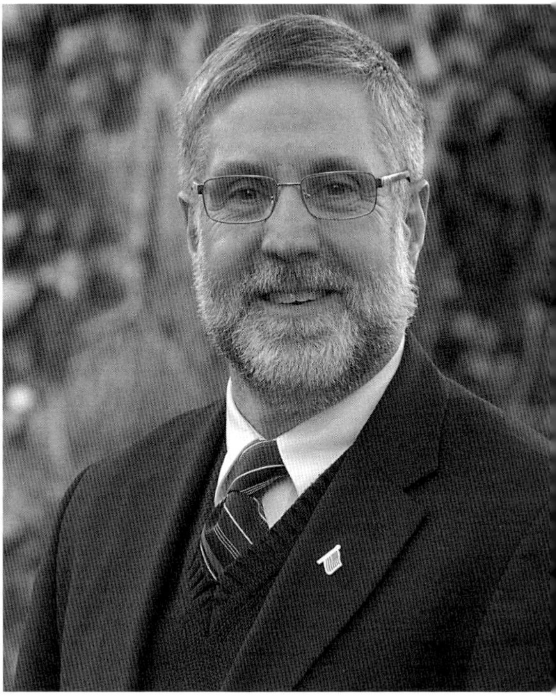

Clerk of the Works
A former manager with Dixon Industries, Louis P. Cirillo has spent most of his life in public service of his hometown, from his eight years on the Bristol Board of Canvassers to a term on the school committee, three terms on the town council, and currently as town clerk, a position he has held since 2004. As town clerk, he also serves as town council clerk, clerk of the probate court, clerk and magistrate of the municipal court, clerk of the board of canvassers, recorder of deeds, and the registrar of vital records. In addition, Cirillo is a past president and life member of the Bristol Historical and Preservation Society, former executive director of the Linden Place Mansion and Museum, an in-demand public speaker, contributing journalist and author, and the 2013 chief marshal of the Bristol Fourth of July Celebration. (Photograph by Richard W. Dionne Jr., courtesy of East Bay Newspapers.)

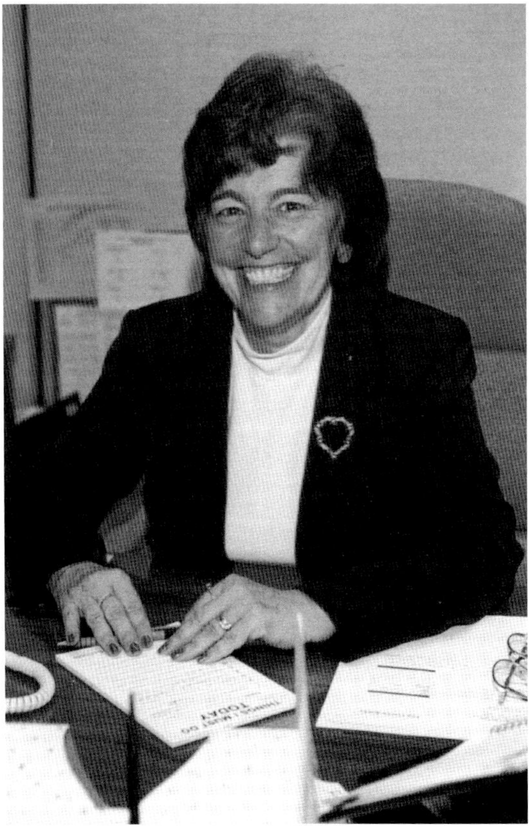

Top of Her Class
Helen "Tina" Barboza can claim a couple of firsts as the first recipient of a doctorate in education though the University of Rhode Island/Rhode Island College joint program and the first female superintendent of the Bristol Warren Regional School District, from 1999 to 2003. But it is not the fact that Barboza was a female superintendent that has earned her so much respect and admiration, it's the fact that she was such an excellent one. Under her leadership, a struggling district improved in every measure, from budgetary deficit to reserve; in student achievement; and in internal morale and community support for schools. Barboza set the district on a winning course that continues to this day. Since 2003, she has been sharing her expertise as an adjunct professor at Providence College, teaching a variety of courses in its educational administration master's program. (Courtesy of Helen Barboza.)

CHAPTER FOUR

Arts and Culture

Despite appearing simple to define, "arts and culture," like people, resist classification. Take the unassailable fact that Champe Spiedel's cuisine and plating are art by any measure. But he's a chef, and restaurants are businesses. Lombard Pozzi, the late architect and preservationist, was a craftsman whose aesthetic made Bristol and surrounding communities far more beautiful than any painting on a wall or a song on a radio ever could. But he was a giving and involved person, so he was shoehorned into the chapter on community. The fact is, no local—let alone a "legendary" one—is as one-dimensional as the words on a page. Even Bristol's slave-trader-in-chief, James DeWolf, was a champion of American independence with a taste for fine architecture. So to turn that lens on the concept of culture, does it make sense that the centerpiece of the culture of this lovely town, a raucous July Fourth celebration, is so multidimensional that it features church bells and song, speeches and services, prayer, passion, and a seeming perpetual piece of performance art? And don't forget the barbecue, beer, and occasional loud explosions and primal screams, heavy with patriotic overtones. Is that culture? In Bristol, the only answer is an unapologetic "yes."

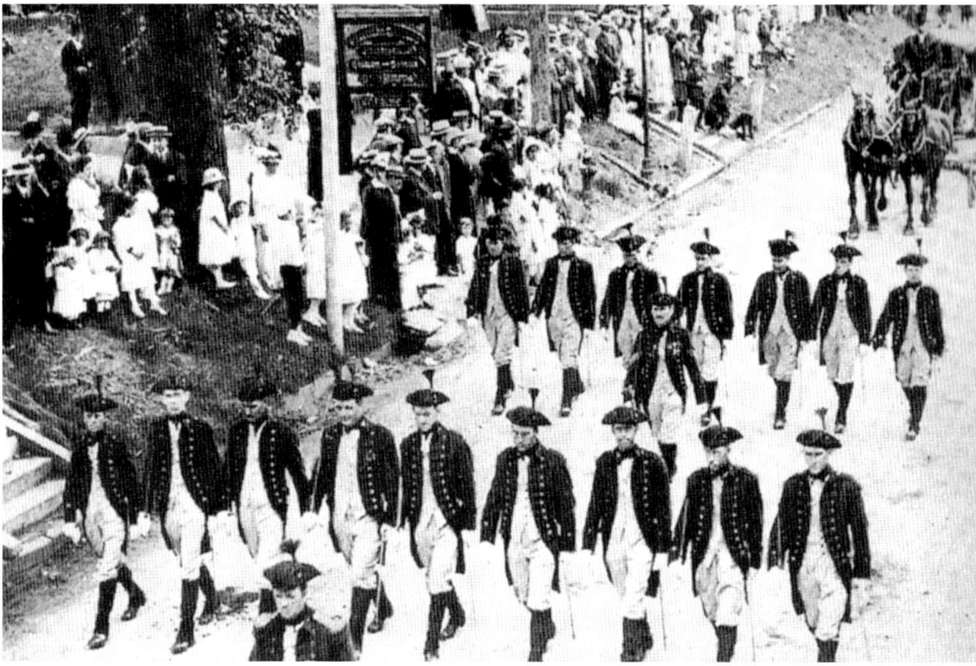

Then and Now, Bristol Loves the Fourth

Mary Gould Almy, a Tory sympathizer of Newport, recorded the following in her diary on July 4, 1775: "This being the first anniversary of the Declaration of the Independency of the Rebel Colonies, they ushered in the morning at Providence [Bristol] by firing 13 cannons, one for each colony we suppose."

That may have been the first unofficial celebration, but the first organized observance of the Fourth was conducted in 1785 by the Reverend Henry Wight, pastor of the Congregational church. It has endured, in one form or another, virtually every year since.

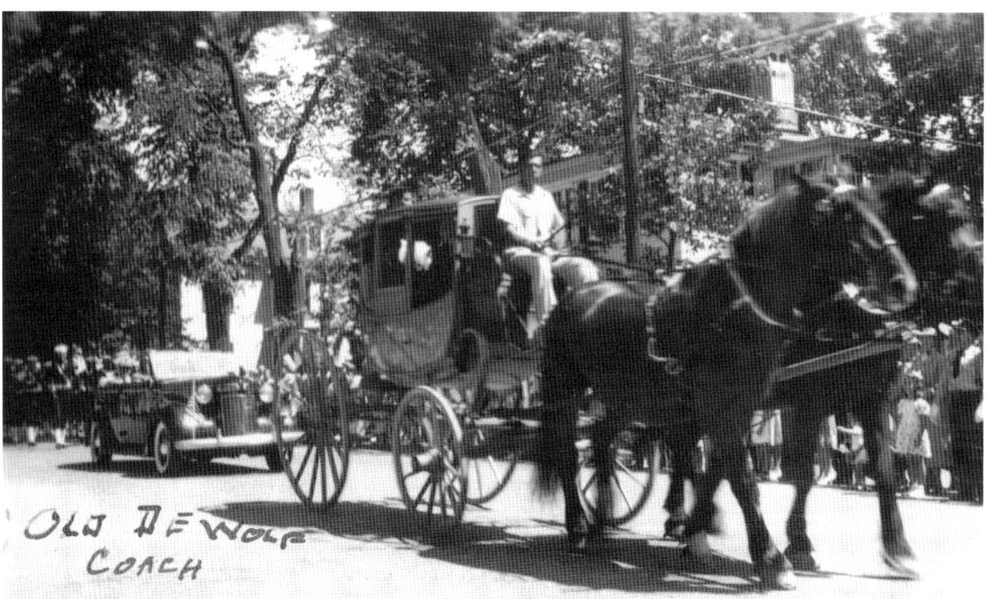

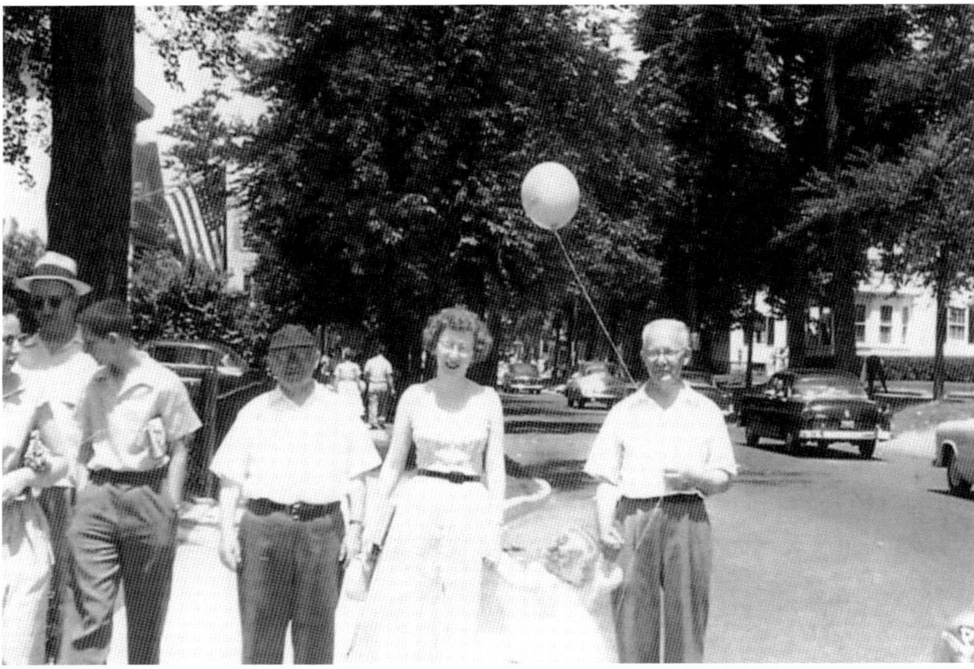

What to say about Independence Day in Bristol? Those who think that this is a holiday to go to the beach, have a picnic, and maybe fire off some firecrackers are from somewhere else. Those who think the Fourth is the greatest (or most exhausting, or both) time of year must be from Bristol. They know it's a time when guests sleep on the floor, fireworks outside the window at one in the morning are expected, batches of chouriço and peppers are mixed in pots big enough to boil a dozen lobsters, and ice is purchased in blocks, not bags. (Opposite, both courtesy of Linden Place; above, courtesy of United Brothers Synagogue; below, courtesy of author.)

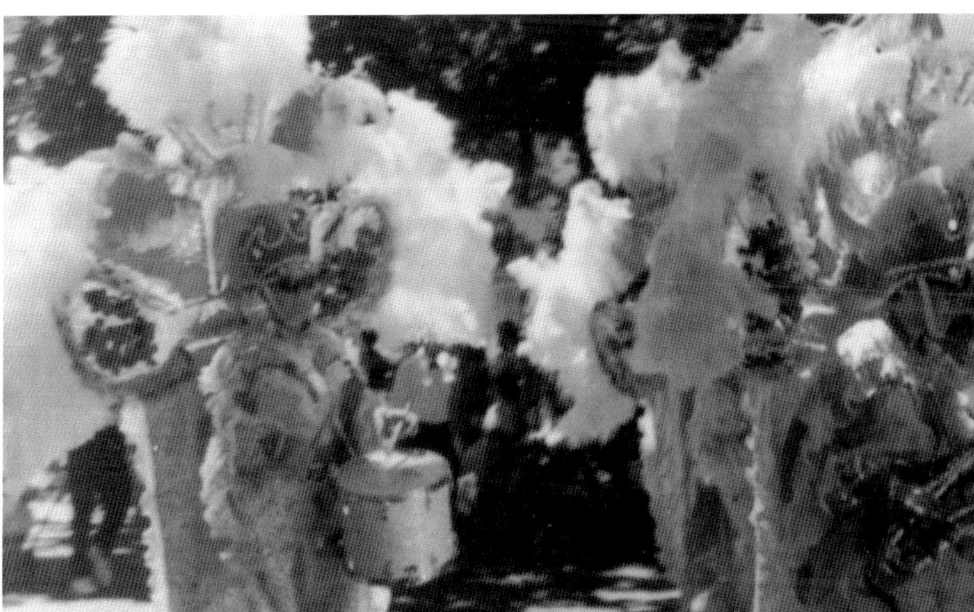

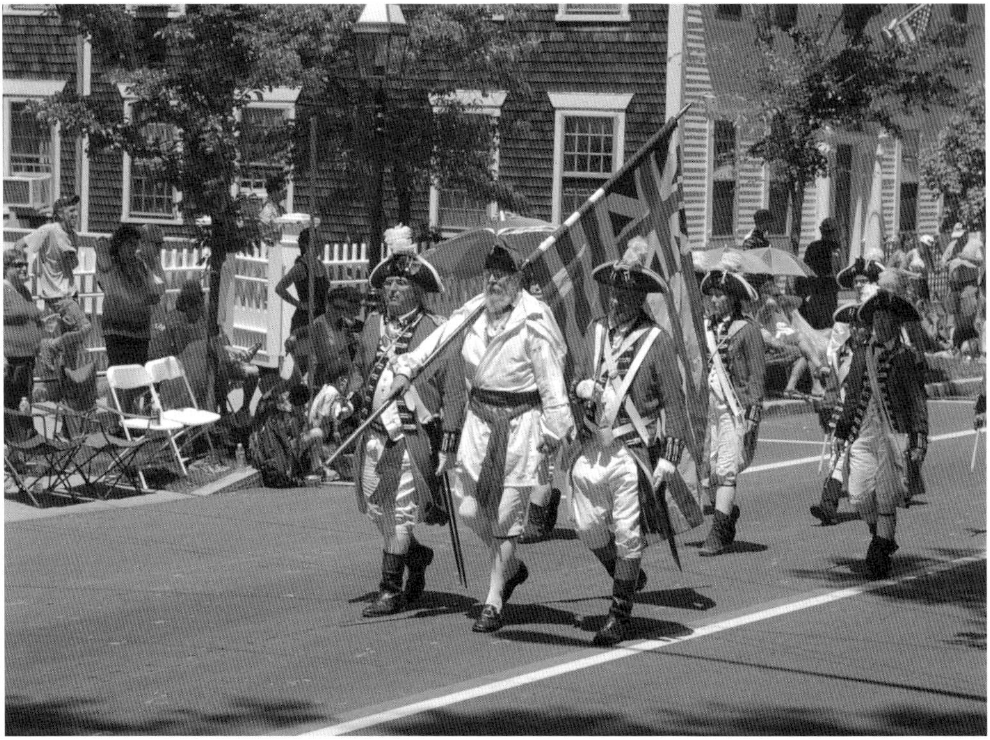

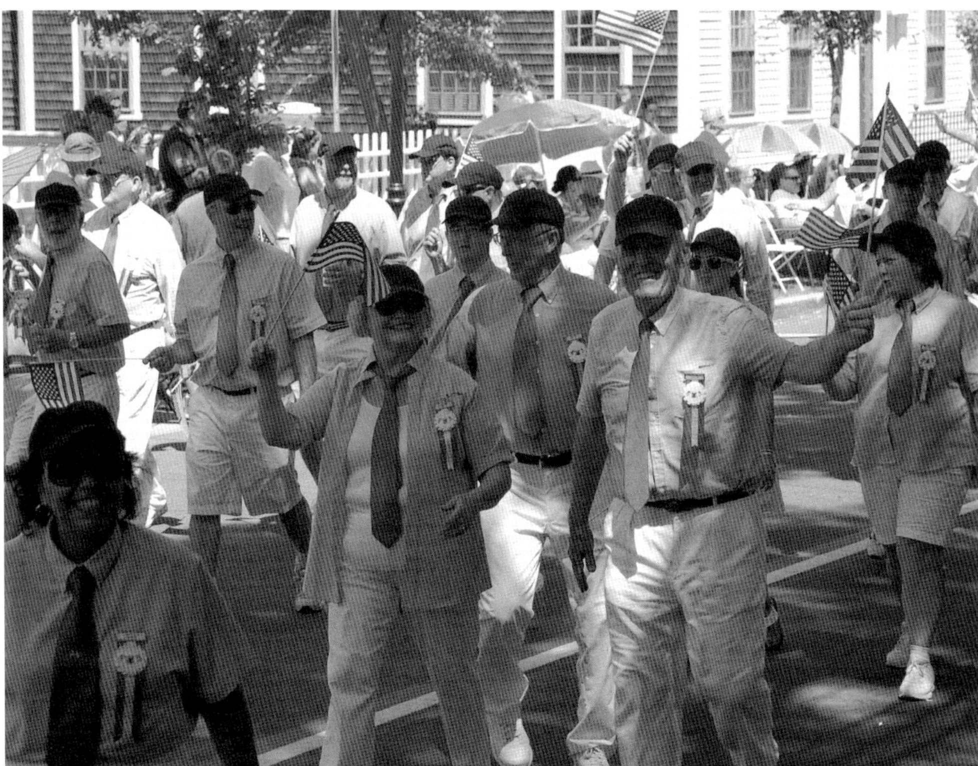

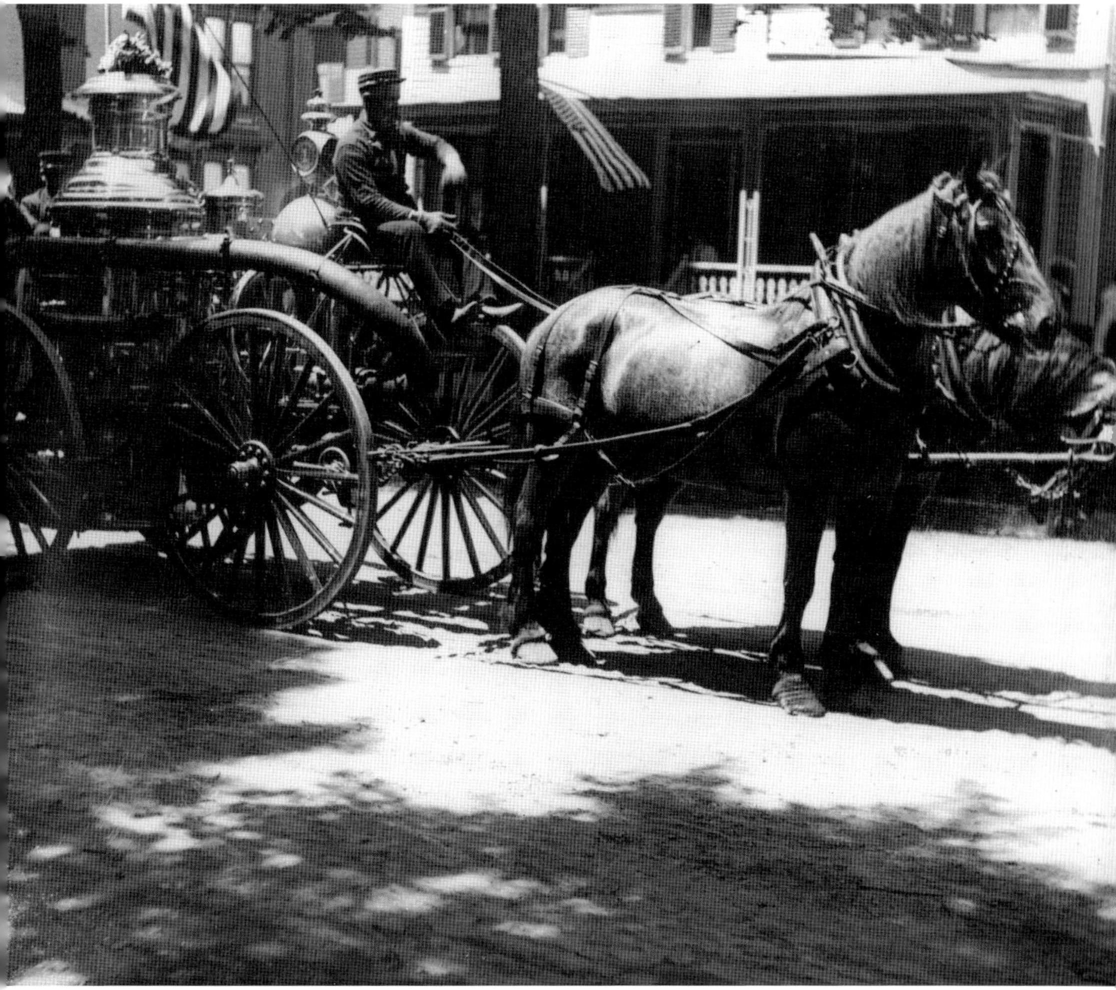

Bristol Loves a Parade

Some things are features of every parade, such as Colonial militia reenactors and a legion of chief marshal's aides, as seen in the photographs on the opposite page. July Fourth is not the only opportunity for a parade, however. Pictured above, a fireman's memorial held every June features trucks including this vintage firefighting apparatus.

Reliance

Maynard Bray and Carlton Pinheiro wrote in *Herreshoff of Bristol*: "Only superlatives adequately describe *Reliance*, until the twenty-first century, the largest single-masted vessel ever built. Her topmast sprit towered 199 feet 6 inches above the water; it took sixty-six men to race her; there was enough square footage in her sails for eight modern 12-Metre boats; her mainsheet measured 1,000 feet in length (it was rolled up on a drum below deck); and she carried over 100 tons of lead ballast in her keel. A marvel of engineering, *Reliance* has lived on as a most appropriate logo for the Herreshoff Marine Museum." (Below, courtesy of Herreshoff Marine Museum.)

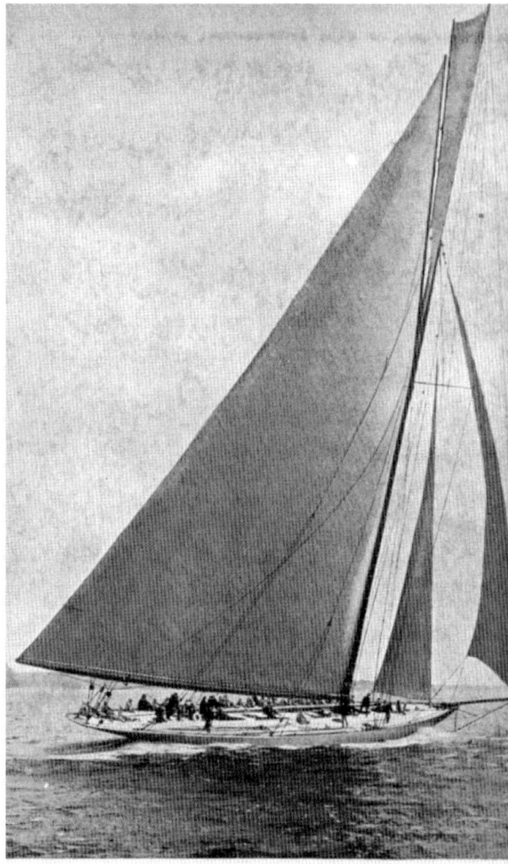

RELIANCE,
Fastest sailing yacht in the world.
Built at Bristol, R. I.

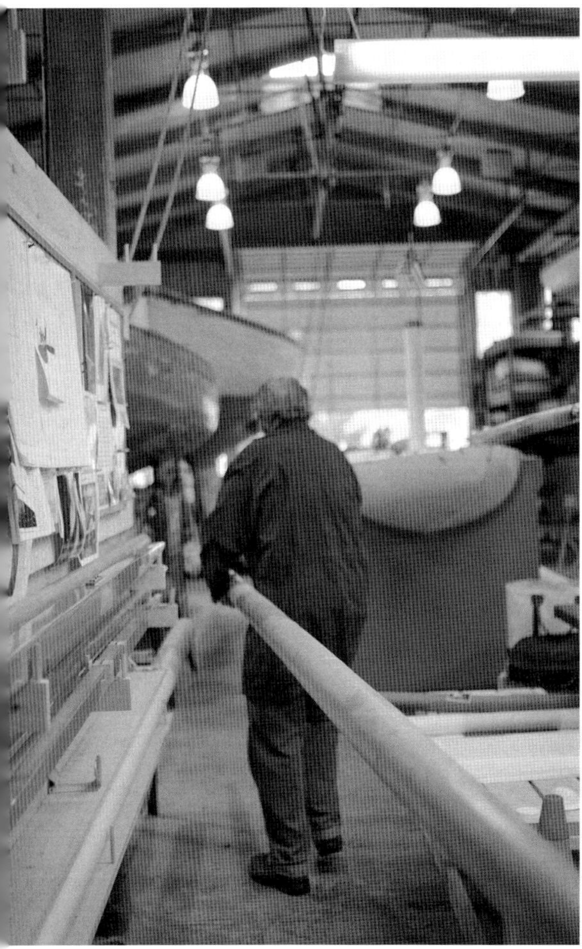

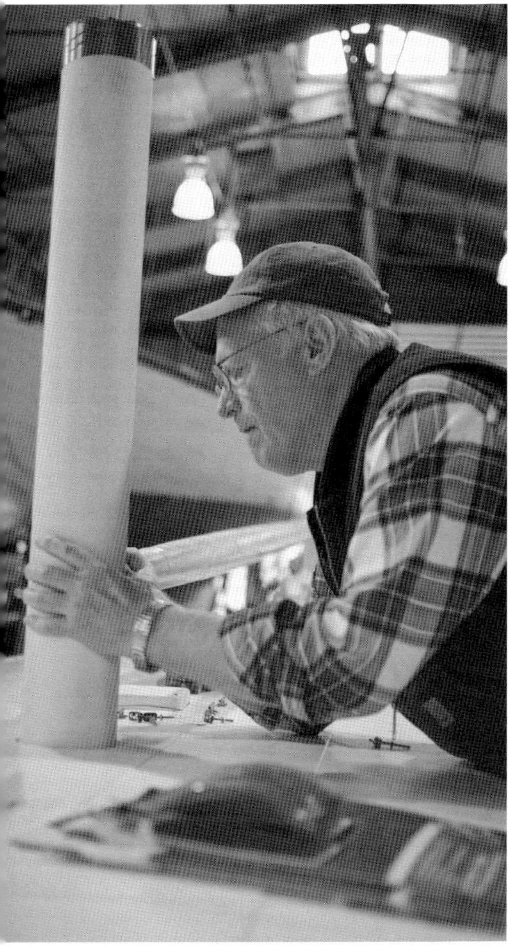

***Reliance* Redux**

A team of volunteers is currently assembling a one-sixth scale model of *Reliance* that will be 33 feet in length and more than 37 feet in height. It will be a fully rigged, static model with sails, destined to become the cornerstone of the Herreshoff Marine Museum's collection and scheduled to be unveiled on the 110th anniversary of the original *Reliance*. (Both, courtesy of Herreshoff Marine Museum.)

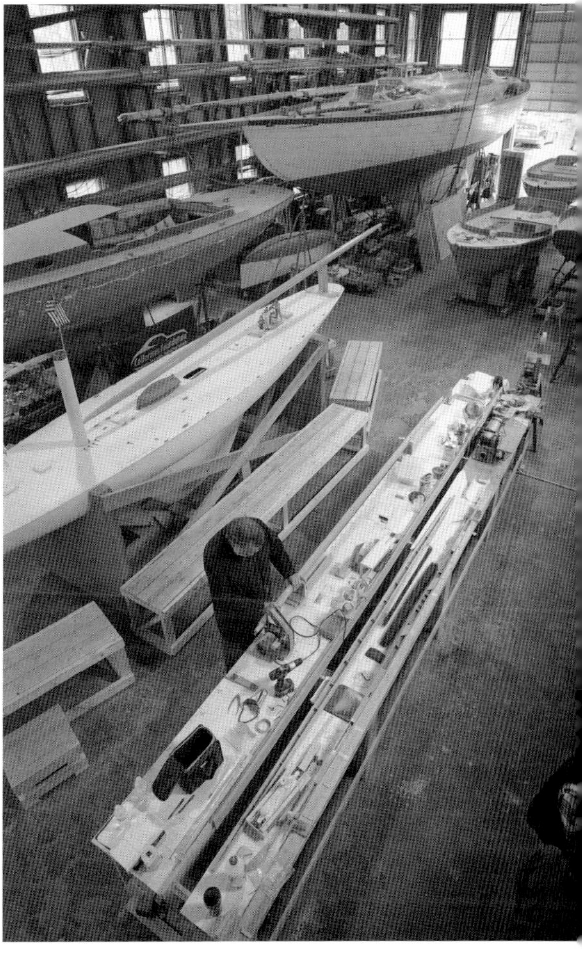

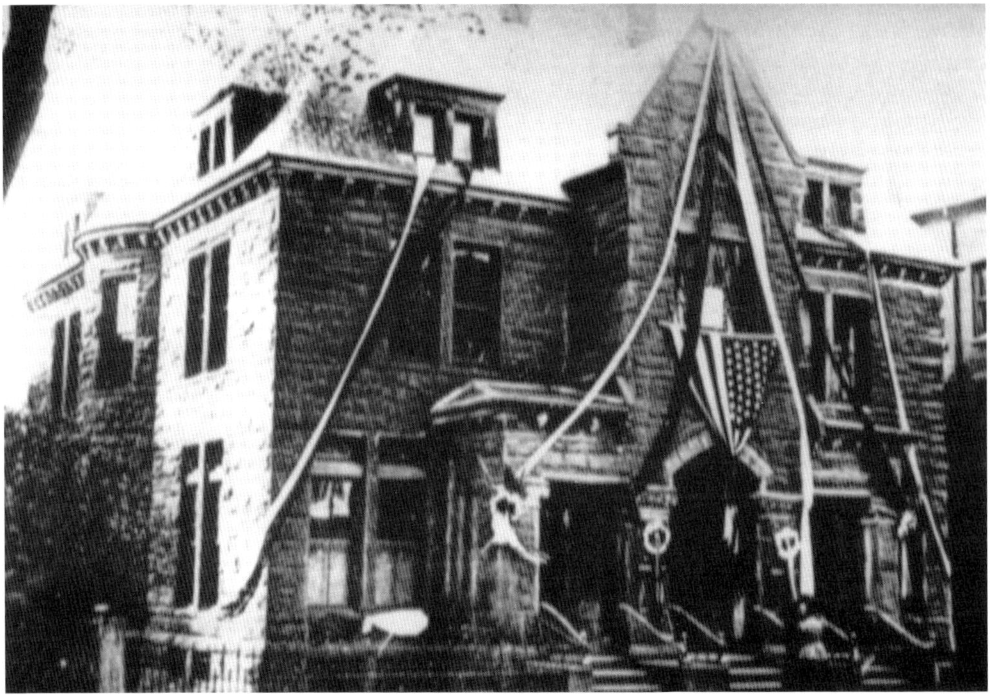

The Hub

The Rogers Free Library anchors the center of downtown Bristol, and over the years, a lot has changed. It was ripped apart by fire in the 1950s, and it was determined that removing the top floor was the best course of action. Since then, the library has more than quadrupled in size, with a beautiful new addition that opened in 2008. (Both, courtesy of Rogers Free Library.)

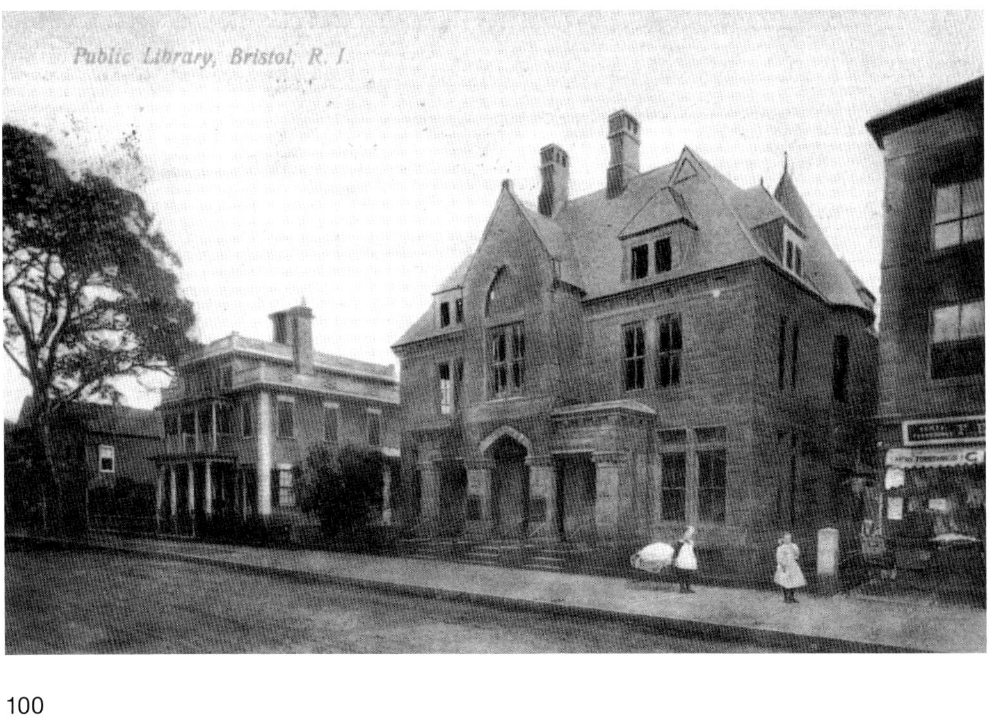

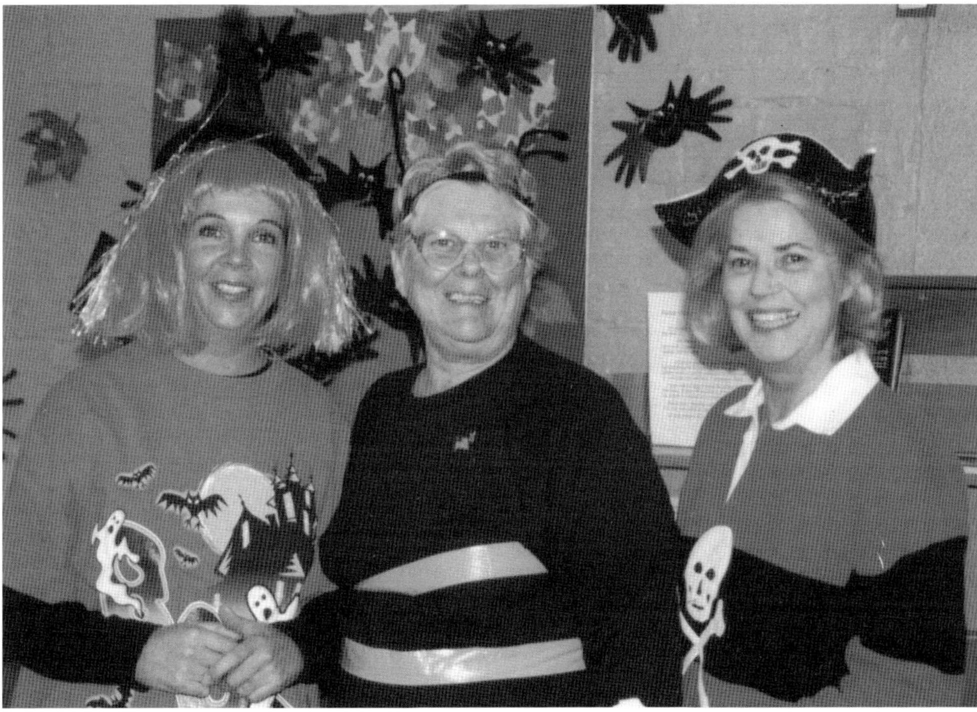

The People
The library includes many memorable personalities over the years, and the names and faces of the Osterbergs, Claudine Fales, and Ned Comstock are familiar to avid readers of the past. Here, (from left to right) Carolyn Carreiro, Arlene McKenna, and Brenda Geremia play dress-up, while the current head librarian, Joan Prescott, takes a break with Santa. (Both, courtesy of Rogers Free Library.)

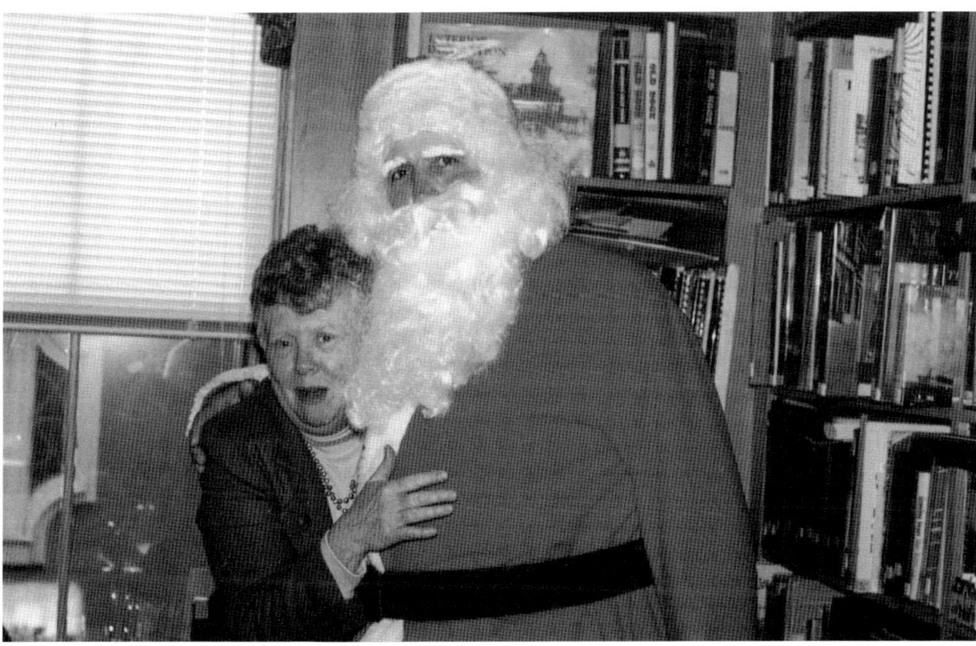

The Children

The Rogers Free Library has always been a wonderful and creative refuge for kids, who over the years have enjoyed countless magicians, puppet shows, craft projects, and, memorably, a lecture on edible insects. This is thanks to all the wonderful librarians, but a special mention is due to Brenda Geremia, who began coming to the library when her boys were young in the early 1970s. It officially became a job in 1976, and since then, she has been responsible for planning and implementing the summer reading programs as well as the display windows. "I've always enjoyed children, the library and the books," Geremia says. "I just fell in love with it." (All, courtesy of Rogers Free Library.)

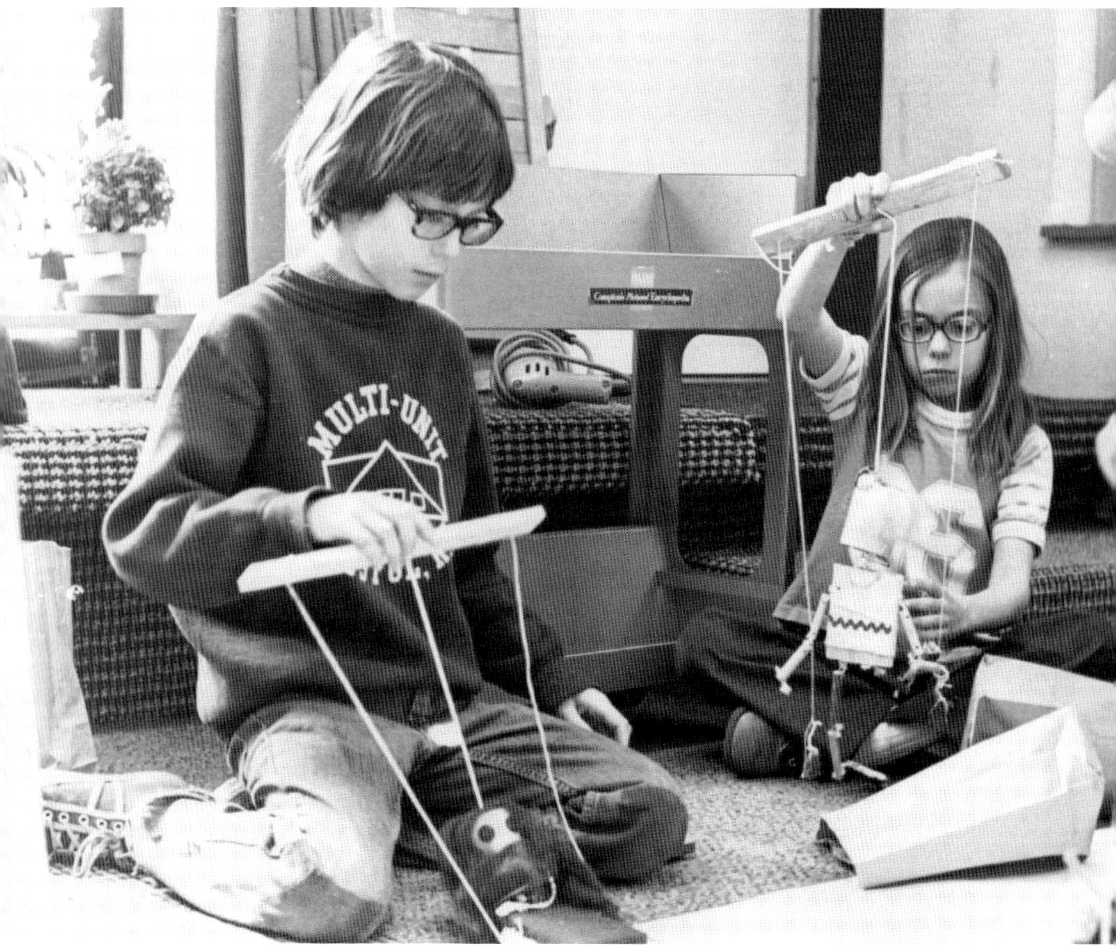

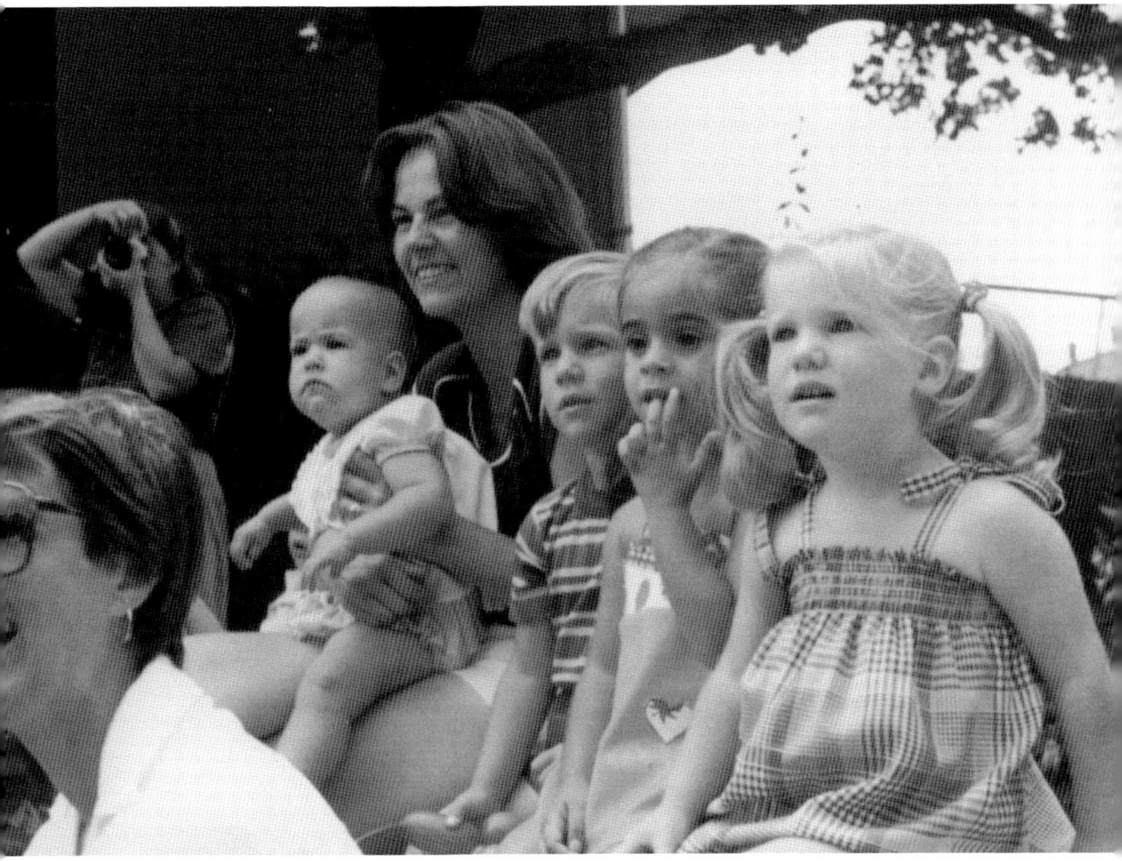

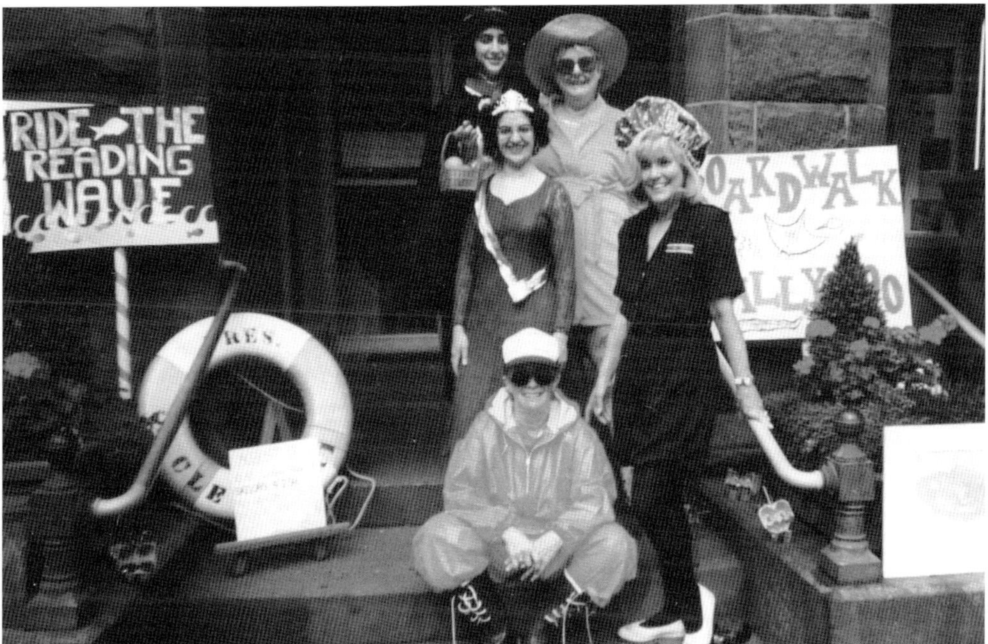
RIDE THE
READING
WAVE

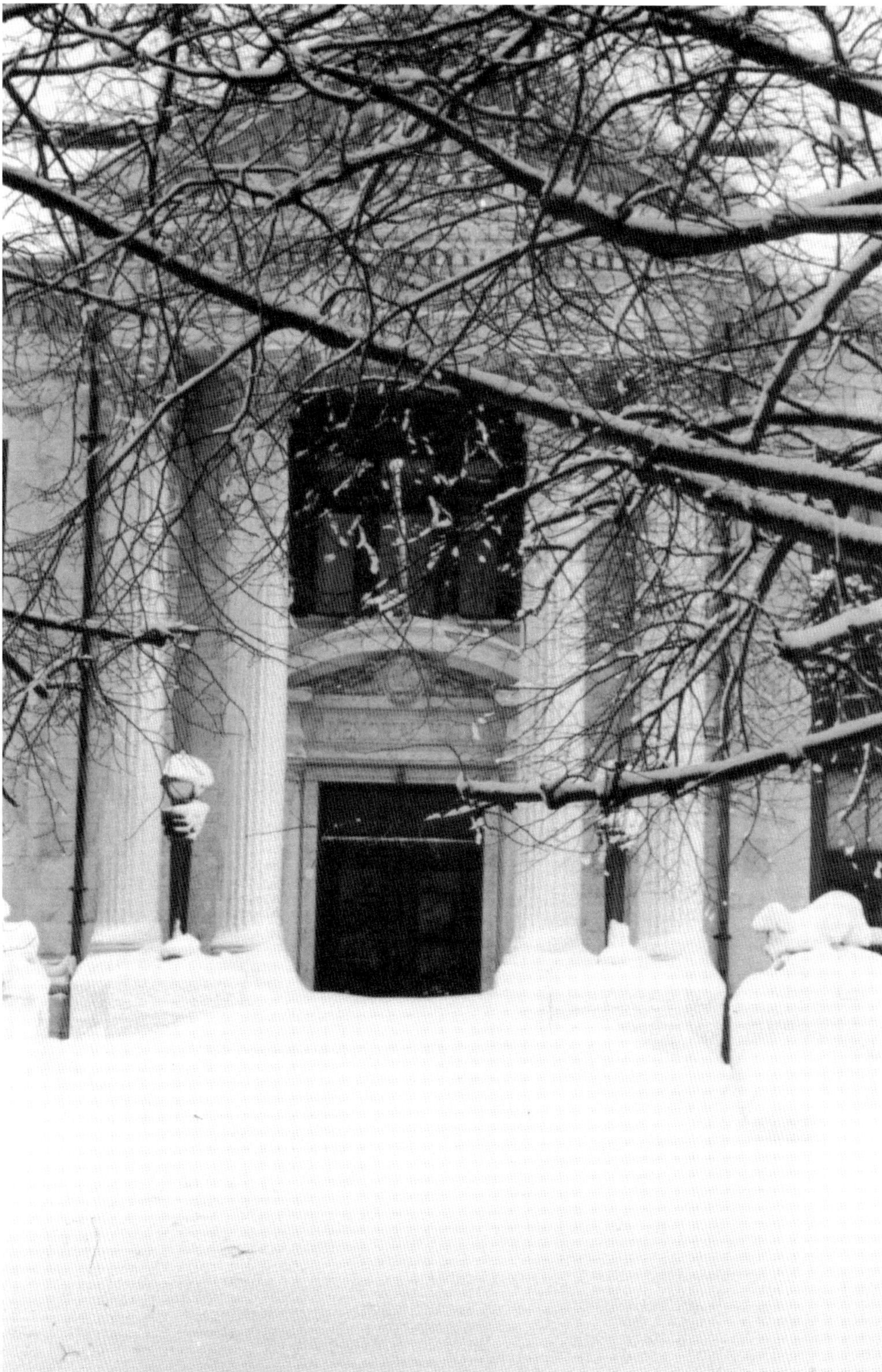

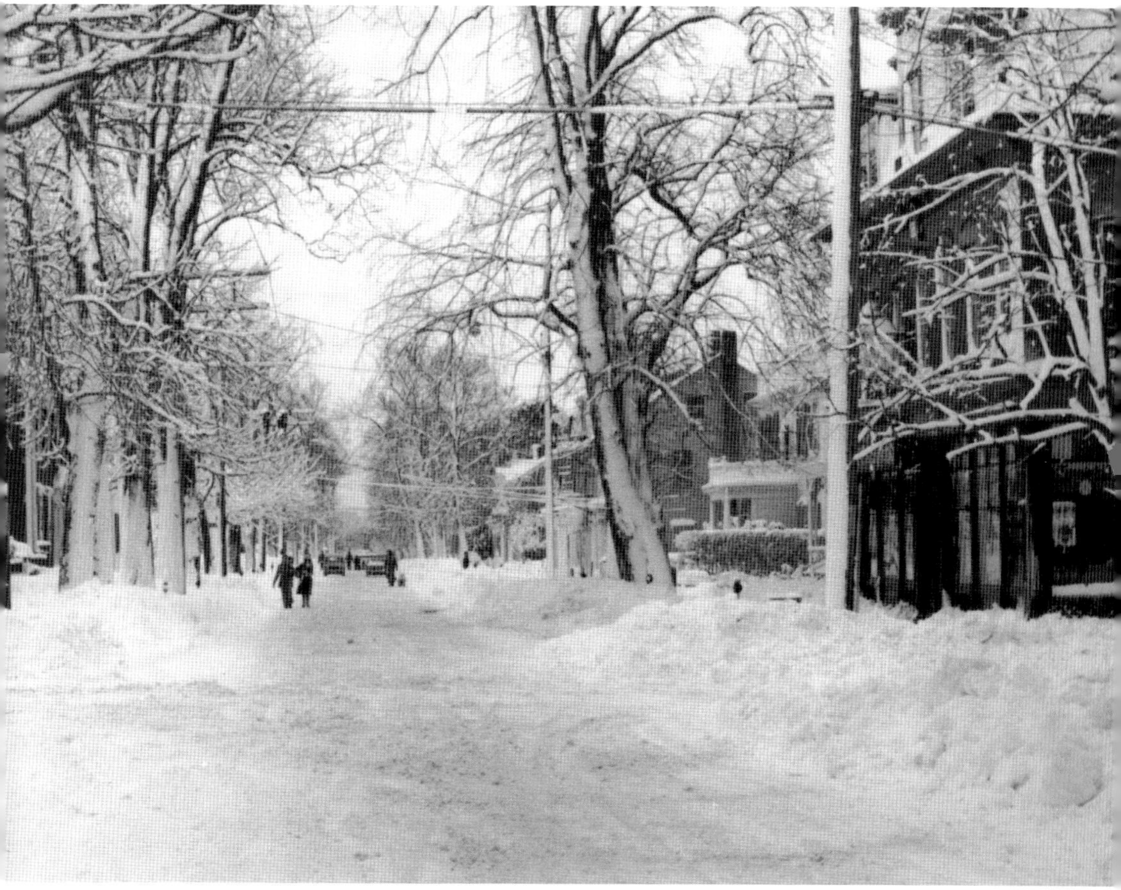

Blizzard!

The blizzard of 1978 hit Rhode Island the first week in February, almost without warning. Children were trapped in schools and on buses, cars were abandoned on the roads, and for a little while, the Northeast came to a standstill. David Barboza was helping to coordinate civil defense efforts in Bristol that day. Here's what he remembers: "Around two p.m. the day of the blizzard, Civil Defense Director Paul D'Amico updated me on the seriousness of the storm. As a major in the National Guard, just activated, he asked that I return as soon as possible to open the operations center. My first major problem was that the town's only ambulance had transported, ironically, the former Civil Defense Director Matthew Capone to RI Hospital and had gotten stuck on Route 195 while returning with Mrs. Capone and Rescue Squad members Lenny Babbitt and Wayne Brown. In traveling around town it was something out of Currier and Ives with no vehicles, people walking and sledding everywhere and candle-lit houses." (Both, courtesy of Rogers Free Library.)

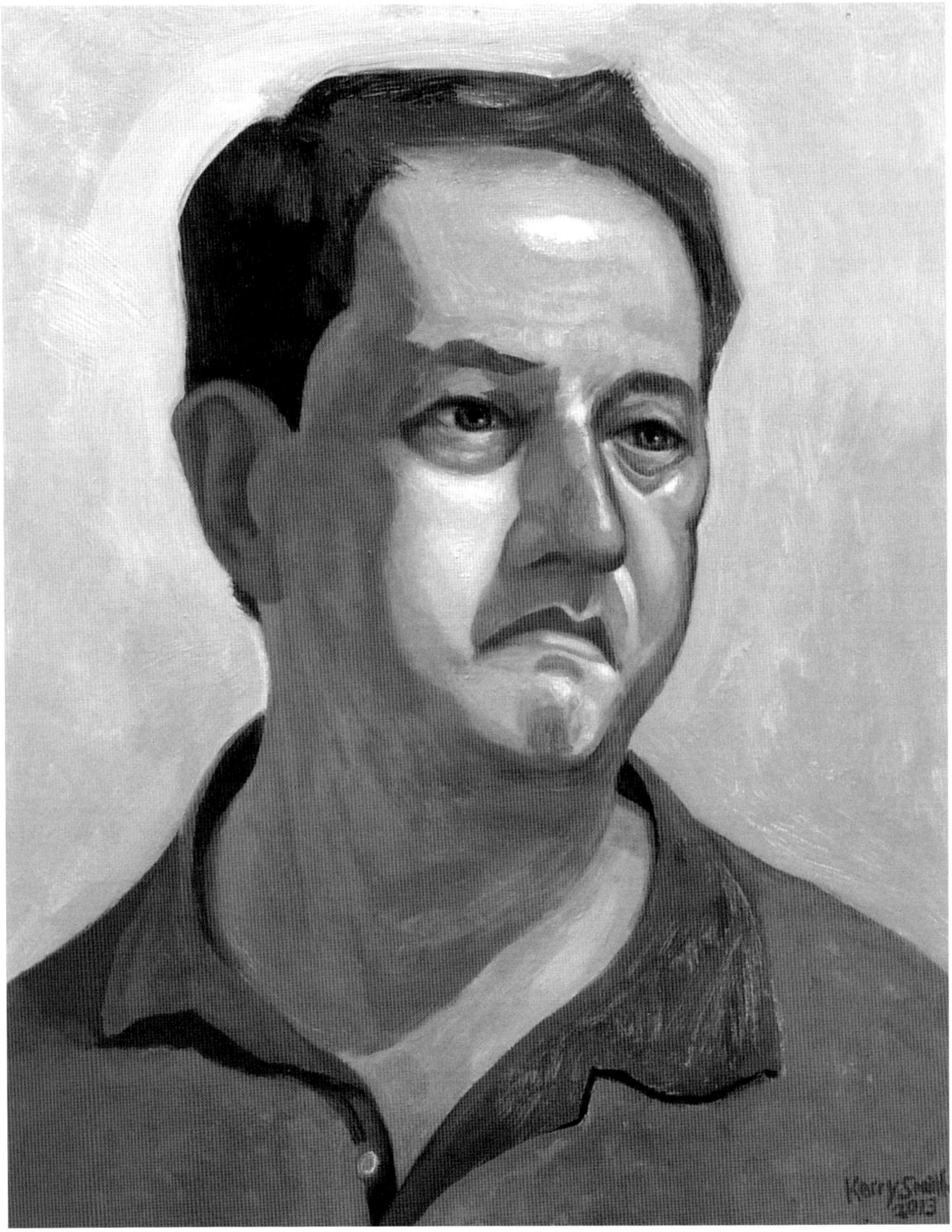

Going with the Flow

David Harrington has had good fortune allowing chance to guide him through life. A longtime Prudence Islander with deep Rhode Island roots, Harrington was educated in architecture and historic preservation. His lifelong appreciation in the arts shaped an interest in music and acting before good fortune introduced him to his current avocation, pottery. Along the way, he lived in Philadelphia, the Virgin Islands, Washington, DC, and now Bristol. Harrington is known for his humor and infectious laugh; this painting, by artist Kerry Smith, shows "my introspective side," Harrington says. "The side nobody sees." (Courtesy of David Harrington.)

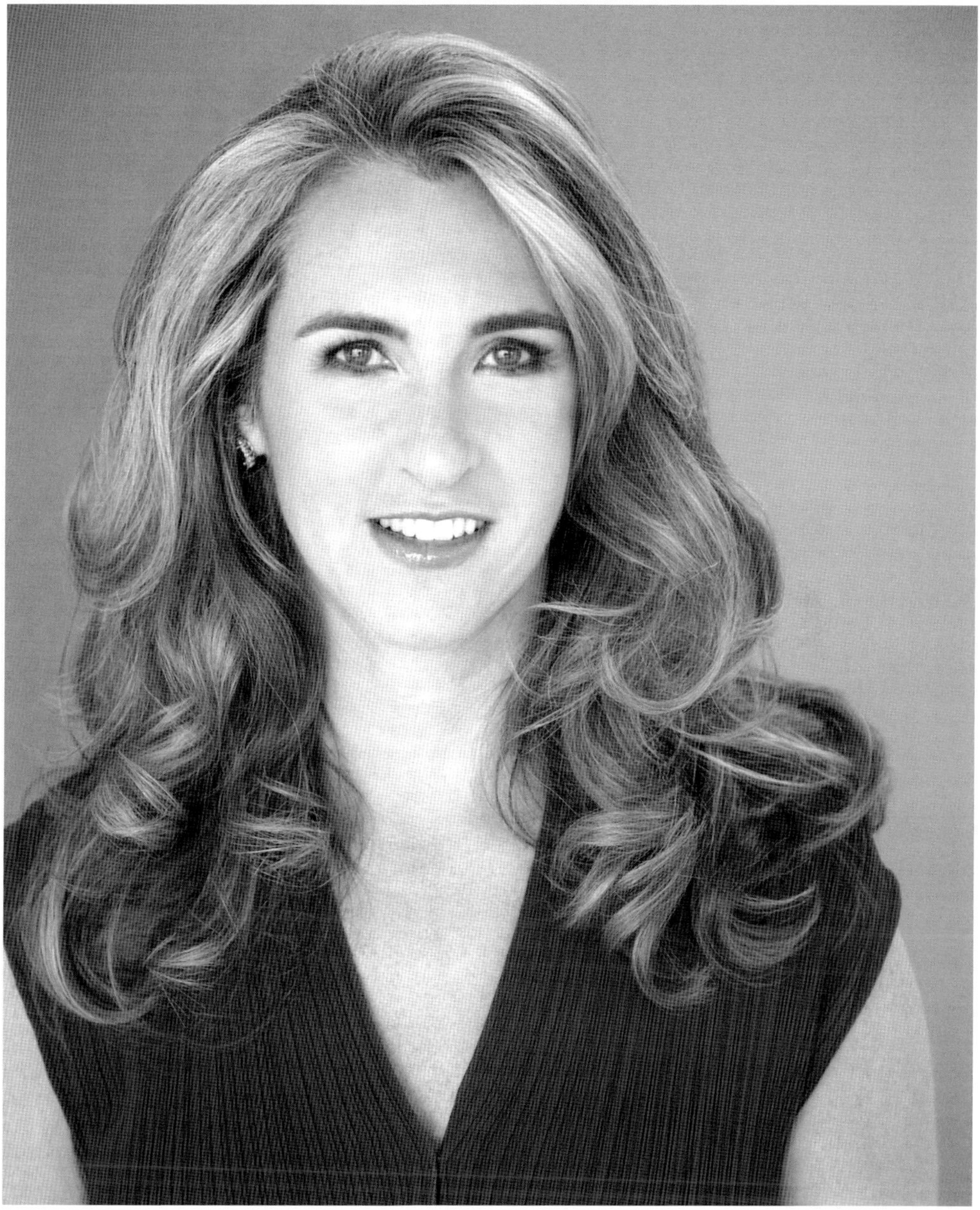

Wonder Woman

Long before she was president and chief executive officer of A&E Networks; long before she was a perennial fixture of the annual *Hollywood Reporter* "Power 100: Top Women in Entertainment" list; and long before she shepherded the miniseries *Hatfields & McCoys* to the highest ratings in cable history (and multiple Emmy Awards), Nancy Dubuc was a Bristol girl who spent her summers sailing Mercurys at the Bristol Yacht Club and swimming in Bristol Harbor. When she is not jetting between the coasts securing deals for A&E's growing portfolio of networks; living in Manhattan, where she and her husband Michael Kizilbash are raising their children Jackson and Alice; or hiding from it all on Nantucket, she can occasionally be found in Bristol, most likely having breakfast at the Hope Diner or grabbing an eggplant grinder from the Bristol House of Pizza. (Courtesy of Nancy Dubuc.)

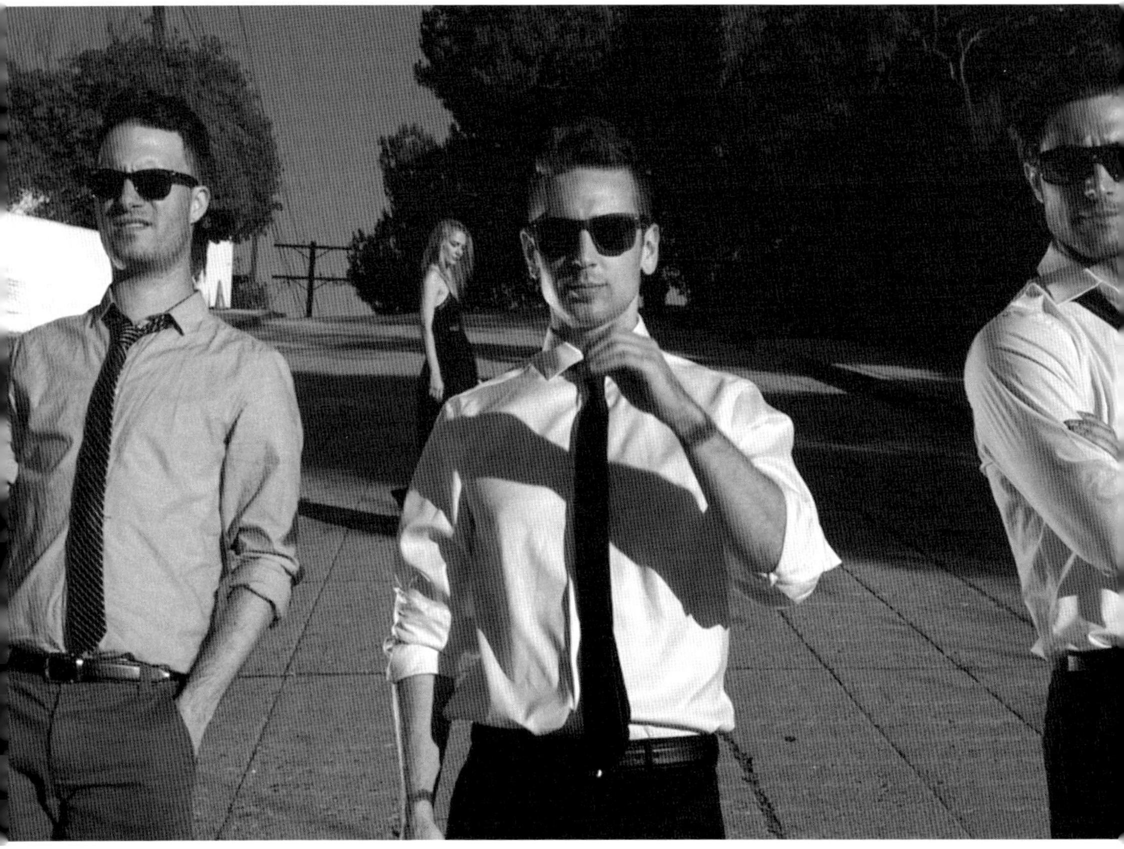

Cable Car, on Track
Not long ago, Bristol residents Ryan Murphy and Nate Mott moved to Los Angeles to see if they could break into the music industry. They began writing soon after landing on the West Coast and before long they met Jack Turner, a native of the United Kingdom and multitalented artist with his own dreams of an acting career. They named themselves Cable Car, and within a year they had written, recorded, and released their first EP, *Ride*. They characterize their sound as Pop&B—a hybrid of pop and R&B that Nate describes as "a collection of Ryan's hip hop drums, Jacks bluesy guitar and my singer songwriter something or other." (Courtesy of Cable Car.)

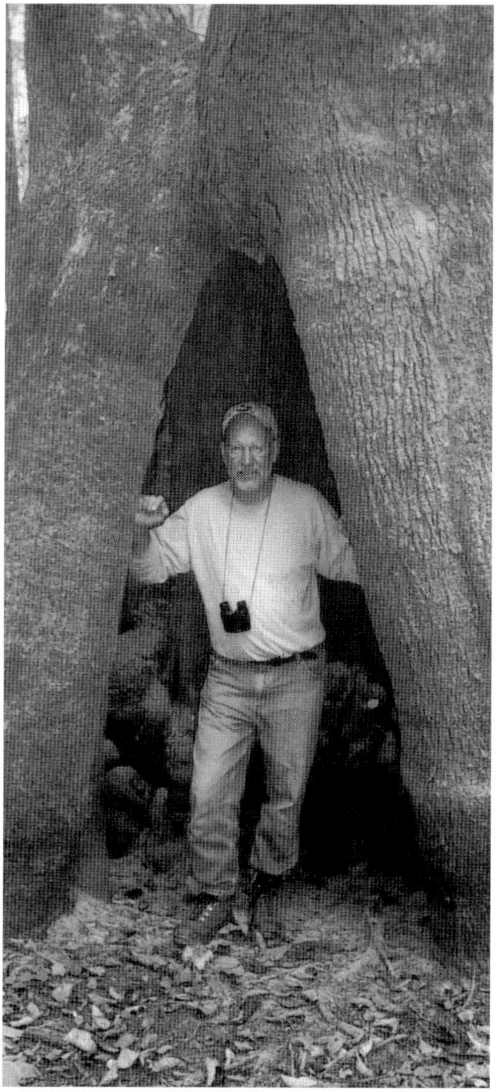

Duck Dynasty

Bristol native Matthew C. Perry has made a life studying the lives of waterfowl, with a special interest in wetland ecology; habitat creation, restoration, and enhancement; and waterfowl ecology and management. Perry is currently editing a book on the history of the US Fish and Wildlife Service Patuxent Research Refuge and the US Geological Survey Patuxent Wildlife Research Center, from which he retired after 40 years of service in 2013. Perry is also involved with several projects writing up past research of waterfowl movements using satellite telemetry, waterfowl food habits, and management of wetlands for optimum wildlife use. (Courtesy of Matthew C. Perry.)

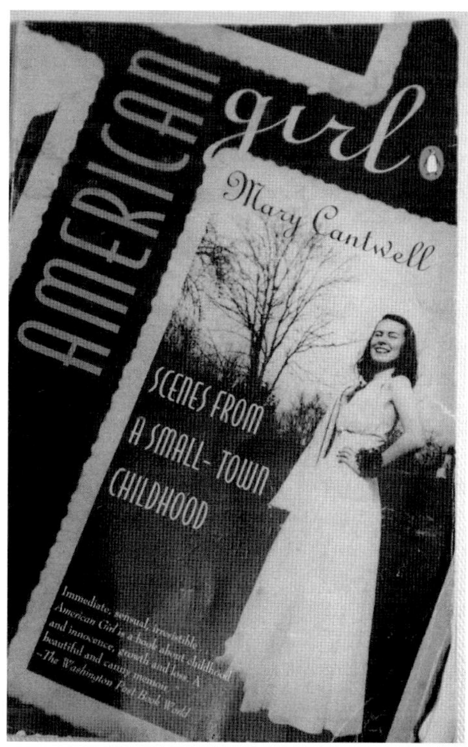

American Girl

Mary Cantwell (1930–2000) was a journalist and writer who spent much of her career in New York City, most notably putting in 16 years on the editorial board of the *New York Times*. But in Bristol, she will certainly be best remembered for her memoir *American Girl: Scenes from a Small-Town Childhood*, in which she masterfully recounted her youth growing up in her family home at 232 Hope Street. Her evocative writing, coupled with her outright honesty and her penchant for producing the perfectly turned phrase, captured the ebb and flow of life in mid-20th century Bristol.

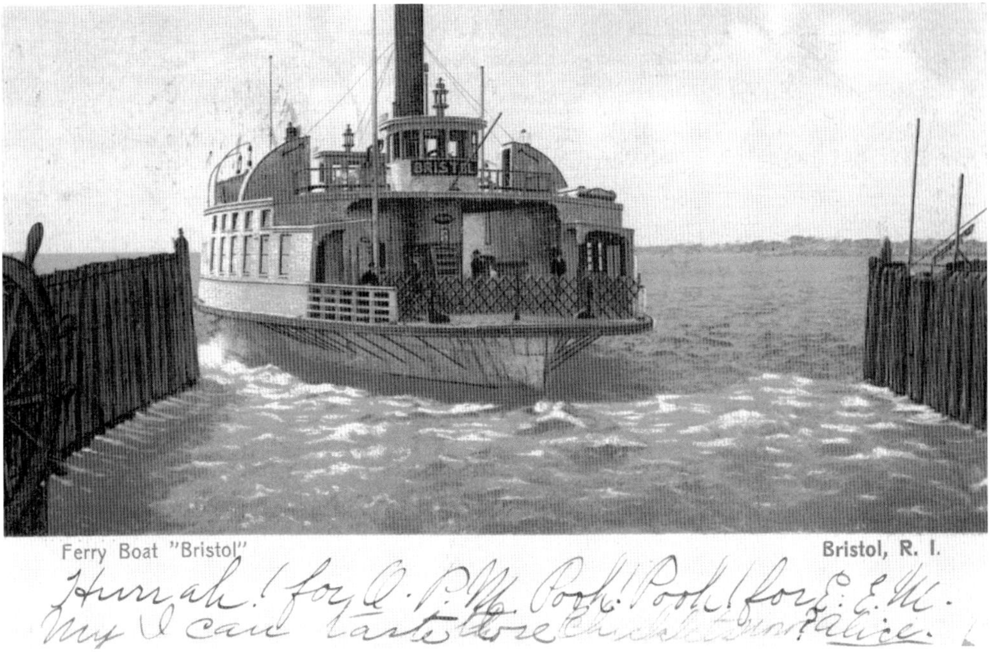

Used to Be, You Couldn't Get There from Here

Before the Mount Hope Bridge opened to traffic in October 1929, people had to take a ferry to get to Aquidneck Island—if ice in the channel didn't prevent a crossing. A bridge was originally proposed in 1920, but construction did not begin until 1927. Four months before it was to open, serious structural problems were discovered, forcing the contractor to disassemble and reassemble portions of the bridge. The graceful span, which accommodates thousands of cars a day, was included in the National Register of Historic Places in 1976.

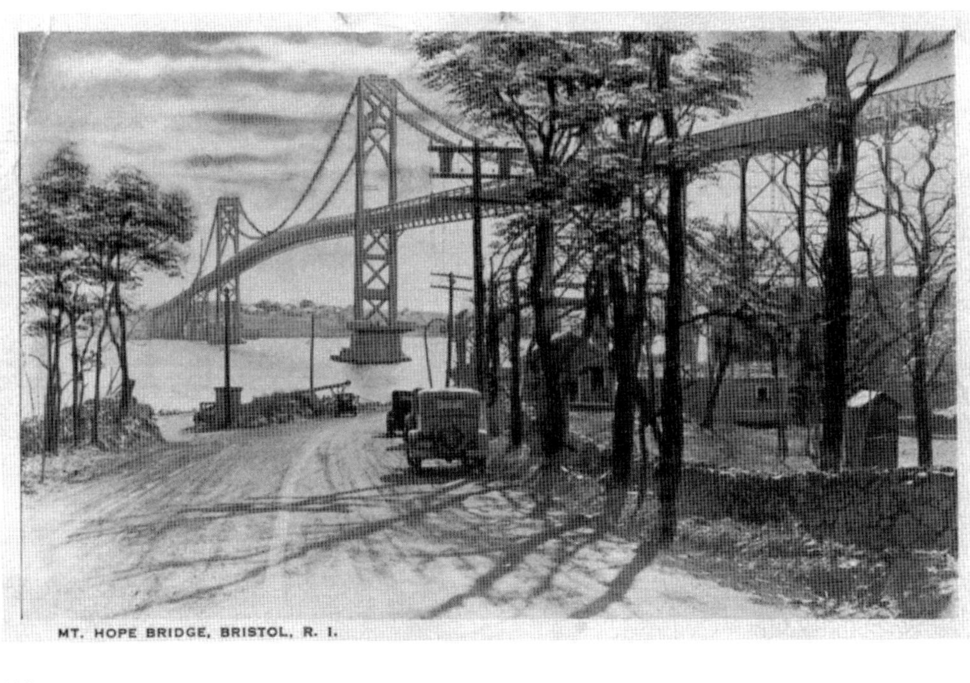

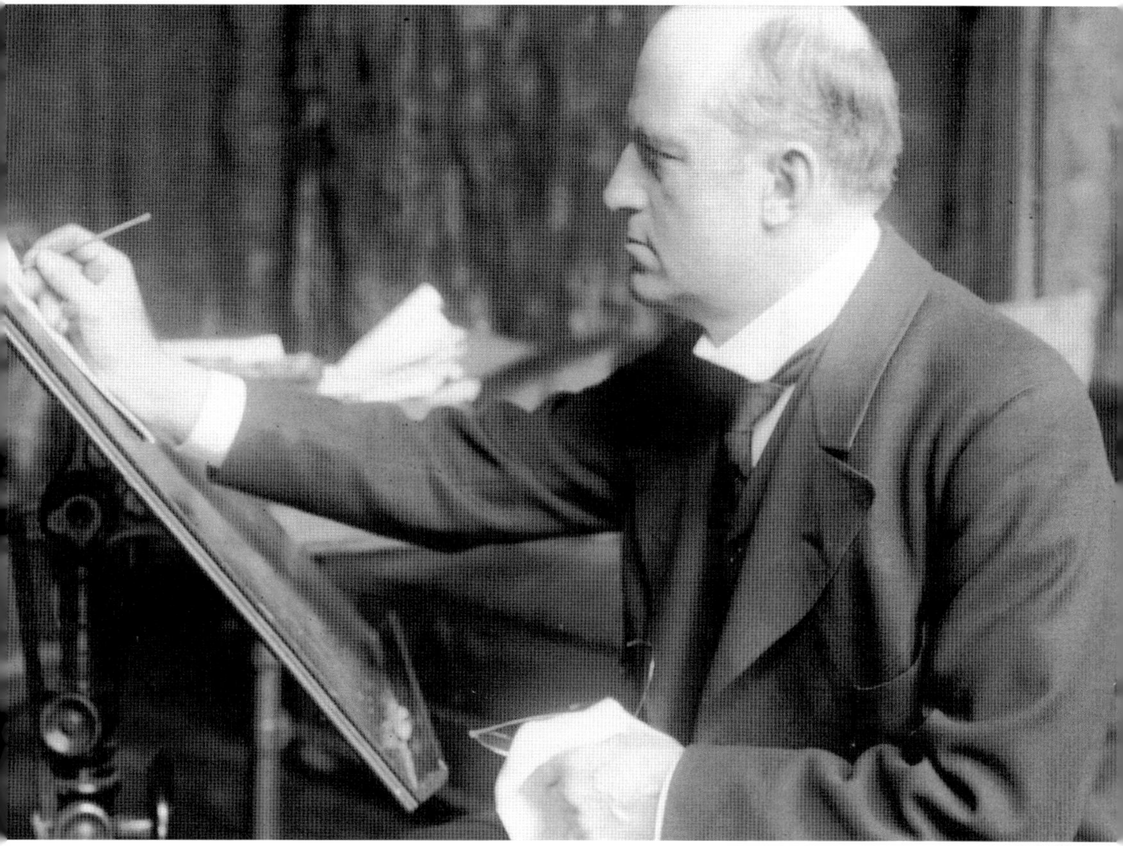

The Illustrator

Charles Dana Gibson (1867–1944) was born into a wealthy New England family from Roxbury, Massachusetts; they summered in Bristol at Longfield, a National Register property on Hope Street at Gibson Road. Interested in art since watching his father cut silhouettes as a child, Gibson was selling his own silhouettes by the age of 12. Apprenticed to sculptor Augustus Saint-Gaudens at the age of 14, Gibson learned that sculpture was not his thing but illustration was. For his first job, he landed with a new magazine called *Life*. He started drawing his iconic "Gibson Girls" in 1890, and they soon became known as the ideal image of a young girl: feminine and uniquely American. (Courtesy of Linden Place.)

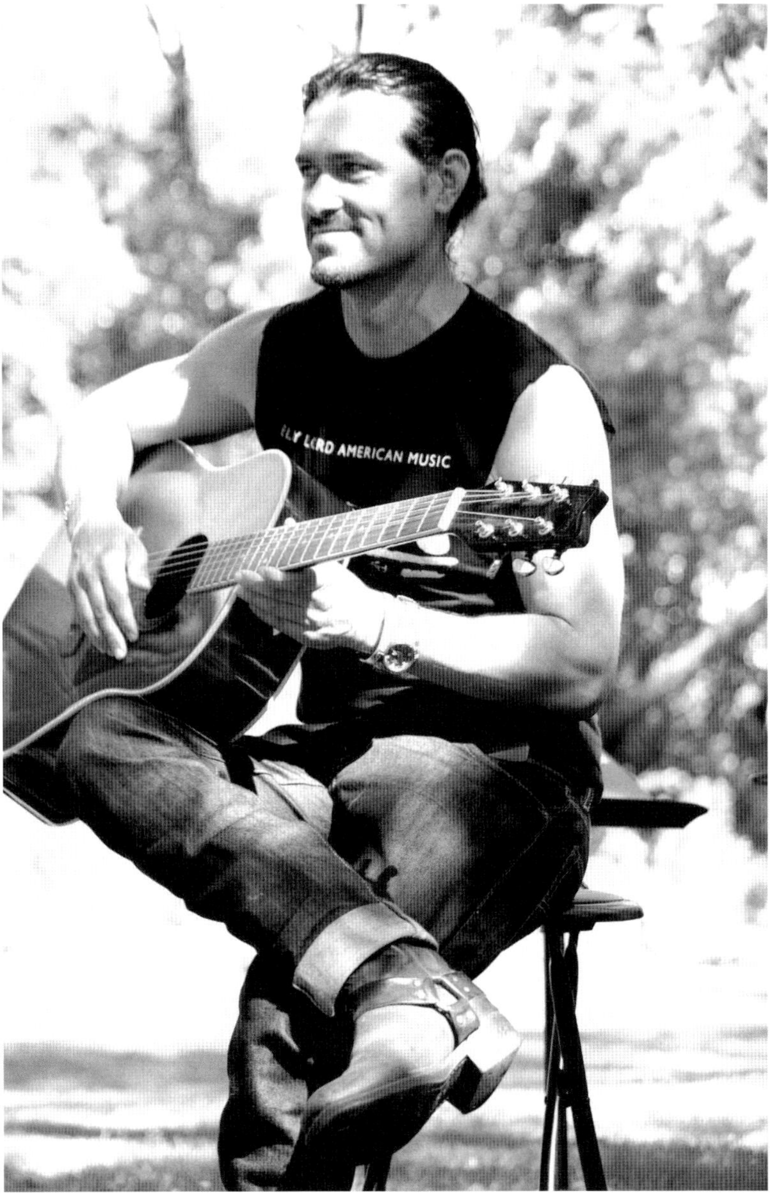

Chasing a Dream
Raised in Bristol and a 1989 graduate of Bristol High School, Billy Lord's typical American life went up in flames when he lost his job in middle management, then everything else—house, savings, and wife—in 2009. Living on friends' couches and in the streets of New York, he worked the night shift on a loading dock. One night, he unearthed an old guitar he hadn't touched in years. He decided to drop everything and follow his passion for music, raising enough money through a Kickstarter campaign to record his debut album, *American Music*. To say that album has been well received is an understatement; Lord's pop/rock/country sound has been compared to Springsteen, Daughtry, and Kid Rock. Lord's story is still being written: he spent much of 2013 traveling over 10,000 miles across the United States on a motorcycle with his guitar strapped to his back and working on his second album, *National Anthem*; a book; and a television show based in his life. (Courtesy of Billy Lord.)

Political Prognosticator

Jennifer Duffy, whose family made their home in Bristol for much of the 1980s and 1990s, is a senior editor for the *Cook Political Report*, where she is responsible for US Senate and governors races. With over two decades in nonpartisan political analysis, she is known nationally as one of a handful of go-to experts on elections and political trends. A frequent public speaker, Duffy served as an off-air analyst for NBC News on election nights from 1996 through 2012. In June 2011, BusinessInsider.com named her one of the 13 savviest political analysts in the country. Though she is now a committed inside-the-Beltway resident, Duffy considers Bristol home and can often be found in the vicinity of the parade's Hope Street midpoint on the Fourth of July. (Courtesy of Jennifer Duffy.)

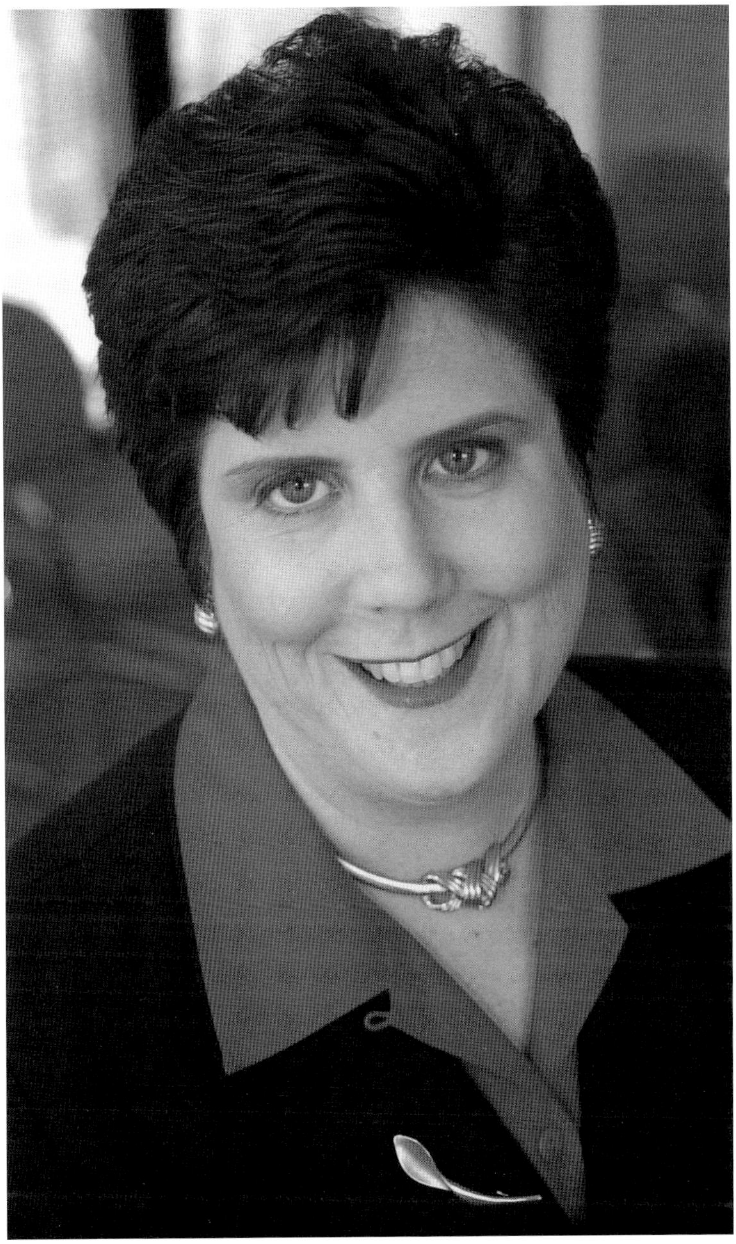

Saving Animals with Her Voice

Allison Argo did not set out to be an award-winning filmmaker of wildlife documentaries; that happy accident came about after she met a gorilla named Ivan who was imprisoned in a Plexiglas enclosure in a Tacoma shopping mall. This inspired the then-actress to get on the other side of the camera and tell Ivan's story. The film that resulted, *The Urban Gorilla* (1990), changed Argo's life as much as it did Ivan's and shaped the majority of her work since. For Argo, whose mother Betsy is a retired Roger Williams University professor and longtime Bristol resident, the appeal is rarely about a species but rather a single animal, whose story speaks to her and helps her shed light on a host of wildlife conservation concerns. Argo believes people would generally choose to treat animals humanely, but they need to be educated as to what is at stake. "How can we do the right thing," she asks, "if we don't know there's a problem?" (Courtesy of Allison Argo.)

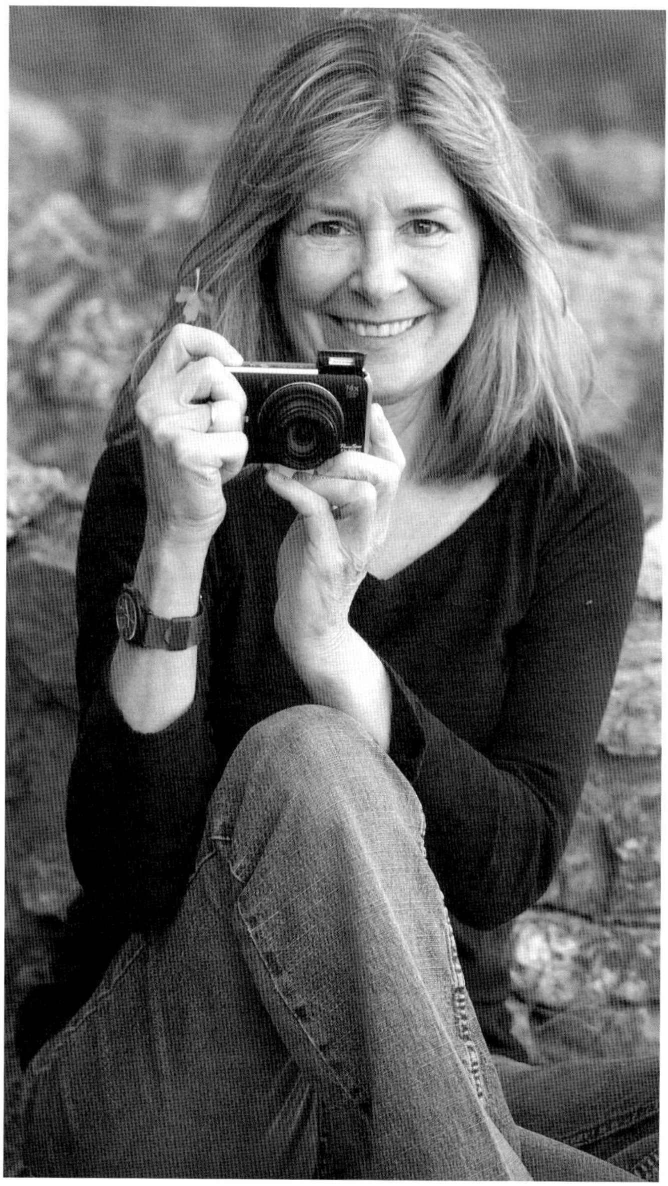

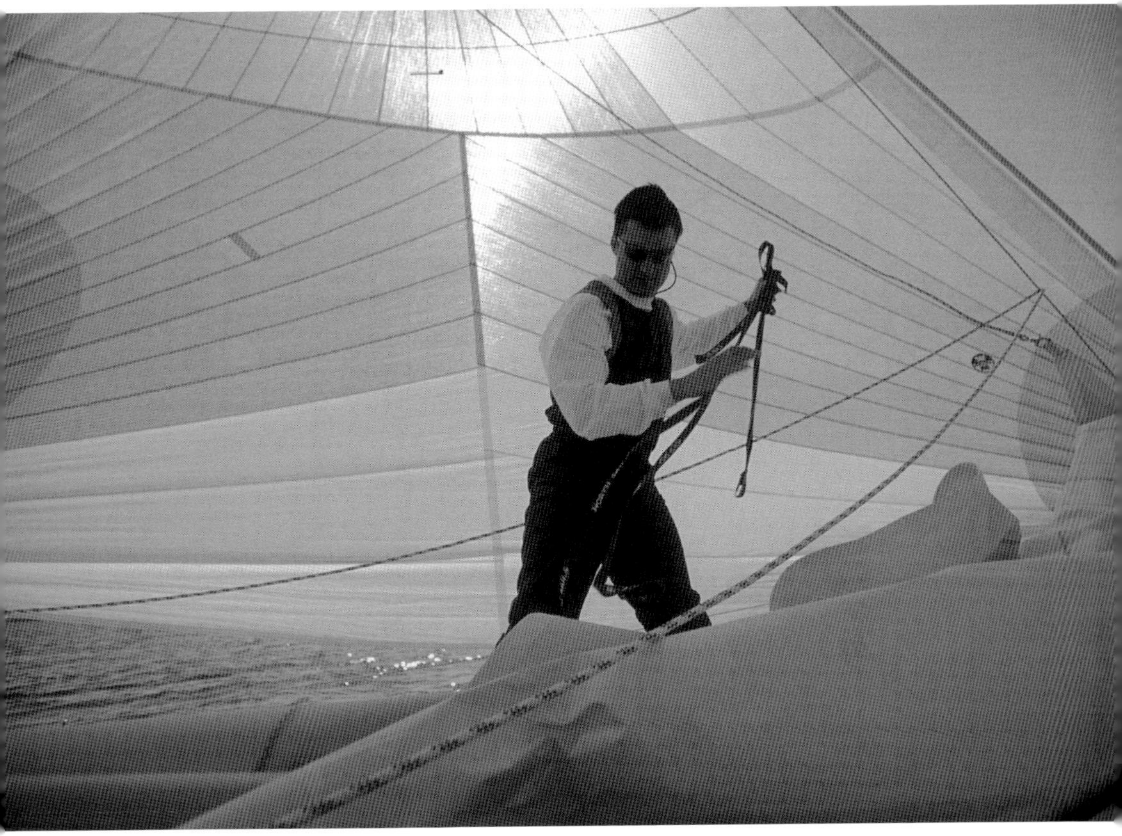

Steel Nerves and Sharp Knives
John Paul "J.P." Mouligne is not what one would call a risk-averse guy. A French native who was raised in Paris, Mouligne spent a number of years in the late 1970s and early 1980s traveling through Europe performing what he euphemistically refers to as a "juggling act." In reality, it was knife-throwing duo, with a live, and very brave, female target. When that career ran its course, he and his brother came to the United States to launch their own composite manufacturing interest, and Mouligne lived on a boat for nearly seven years. A largely self-taught sailor, he developed an interest in singlehanded distance racing and before long had secured sponsorship and started winning transatlantic races. In 1998, construction began on the *Cray Valley*, a 50-foot, purpose-built vessel with which Mouligne won the 1999 Around Alone solo circumnavigation of the world, a race run over the course of four grueling legs. While living on his boat in 1985, Mouligne met Kate, a waitress at a local restaurant who, Mouligne claims, was not all that interested in him at the time. By the time they became reacquainted in 1992, Kate had had a change of heart, and they married in 1993. The Moulignes live in Bristol with their two children, and J.P. is looking forward to his seventh transatlantic crossing, just for fun, scheduled for the summer of 2014. (Photograph by Billy Black, courtesy of Joyce Black.)

Painting History

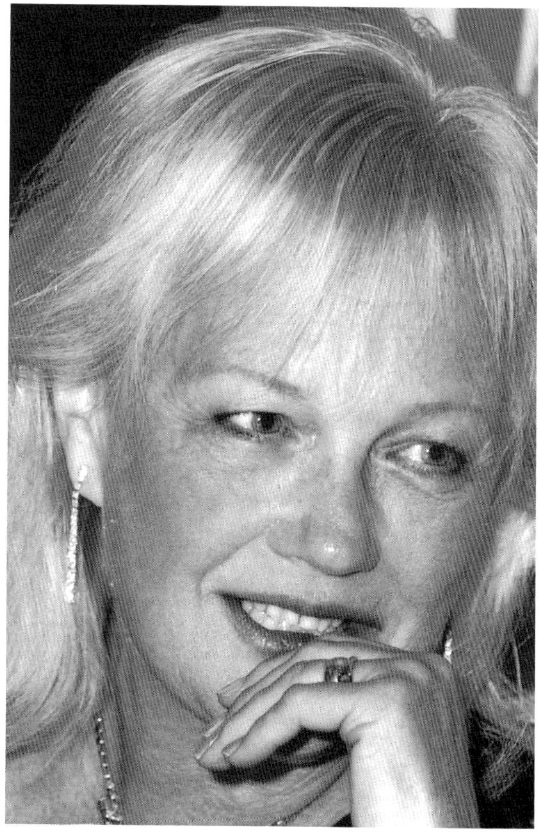

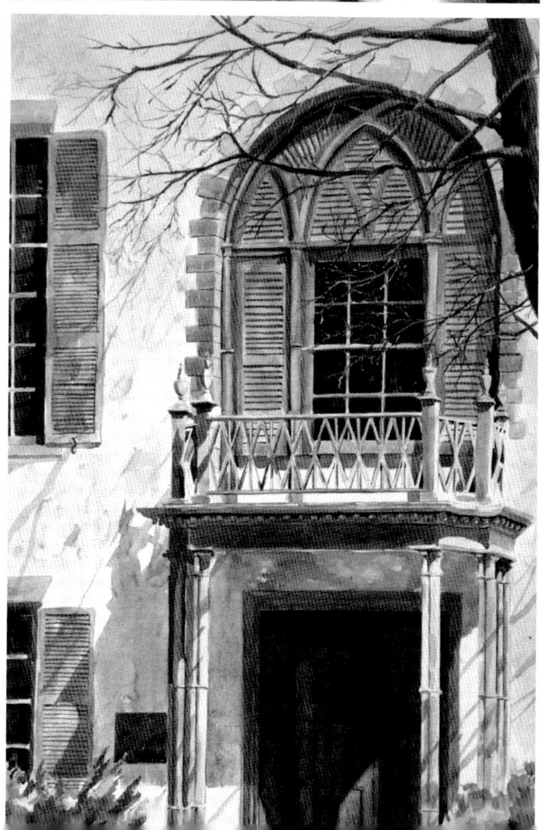

Painter and graphic designer Janet Schulz returned to watercolor, her real love, in 1990. Since then, she has worked almost exclusively painting watercolors, specializing in architecturally detailed paintings of private residences, as well as historic and commercial buildings. Her inspiration comes not only from the structure she is painting but also from the feeling or mood of the setting, concentrating on light and shadows, rather than the object itself. Schulz has gained a widespread reputation for her watercolor house portraits, having painted the homes of people across the United States and in France, England, and Switzerland. She has also been commissioned by historic and preservation societies to paint architectural scenes which are, in turn, offered as originals or reproduced as limited-edition prints. Janet has been connected to Bristol since she moved to Rhode Island in 1975 and has spent many years admiring the historic beauty of this quaint New England town. The extraordinary brilliance of light and shadows on the fine architectural details of Bristol's homes and buildings has always intrigued Schulz. Her quest has been capturing the purity of this light, as she has with this depiction of the historic Bristol Courthouse. (Both, courtesy of Janet Schulz.)

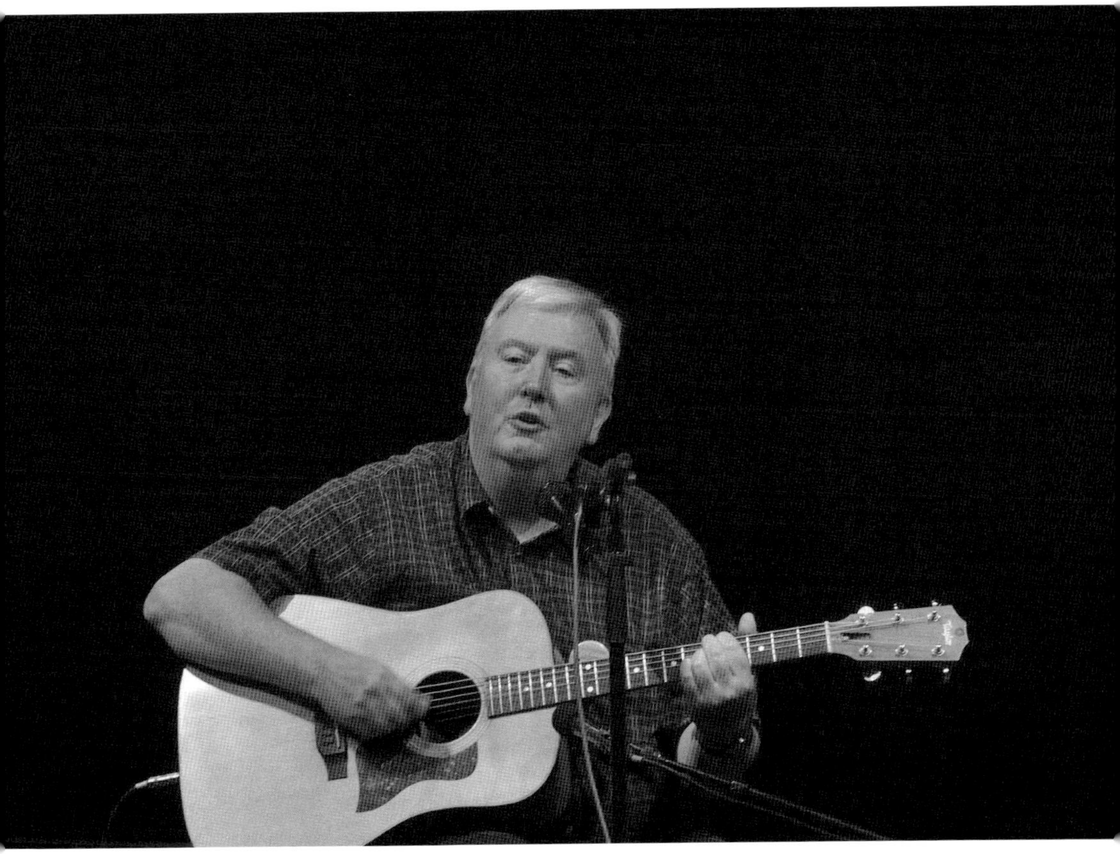

Emerald Islander
Robbie O'Connell was born in Waterford, Ireland, and grew up playing guitar in his parents' County Tipperary hotel. He enrolled at University College Dublin after a year touring the folk clubs in England and worked as an Irish entertainer in the United States during school breaks. O'Connell joined the Clancy Brothers in 1977 and since then has performed both solo and as a member of the Clancy Brothers & Robbie O'Connell, among other groups. O'Connell has appeared at almost every major US venue from Carnegie Hall and Lincoln Center to the Cerritos Center for the Performing Arts in Los Angeles and internationally from Denmark and Germany to Bolivia, Ecuador, and Nicaragua. (Courtesy of Robbie O'Connell.)

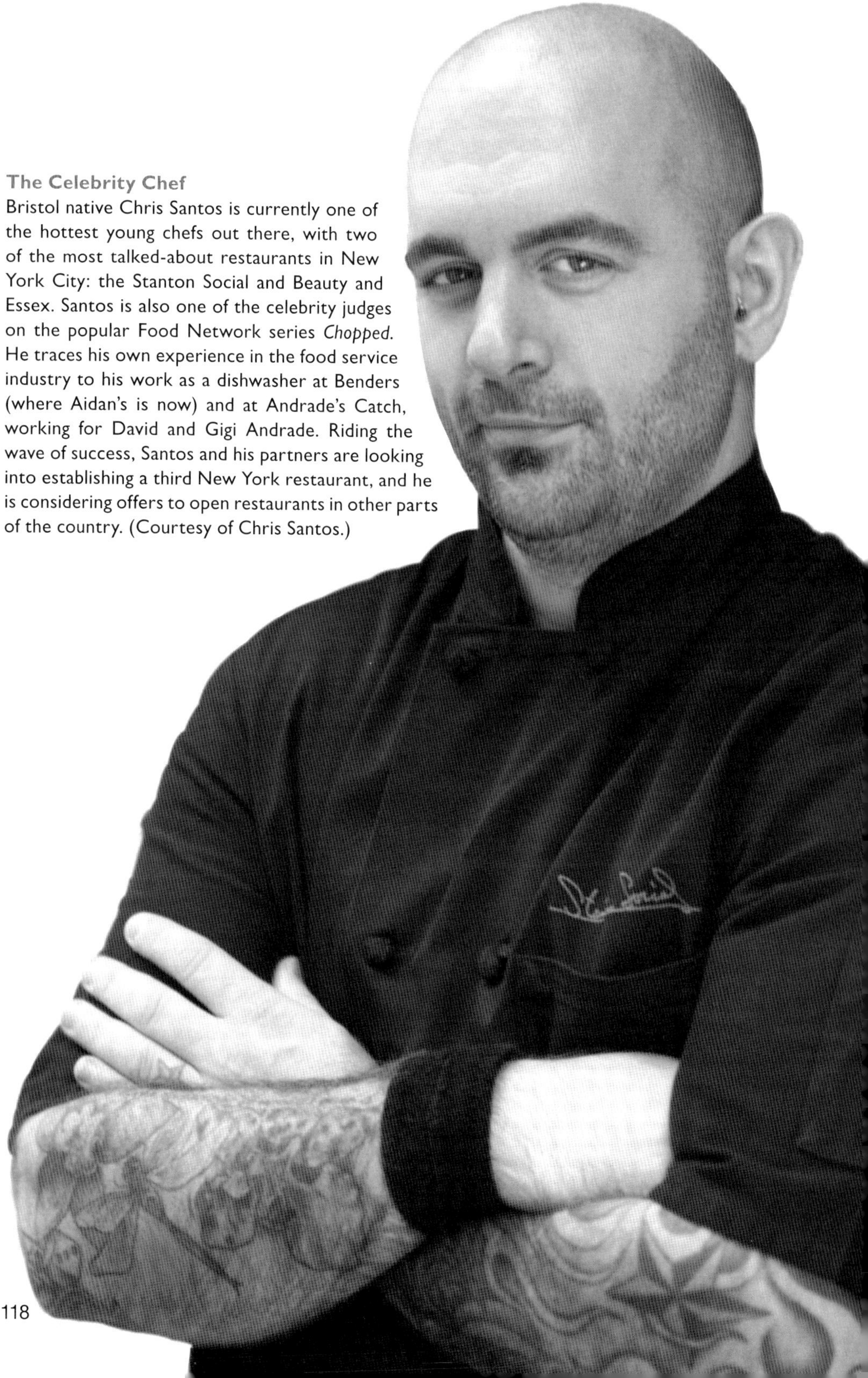

The Celebrity Chef

Bristol native Chris Santos is currently one of the hottest young chefs out there, with two of the most talked-about restaurants in New York City: the Stanton Social and Beauty and Essex. Santos is also one of the celebrity judges on the popular Food Network series *Chopped.* He traces his own experience in the food service industry to his work as a dishwasher at Benders (where Aidan's is now) and at Andrade's Catch, working for David and Gigi Andrade. Riding the wave of success, Santos and his partners are looking into establishing a third New York restaurant, and he is considering offers to open restaurants in other parts of the country. (Courtesy of Chris Santos.)

Faithful Educator

Fr. Jonathan DeFelice stepped down as president of St. Anselm College in 2013, at the time the longest-serving college president in New Hampshire. He left an indelible positive impact on the institution he led for more than two decades, expanding facilities and faculty and overseeing the introduction of a number of new majors from fine arts to environmental science to communication. Raised in Bristol and a communicant of Our Lady of Mount Carmel, Father Jonathan graduated from the Portsmouth Priory (now Abbey) and was a member of the St. Anselm class of 1969 before professing solemn vows as a Benedictine monk in 1973. He was ordained a priest in 1974 and is a founder of the Association of Benedictine Colleges and Universities. Father Jonathan, who maintains strong family ties to Bristol, hopes to return to St. Anselm in some capacity following a year's sabbatical in New York and Italy.

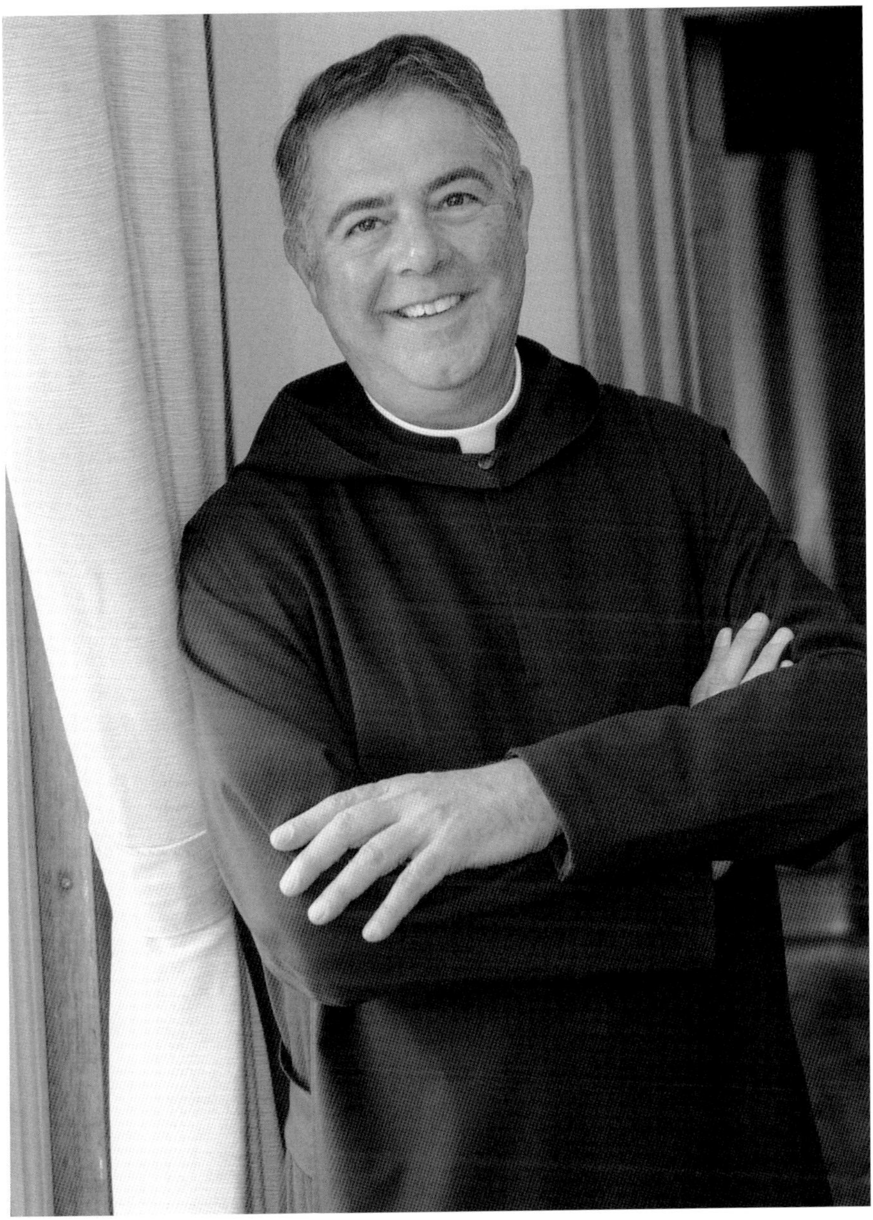

When Gatsby Came to Town

John Drew Colt, known as "Jack," was one of Ethel Barrymore's three children along with brother Samuel and sister Ethel. An actor himself (though of significantly lesser fame than his mother and her siblings), Jack's primary credit was in the 1947 film *A Double Life*.

Jack was Linden Place's owner of record in 1974 when the house was featured in a scene from *The Great Gatsby*, portraying Daisy Buchanan's childhood home, with Robert Redford and Mia Farrow dancing on the Hope Street sidewalk during the nighttime shoot. Less than a year later, Jack died at Linden Place at the young age of 61, due in part to complications from alcoholism. (Both, courtesy of Linden Place.)

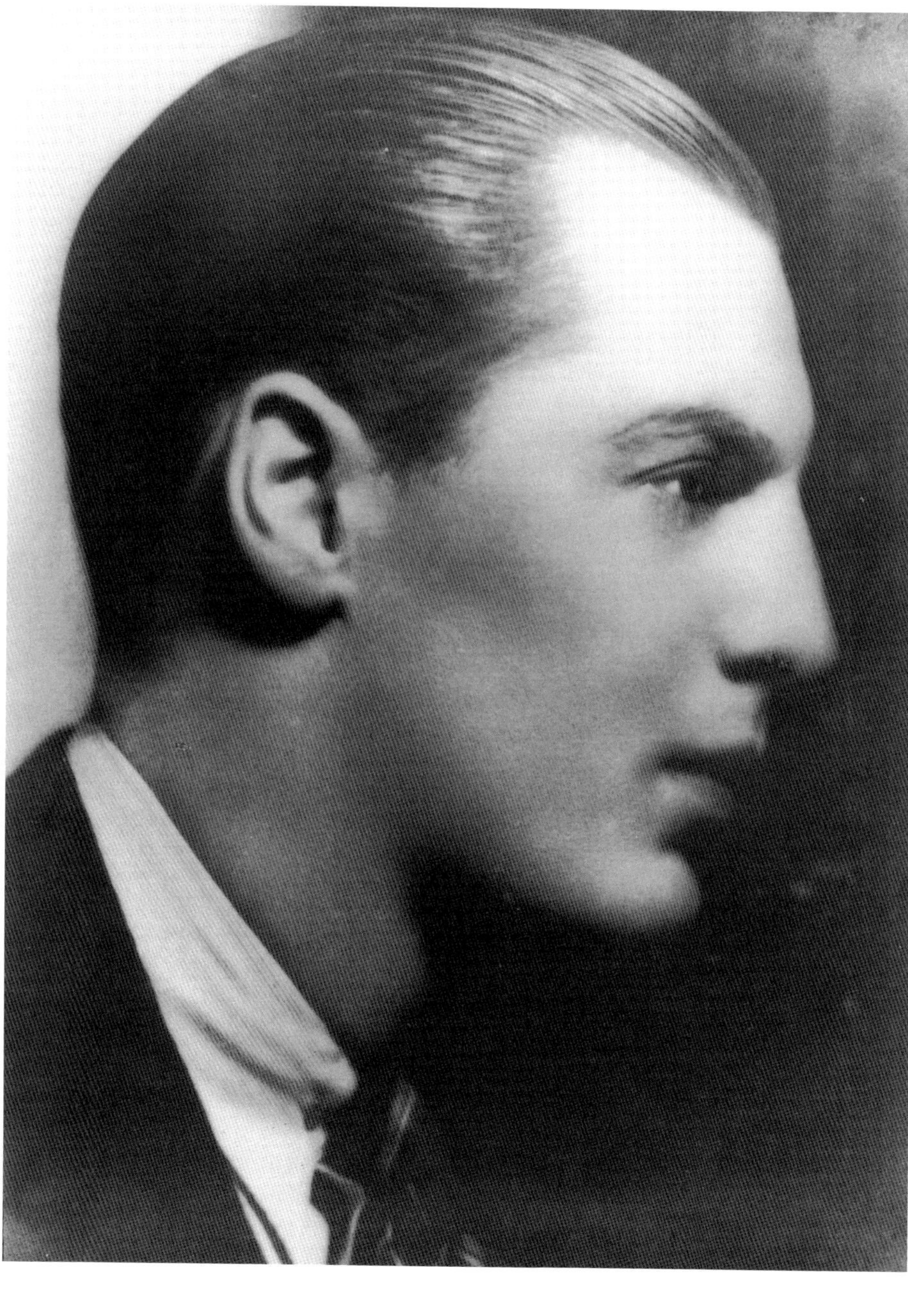

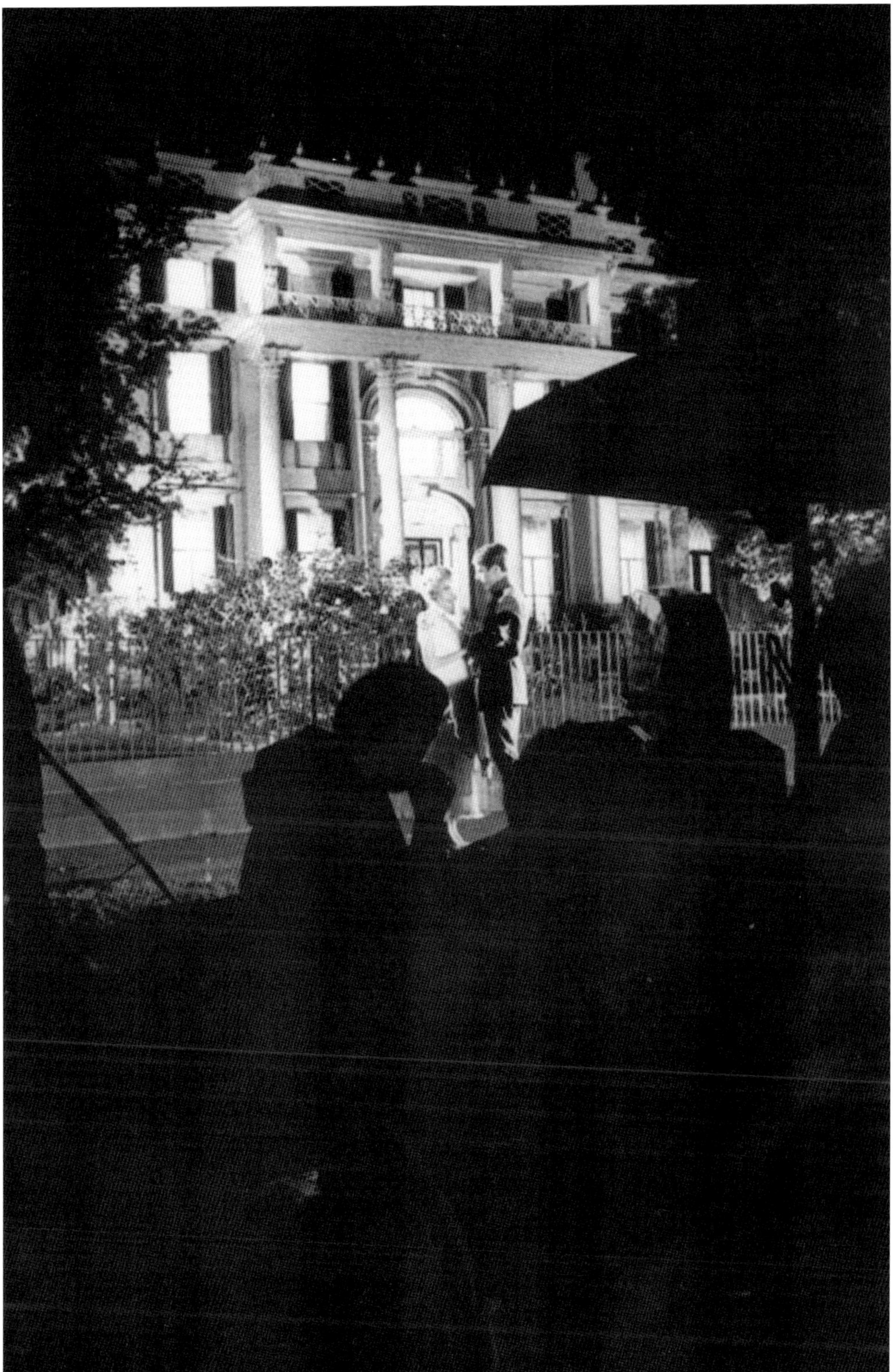

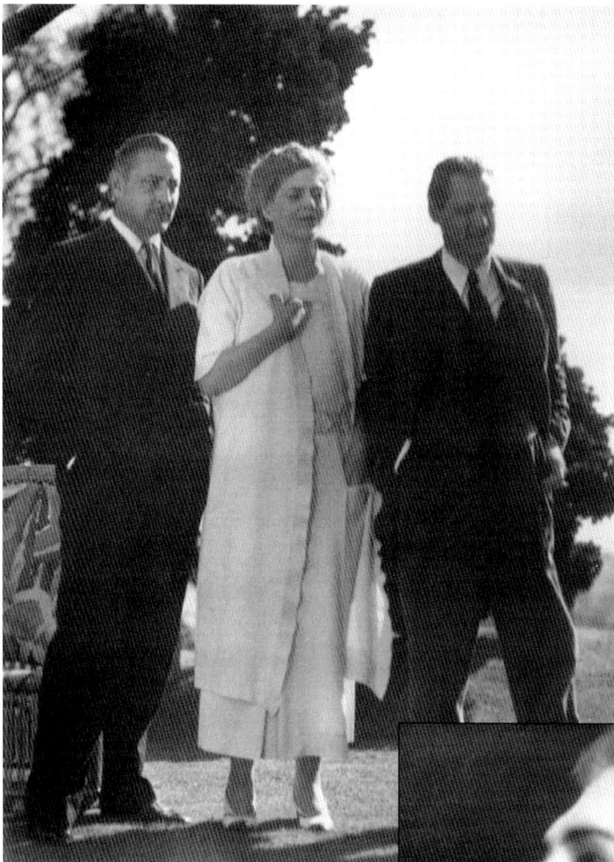

Bright Lights on Bristol
From her first Broadway appearance in 1895 to her last film role in 1957, Ethel Barrymore became a legend of stage and screen, along with brothers John and Lionel. It was her marriage to Russell Colt, and with it the family home at Linden Place, that brought the Barrymores to Bristol. (Both, courtesy of Linden Place.)

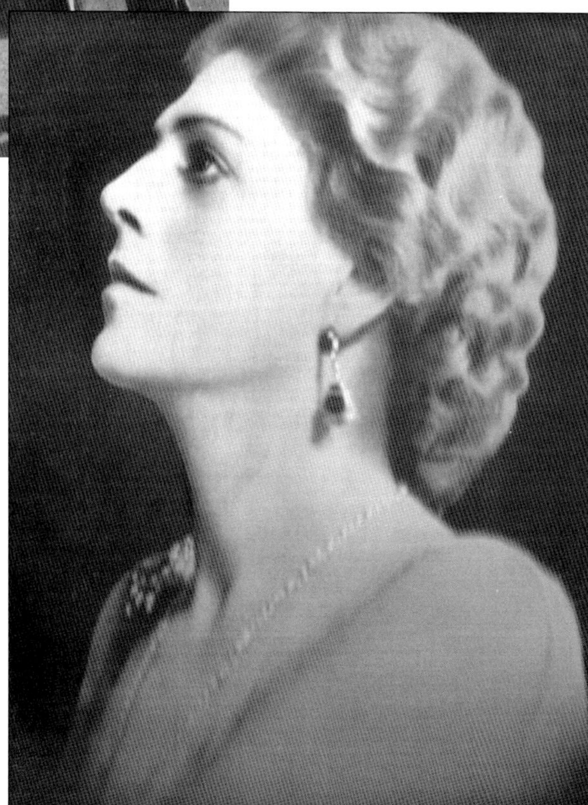

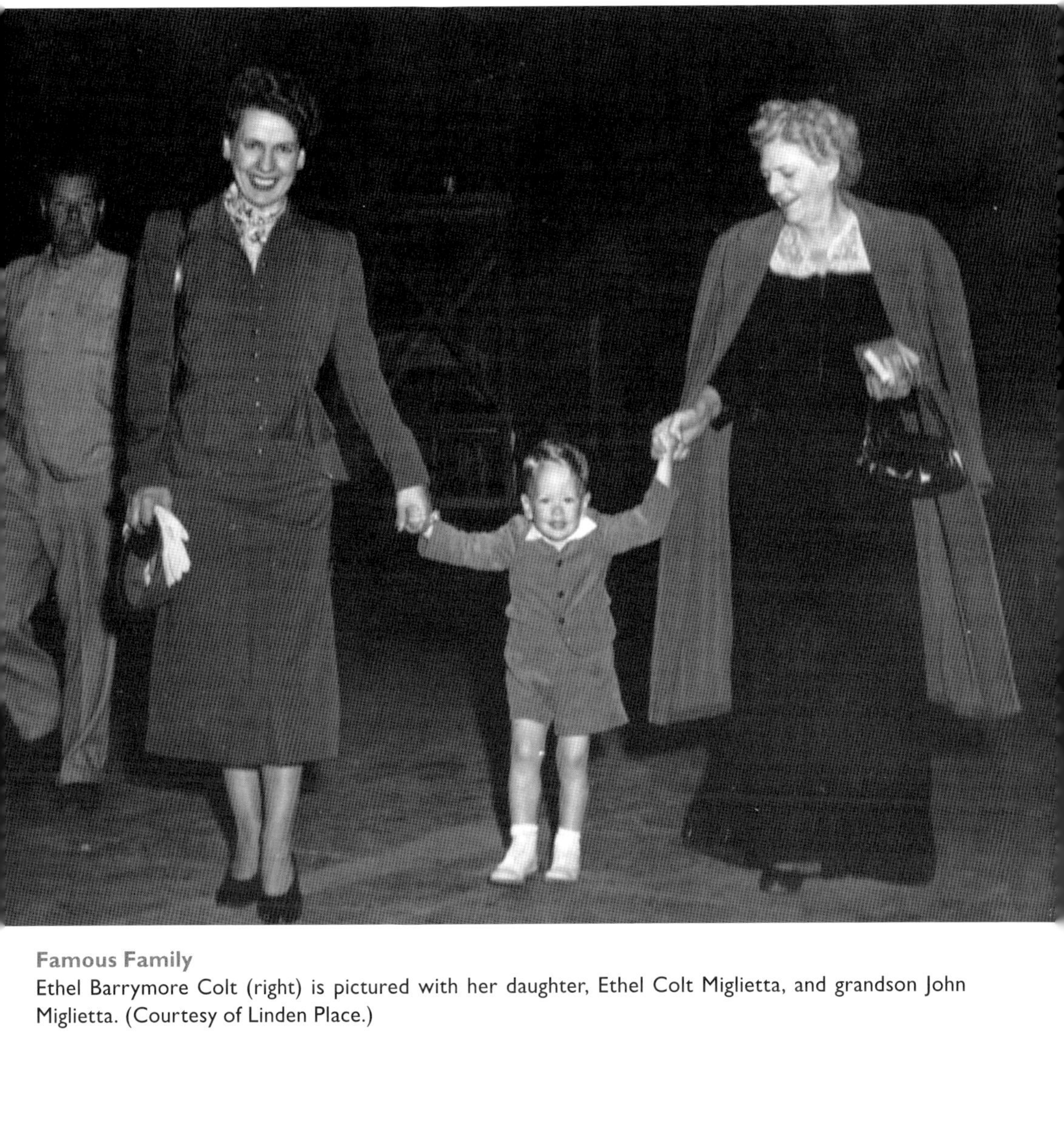

Famous Family
Ethel Barrymore Colt (right) is pictured with her daughter, Ethel Colt Miglietta, and grandson John Miglietta. (Courtesy of Linden Place.)

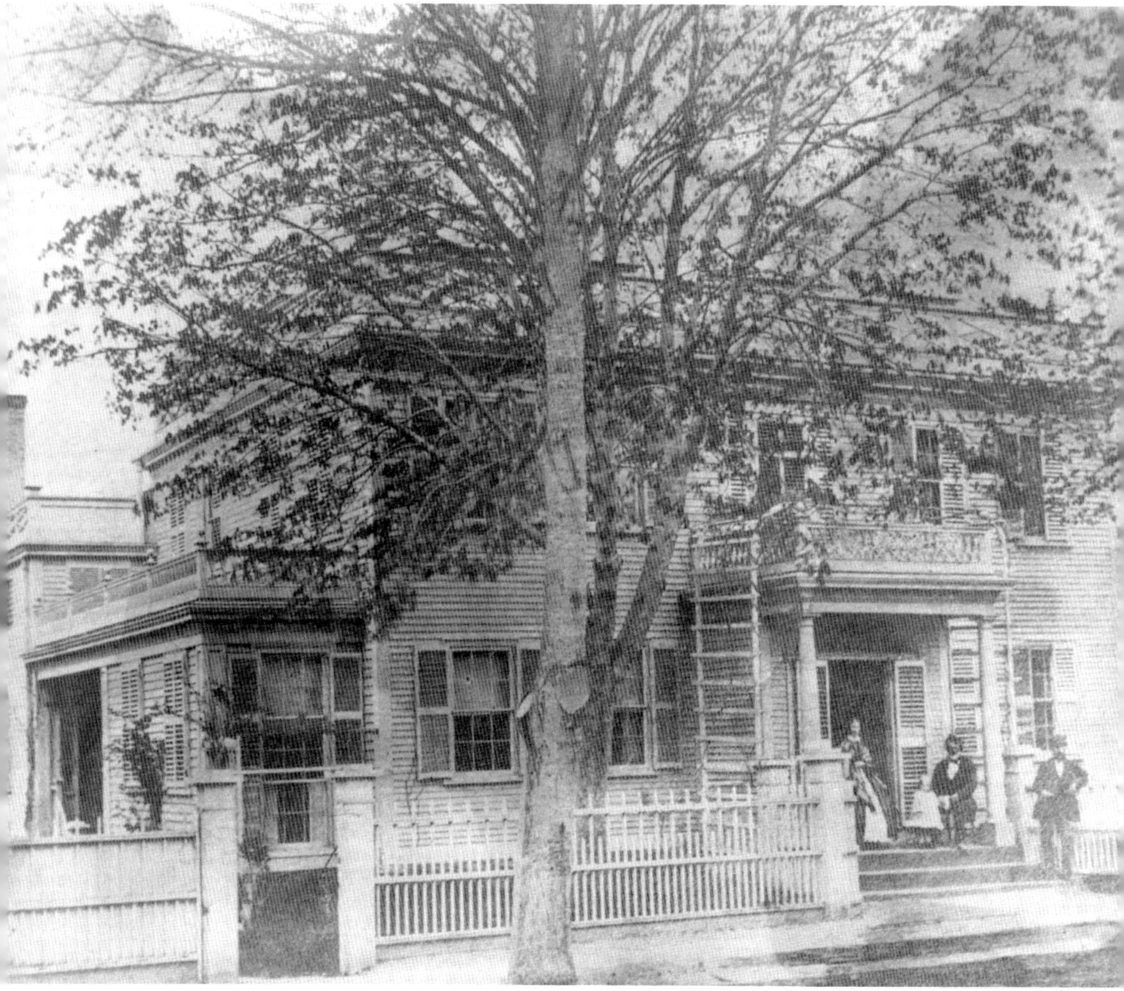

America's Architect
Russell Warren (1783–1860) was among the best-known 19th-century architects and a master of both the Federal and Greek Revival style, which was reaching the height of its popularity at the time Warren was most active. Born in Tiverton, Warren was working out of Bristol by the beginning of the 19th century. He is responsible for some of the most lovely and iconic buildings in the region, including the Arcade in Providence, Linden Place, the Bristol Statehouse, St. Mark's Episcopal Church in Warren, the New Bedford Public Library, and Longfield. Pictured is another of his masterpieces, Four Eagles. It survives, in immaculate condition, less than two blocks south of Linden Place on the opposite side of Hope Street. (Courtesy of Cathy and Garry Holmstrom.)

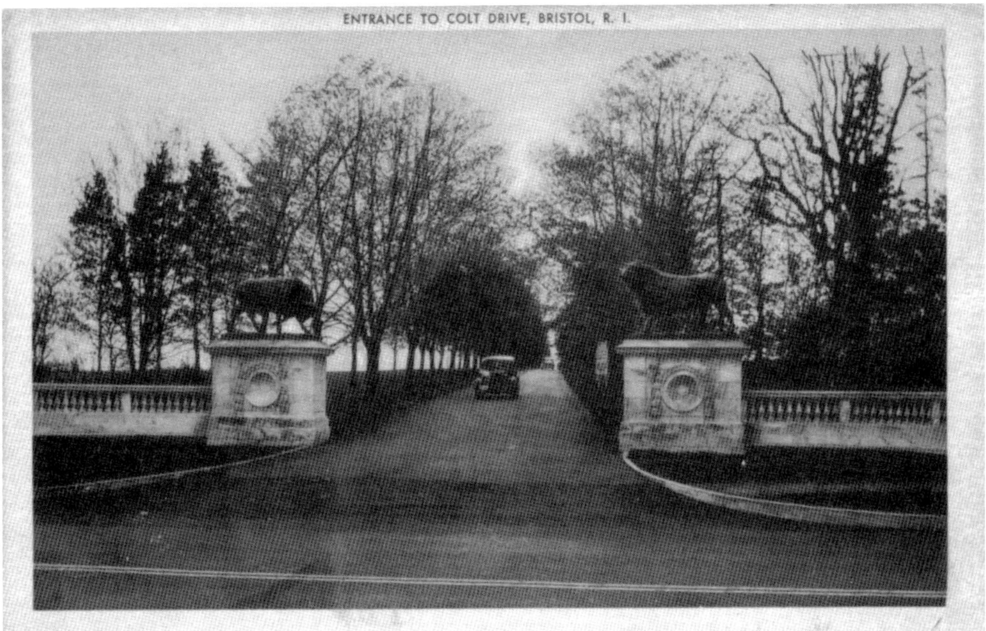

Conrad and Pomeroy

The two bronze bull statues, designed by French sculptor Isidore Bonheur, that guard the entry to Colt Park have suffered a few indignities over the course of the years but none as disconcerting as when they seemgingly vanished in 2000. It was for a good cause, fortunately, as they were removed for repair and conservation. They were returned to their rightful spot in the spring of 2001 and rededicated on August 21. (Both, courtesy of Linden Place.)

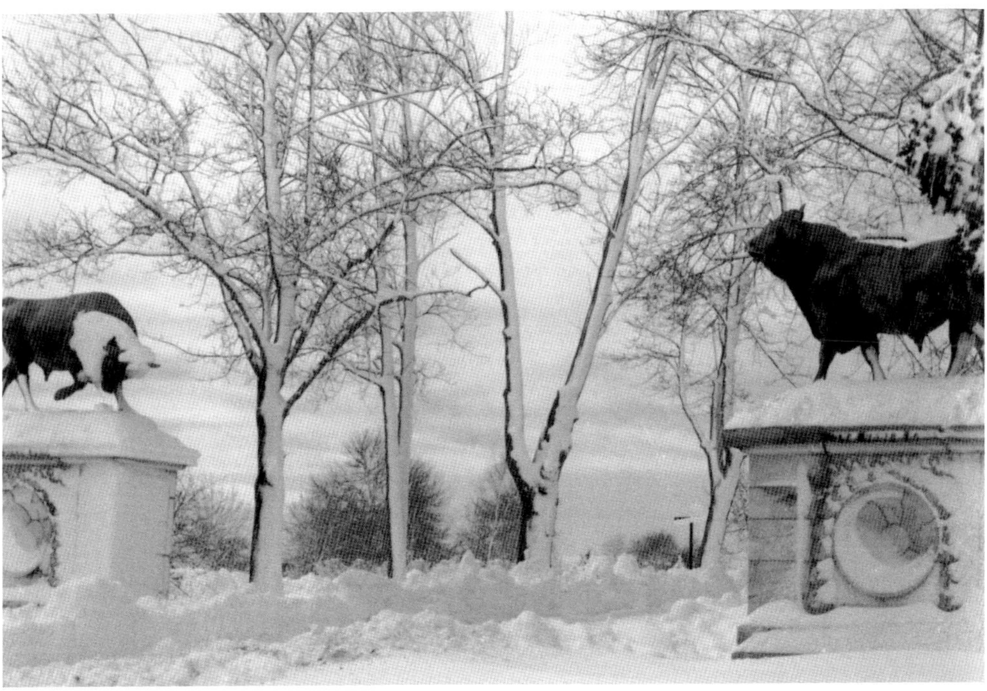

INDEX

LEGENDARY
LOCALS

AN IMPRINT OF ARCADIA PUBLISHING

Find more books like this at
www.legendarylocals.com

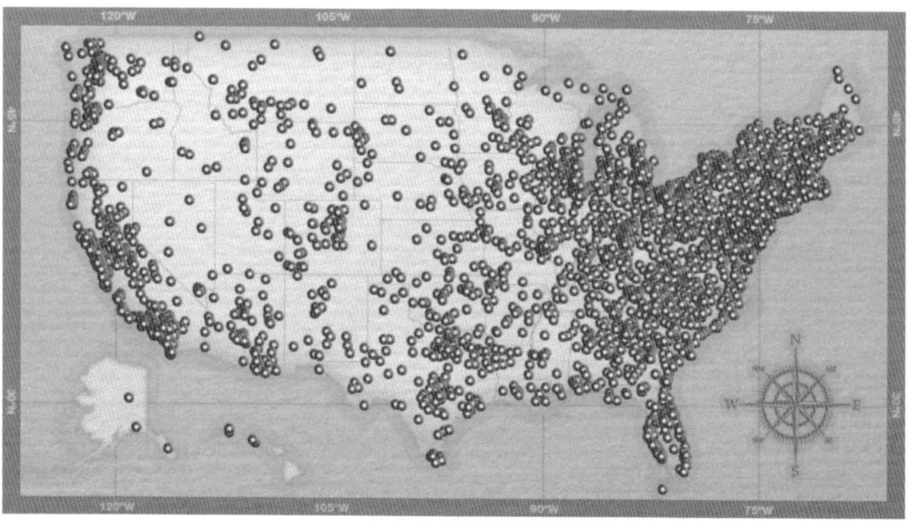

Discover more local and regional history books at
www.arcadiapublishing.com

Consistent with our mission to preserve history on a local level, this book was printed in South Carolina on American-made paper and manufactured entirely in the United States. Products carrying the accredited Forest Stewardship Council (FSC) label are printed on 100 percent FSC-certified paper.

MADE IN THE USA